St. Mary's Cathedral

St. Mary's Cathedral

1858 - 1958

BY

John H. Davis

A history of St. Mary's Episcopal Church, Memphis,
which became the Cathedral of the Diocese of
Tennessee in 1871.

Published By The

CHAPTER OF ST. MARY'S CATHEDRAL
(GAILOR MEMORIAL)

Memphis, Tennessee

1958

Library of Congress
Catalogue Card Number 58-10083

Manufactured in the U.S.A. by McCowat-Mercer Press, Inc.,
Jackson, Tennessee

DEDICATED

TO

*The glory of God and in memory of
all who have labored in this Church in
the service of Christ during the past
hundred years.*

Table of Contents

Appendices

Table of Contents (Continued)

List of Illustrations

List of Illustrations (Continued)

PREFACE

ABOUT THREE YEARS AGO the Cathedral chapter began to consider a Centennial program and celebration. At that time Dean Sanders and some chapter members mentioned that it might be an appropriate time for a Cathedral history. Informally, they suggested that I might be the one to attempt the task (since I "professed" history). I felt some hesitancy about undertaking this assignment since I was a relative newcomer to Tennessee and to the Cathedral, with no training or experience in local or church history, and with a full schedule of teaching and of other activities. But the idea of a centennial history intrigued me, and on January 1, 1956, I set to work to explore sources and to see what could be done.

I soon found that the records of the Cathedral were in a very chaotic state. Some early vestry books were lost, others were kept in such a variety of places that it seemed almost impossible to locate them. Fortunately, with the help of Miss Ellen Correll, who has been so long and so intimately connected with the Cathedral, and who knew the various closets, shelves, and vaults in which records were stored, most of the vestry and chapter minutes were located. Miss Correll had also kept a scrapbook of newspaper clippings and had preserved through the years various old programs, pictures, and documents which might otherwise have been lost. Fortunately, too, the diocese moved its file of Convention *Journals* to the vault at about the time my search was beginning. The Cathedral had preserved old copies of the *Chimes,* but these were in a sad state of disarray and would have been virtually unusable but for the valiant labor of Mrs. W. Clark Williams, who ordered them in sequence for me.

These, then, were the main sources for my narrative. I would have liked more—especially the records of Guilds, Men's Council, the Church School, etc.—but unfortunately for the completeness of the history, too little attention has been paid to the keeping and preserving of our records; and I hope that one by-product of this attempt will be that in the future more care will be given and that the historian of the second century will have an easier time. It is customary in most historical works to employ footnotes to give references to the sources of ideas and quotations employed in the text. Since, however, the sources of my quotations (Convention *Journals,* chapter *Minutes,* the local press, the *Chimes*) are generally self-evident from the context, I have used footnotes mainly for biographical sketches, additional quotations or explanations which might clutter the text.

Once launched into the projected history, my interest grew and my main problem became one of finding time, for although notes can be taken in spare moments it is harder to compose without consecutive time. As the manuscript progressed, I inflicted it—or parts of it—on several long-suffering readers who assisted me by detecting errors in names, facts, spelling and English. For this task I thank the Dean, Mrs. Thomas Lill, Miss Correll, Mr. Jack Carley, Mr. Moody, Mr. J. M. Patten, Canon James R. Sharp, Professor Danforth Ross and my wife. I am sure that many errors and omissions will still be found, for which I accept responsibility.

One never plunges into a job like this without the kindly assistance of many people. I gained certain valuable insights from conversations with some of the older members of the congregation (and since I have called them old, they might prefer to remain unnamed). I am indebted to the Rev. Holly Wells and to Mrs. James Craik Morris for long and informative letters on the work of Dean Morris; and to Sister Frideswide, Mother Superior of the Order of St. Mary, for her letters on the work of the Sisters. I owe a very deep debt of gratitude to Miss Nadia Price for assuming the responsibility of collecting and making the pictures used in the volume; to Mr. William Barr for volunteering to have the manuscript typed for the printer by his three efficient secretaries, Mrs. Mairuth Phillips, Mrs. Frances Johnson, and Mrs. Georgia Zoffka; and to Mr. Seale Johnson of the McCowat-Mercer Press for his kind suggestions and assistance in all stages of the book-making; and finally to the Chapter for underwriting the publication of the history, virtually "sight-unseen."

JOHN H. DAVIS

Lent, 1958.

St. Mary's Cathedral

CHAPTER I

BEGINNINGS

1. THE STATE

THE EPIC STORIES of the westward thrust of settlers into Tennessee, of the foundation and development of the city of Memphis, and of the establishment and growth of the Episcopal Church in the state have frequently been told. Since, however, the interweaving of these three factors forms an indispensable preamble to the story of St. Mary's Cathedral, a brief resumé of the main features of these movements must constitute our starting point.

Recent historians of the westward movement have tended to shatter some early illusions about the nature of the sturdy frontiersmen and pioneers, and have, perhaps, substituted too strongly the impression that the motivating force of the movement was mainly landjobbing and speculation. Certainly even before England wrested the Mississippi Valley from the French in the Seven Years' War (1756-63), there were prominent groups of Virginians and North Carolinians who realized the possibilities for fortune in the transmontane region; who formed companies for its exploration, and who sent agents and surveyors to spy out the land.[1] George III by issuing the "Proclamation Line" attempted to stop emigration at the Alleghenies and in some degree to protect the Indian region,

---

1. T. P. Abernathy, *From Frontier to Plantation in Tennessee.* (Chapel Hill, 1932) Chapt. 2, gives the names of the four most prominent 18th century companies. In Virginia, the Loyal Land Company (William Preston, John Donelson, Andrew Lewis); a company organized by Patrick Henry; in North Carolina, companies headed by William Blount and Richard Henderson.

but after treaties were made with the Cherokees in 1768 and 1770, settlers from Virginia ignored the line and pushed across the mountains into the Holston River region, while others from North Carolina invaded the Watauga district. The latter were led by James Robertson, who became the founder of the Cumberland settlements and of Nashville (1779). In fact, investigators have shown that most of the leading figures in early Tennessee history, the Seviers, the Campbells, the Donelsons, William Blount, James Robertson, Andrew Jackson, and others of their type, were a fairly close-knit group. They had in common (1) a background of Scotch-Irish ancestry, for most were descendants of the groups which settled the Valley of Virginia and the Mecklenburg district of North Carolina; (2) a Presbyterianism which produced a passion for "Liberty" and a belief in legality and in constituted authority; and (3) a canny acquisitiveness involving the knowledge of how to manipulate legislatures and obtain choice land grants and how to purchase others from the unwary. Professor Abernathy clearly distinguishes between two types of Tennessee frontiersmen (although in the very early years they may have appeared to live in much the same style). One group—the above mentioned—came to seek fortune and fame. The other composed mainly of shiftless men from the back country of North Carolina came to escape debts or find a place to live. The former "bought land as soon as it was put on the market and often staked out claims long before that time, while the other rarely acquired property. These were the perpetual squatters of the back country . . . who attached themselves like parasites to the westward-moving caravan."

We need not trace the trials and vicissitudes of the early settlements in East and Middle Tennessee. Population estimates show the rapidity with which the region was filled by families from the east who struggled across the mountains in an almost continuous stream. From 1790-1800 the population increased from 35,000 to over 100,000; and by 1810 rose to over 250,000. Many of the events from the close of the Revolution until Tennessee became the sixteenth state (1796), such as the formation of the transient state of Franklin, and secret negotiations between leading politicians and Spain, were but minor maneuvers in the eternal struggle for land. Even after Tennessee gained statehood, there followed a long period of litigation with the United States and North Carolina over land claims. Legislation in 1806 seemed to settle this matter, when Tennessee agreed to satisfy North Carolina's claims and to surrender to Congress the Western District, which at the time was still in the possession of the Indians.

2. MEMPHIS

It is this Western District, the region between the Tennessee and Mississippi Rivers, which concerns our story, since it is the location of Memphis and the Cathedral. As already noted, this region became a Congressional reservation in 1806, but with rising cotton prices in the early 1800's, and with the prospect of exhaustion of the lands available for the satisfaction of North Carolina warrants, pressure was building up for opening the region. By 1818 the Tennessee delegation in Congress was able to get an act passed to open this reservation.[2]

As invariably happened, the best land had long since been taken up by the foresighted. Thus, for example, the grants for the land on which Memphis now stands—the John Rice and John Ramsey tracts of 5,000 acres each—were originally entered in the land office in Hillsboro, North Carolina, in 1783. By the time the Indians were dispossessed (October 19, 1818), these grants, after many involved negotiations, had come into the possession of John Overton, who held one half; of General

---

2. Abernathy, *Op. Cit.*, 252. In 1806 Tennessee had not gained permission to dispose of this land in her name, but for the satisfaction of North Carolina warrants. Tennessee proceeded to complete the survey, create townships, districts, and land offices.

James Winchester with a fourth; and of Andrew Jackson and William Winchester, who held one eighth each. (Jackson for political reasons later withdrew from the group, getting $5,000 for land he had obtained for $25). By May 1, 1819, the proprietors named, surveyed and laid out the infant town of Memphis. The site chosen was the northwest corner of the Rice tract. A promenade, a series of streets and squares— Auction, Court, Exchange, Market, named in anticipation of their expected function—and 362 lots were marked off for sale.

Although according to one Memphis historian, "details concerning the paternity of Memphis are obscure," there is little doubt that the nurse and guardian of early Memphis was the redoubtable John Overton. This astute man, a power in Tennessee politics, and its wealthiest citizen, was determined that his venture would succeed. As chief proprietor, his agent in Memphis was Marcus Winchester. Overton was determined to anticipate his rivals. "We must not," he wrote James Winchester, "let the owners of property on the bluffs of the Mississippi above us be beforehand in laying off towns, as it might damp the sale of ours." In the state legislature (1819) he pushed through the creation of Shelby County and had it stipulated that the court was to be held on the Chickasaw Bluff.[3] He also launched a widespread publicity campaign, and tempting notices of the sale of lots were placed in papers as far removed from Memphis as New Orleans, Natchez, St. Louis, Louisville, and Cincinnati.

The hopes of the proprietors for a quickly growing and flourishing town were not, however, immediately realized. In fact it was not until after 1840 that the infant community surmounted early dangers and ceased to be described as a "tough and uninviting hole, overrun by the scum of the river." The

---

3. The court was held on the bluff until 1827, and then at Raleigh, which was made the county seat in 1825 and so continued till after the Civil War. Overton suggested using "one to two hundred gallons" of whiskey to influence the commissioners who chose the site. State politics were consistently "anti-Memphis" during its early years.

early woes of the town stemmed from several sources. Memphis was not virgin territory. DeSoto may not have crossed here, but by the early 18th century the French had outposts on the bluffs named at various periods Ft. Prudhomme, or Ft. Assumption, for their campaigns against the Indians. After the French departed, for a brief period Spain had a fort. When Spain finally ceded this to the United States, the fort was renamed Ft. Pike, but this was soon replaced by a nearby fortification, Ft. Pickering (1796-1819). For quite a long while a small colony of soldiers, traders and squatters had lived on lands which in most cases they had bought from the Indians, but which were now taken over by the proprietors. Thus in the formative years (1820-1840) the proprietors had to face hostility or rivalry from several quarters: from the local squatters ably led by the famous trader and town character, Ike Rawlings (in many cases the proprietors tried to avoid hostility here by the granting of lots); from those opposed to the act of incorporation (1826), since this involved higher taxes; from the rivalry of other developers, either those close by, like South Memphis (producing what became the Sodom-Pinch feud), or from the McLemore interests still further south at Ft. Pickering. Then too there were also rival West Tennessee communities, such as Randolph and Raleigh. Thanks to the continuing interest of Overton and to the ability of his agent, Marcus Winchester, the infant community did survive these dangers, as nearby rivals were incorporated, and distant ones surpassed.

3. The Church Comes to Tennessee

There is considerable difference of opinion as to whether early Tennessee was a godless or a religious settlement. Those holding the former view (and they are numerous) point out that in the "back country" of the eastern states, from which most settlers came, many were completely indifferent or untouched by religion; that even the seaboard settlements were deistic or anti-religious, and that the difficulties of creating a new home and life in the wilderness meant that even had some arrived with early religious training, there was little or no chance of keeping it alive in the new surroundings. Others maintain that the more able and substantial settlers did come of Scotch-Irish stock and did bring their religion into the new region, pointing to the early academies and log-cabin colleges which they established, and to the Presbyterian desire to insert religious qualifications as requirements for voting and office holding into early constitutions. Baptists and Methodists, who had already done work in frontier regions of the eastern states, were to be found in Tennessee by the early 1780's. The itinerant Baptist preacher who could combine hot-gospeling with secular pursuits, and the Methodist system of circuit riders were more adapted to frontier life, to reaching into remote places, and to people with little or no education, than were the more conservative religious bodies. The Great Revival of the early 1800's, which created the new and widespread institution of the "camp meeting," succeeded in diffusing a popular but narrow type religion through the state. Memphis was one of the last communities to be reached. There seem to have been no ministerial representatives of any denomination in the Bluff City until 1822, when a Baptist and a Methodist held meetings. The first Presbyterian parson arrived in 1823, and the first Episcopalian about ten years later (1832).

Episcopalians of today are often at a loss to understand why, during the first fifty years and more of the great westward movement (1770-1825), not a single Episcopal church or clergyman was to be found in Tennessee. The reasons are numerous and complex.

The Anglican Church, even in colonial days, labored under certain handicaps. First of all, there was lack of direct episcopal oversight, since American churches were under the control of the Bishop of London. This meant that no confirmations were possible in this country, and that young men seeking ordination had to make the long trip to England. The northern and predominantly Puritan colonies were hostile to Anglicanism, though in spite of this the Church managed to obtain a firm hold in Connecticut. The Church was also fairly strong in the middle colonies, but was disliked by many because of its strong dependence upon royal governors and their entourage. The Church in Virginia was in a weak state in the 18th century, suffering from the prevalent deism, and from the fact that state support (glebes, tithes) aroused complaint. The Revolution brought about a real crisis. Though most southern clergy tended to take the revolutionary side (in Virginia, for example, only a fifth of its 120 clergy were definitely Tory) and many clergy and most of the lay leaders were for separation, many northern clergy and laymen were loyalists who were forced to return to England or to emigrate to Canada, thus leaving the Church in a very weakened condition and with an un-American reputation. Once the break with England was completed, the scattered and motherless churches had to set about reorganization, bereft of most of their former sources of support. It is well known how Samuel Seabury, an ex-Tory from Connecticut, went abroad in 1785 and secured consecration as bishop from the hands of the Scottish Church. In his absence William White, rector of Christ Church, Philadelphia, proposed the idea of a federal union of churches. His efforts, seconded by those of William Smith of Maryland, led to a meeting of some representatives in Philadelphia, in 1785, which in turn led to the famous General Convention of 1789 which adopted a Constitution, Canons, and the American Book of Common Prayer, and created a federation of state churches. Before this Convention met, White and Samuel Prevoost of New York had been consecrated in England by the Archbishop of Canterbury. Within ten years of the Convention, bishops were consecrated and dioceses created for Virginia (1790), Maryland (1792),

[7]

and Massachusetts (1797). Unfortunately, no new outburst of activity accompanied these necessary moves. It took time for the new bishops to learn their duties and consolidate their positions. Many became discouraged and gave up the effort. The result, as one Church historian puts it, was that "for twenty years after the convention of 1789, the Episcopal Church, its strength seemingly spent by the tremendous effort at reorganization, lapsed into lethargy and inaction. Spiritual vitality was at a low ebb . . . The Church during these two decades received little or no inspired leadership from its first bishops."

A combination of the above circumstances, coming at the time when the great western migration was on, accounts for the lack of frontier activity. Fortunately the situation improved in the early 1800's. A new and more progressive leadership developed in the Church, associated with the names of Bishops Hobart, Griswold, Chase, Moore, and Ravenscroft. Colleges and seminaries were founded, and the Domestic and Foreign Missionary Society established (1821). This new and active period coincides with the beginning of the work in Tennessee.

4. The Church Comes to Memphis

By the mid-twenties, there were undoubtedly many settlers with Episcopalian backgrounds among the nearly half-million inhabitants in the new state. But if they worshipped in church, they perforce had to do so with other denominations. The first two Episcopal clergymen in the state seem to have been a young deacon from Philadelphia, the Rev. John Davis, who was sent by the Domestic and Foreign Mission Society, and who labored, none too successfully, in East and Middle Tennessee from 1826 to 1829, before departing to Alabama; the second was James Hervey Otey, who later became the first bishop and, one might add, the patron saint of Tennessee Episcopalians.

Otey's story has often been told, but anyone studying an Episcopal Church in Tennessee founded prior to his death

[8]

(1863) must begin with him. A Calvinist might cite Otey as an example of God's providence in providing the right man for the right hour; and as Canon James R. Sharp, the Nestor of the Diocese, has remarked, "his Journal should be made compulsory reading for all Tennessee clergymen." Especially is this true for anyone who might be inclined to self-pity at his difficulties, for when one reads the dangers and discouragements which Otey faced, those of the present generation pale into insignificance.

James Hervey Otey was born in 1800 in Bedford County, Virginia, on a farm near the Peaks of Otter. He was the youngest of twelve children. His family was of some importance in the community, his father having served in the Virginia legislature, but they seemed to have been members of no religious denomination, a condition not unusual among the frontiersmen of the time. The family also had a reputation for great physical stature. At sixteen the tall and rather ungainly James was sent to the University in Chapel Hill, North Carolina. He was six feet four inches in height, and so swarthy that he was usually called "Cherokee" by his fellows. He did well in college, received his bachelor's degree in 1820, and remained at the University for another year as a tutor or instructor. In 1821 he married Elizabeth Pannell of Petersburg, Virginia, and ventured west into Tennessee to teach in a boys' school in Franklin. After a year or two here, he returned to North Carolina to accept the post of principal of the school at Warrenton. This return marked a turning point in his life, for under the influence of John Anderson and William Green (an ex-classmate, then a priest, and later Bishop of Mississippi), he was baptized. A little later, on May 8, 1824, he was confirmed by Bishop Ravenscroft in St. John's Church, Williamsboro. No doubt with the religious needs of Tennessee in mind, he decided to enter the ministry and was ordained deacon on October 10, 1825.

What brought about Otey's conversion and call to the

[9]

ministry has long been a moot point among his biographers.[4] Most are agreed that somewhere in his early teaching career he was confronted with the necessity of conducting religious exercises for his students, and in this way discovered the Book of Common Prayer. He is therefore cited as an outstanding example of "Prayer-Book conversion." Canon James R. Sharp, in his fine chapter on Bishop Otey in the *History of Christ Church,* points out that there are too many discrepant views as to where this Prayer Book discovery took place to make it a certainty, and he speaks of it as the "Prayer-Book legend."[5] Otey's years in Warrenton were productive of other consequences, for it was here that he came to know the Alstons and the Andersons. Both families migrated to Tennessee in the late twenties and established large plantations, the Alstons near Randolph, and the Andersons and their mother-in-law, Mrs. Mary H. Gloster, at LaGrange. Both families became, as we shall see, the principal supporters of the Bishop and of the Church in the Western District.

Late in 1825 the newly ordained deacon and his wife returned to Franklin where he resumed teaching at Harpeth Academy. He organized a church here (St. Paul's) and on foot, by mule or horseback, travelled to nearby Columbia and to Nashville to gather the groups which founded the churches in those places. In Columbia he was for a while assisted by the Rev. John Davis.[6]

---

4. Bishop Otey, in his address to the Convention in 1848, when reporting the death of John Anderson of LaGrange, seems to give him credit for his conversion: "He was in Christ before me and to his meek, but instructive conversation, to his exemplary deportment witnessed 25 years ago, do I now feel that I am greatly indebted under God's blessing, in being turned away from the love of the world and to seek Christ and the peace he alone can give."

5. See *History of Christ Church* (Nashville, 1929), 51-56. Bishop Gailor, in his sketch of the Church in Tennessee in *Tennessee Churchman* (Gailor Memorial Edition), 33, says the "Prayer Book" episode was in Tennessee and even gives the name of the gentleman who gave him a copy, Mr. James H. Piper, who as a boy tried to carve his initials beside those of George Washington on the Natural Bridge of Virginia.

6. E. Clowes Chorley in a pamphlet, *How the Church Came to Our Country,* says that in 1827 Davis preached in the court house in Knoxville and wrote, "I organized a church on Easter Mondoy." This later wilted for he said

Otey revisited North Carolina in 1827 to be ordained to the priesthood (June 7th). The first Episcopal visitation to Tennessee was made in 1829 by Bishop Ravenscroft, and on July 1st and 2nd, in the Masonic Hall in Nashville, the first Diocesan Convention was held with three clergymen, Otey, Davis, and the Rev. Daniel Stephens (brought by Ravenscroft), and six laymen in attendance. These represented four parishes, and possibly fifty communicants. The next two conventions, 1830 and 1832, were also under the supervision of visiting bishops (Meade of Virginia, and Ives of North Carolina), and during these years a few more clergy were brought into Tennessee by the bishops or were sent by the Missionary Society.[7] Thus by the time of the fourth convention (June 27, 1833), the one which chose James Hervey Otey as bishop, there were under his supervision but five priests, three deacons, one church building, and about a hundred communicants. Otey journeyed to Philadelphia to the General Convention for his consecration, which took place in Christ Church on January 14, 1834. Bishop Doane of New Jersey preached the sermon, in which we find these words:

> There is a common notion that Bishops are stately persons, and that large salaries, noble edifices, and splendid equipages are somehow an appendage to their office. But here is a Bishop who has never had a church to preach in and has never had a living at the altar, but has been obliged to labor for his children's bread in that laborious, though most honorable, vocation of teaching; spending five days out of seven in a school, and for years has not had a month's relaxation.

Significant for our story is the fact that prior to his election, in 1831, Mrs. Mary Gloster and her son-in-law John Anderson,

that at Knoxville, "the people were more interested in politics than in religion." He also visited Kingston, Nashville, Franklin, and Columbia. In another report he wrote: "I found the Episcopalians rejoicing to have services." From Columbia he reported that many men of wealth and influence "would receive a missionary very joyfully and treat him with great kindness." He felt that prospects were dim at Nashville. He and Otey organized the congregation at Columbia. Davis was dismissed from the ministry in 1834 by the Bishop of Pennsylvania the year Otey was consecrated.

7. These were: George Weller, Samuel Litton, Thomas Wright, and John Chilton (the first priest to be ordained in Tennessee).

old Warrenton friends, now comfortably established at LaGrange, made the forbidding two-hundred-mile trip on horseback to Franklin to persuade Otey to come or to send a clergyman into West Tennessee. Thus the first "mission to the west" was organized. Otey asked aid of the Domestic and Foreign Mission Society, and sent John Chilton, Samuel Litton, and Thomas Wright into the Western District. Their journey in 1832 led to the formation of parishes in Clarksville, Paris, Jackson, Brownsville, LaGrange, Memphis, and Randolph.

The Rev. Thomas Wright, a North Carolinian sent to Tennessee by Bishop Ives, was the first Episcopal minister to reach Memphis. He came west in the summer of 1832. He stopped with the Andersons and Mrs. Gloster at LaGrange; and from this visit Immanuel Church was organized.[8] He pressed on to Memphis, and on August 6th met with the group which became the nucleus of Calvary.[9] He then visited the Alston plantation near Randolph.[10] From here he wrote his wife on August 11, 1832, a letter which gives a lively impression of his activities:

> At Memphis, a town of 1200 inhabitants, I organized a Church of most reputable material. Much praise is due to Thomas Brown who aided me in all my exertions, and who was particularly useful in conducting the service. Indeed at first he was the only one to respond, and I shall never forget his kindness and shall always think with him that the hand of God was visible in the foundation of the church at Memphis . . . In four weeks, God willing, I shall visit the place

8. The Andersons, John and George, came to LaGrange in 1827. Mrs. Anderson's mother was Mary Hayes Gloster, then a young widow who had a son Arthur. She lived with them until her death in 1854.

9. The Rev. Philip Alston's list of the first ten members of Calvary is as follows: John Boothe, Thomas Beatty, Lewis Shanks, Samuel Rembert, Mrs. Anna Hart, Mrs. Virginia Skipworth, Mrs. Elizabeth Rose, Mrs. Bray, Mrs. Truelove (listed in the Program of the 90th Anniversary celebration). Though women predominate, the proportion is not as high as one early Presbyterian congregation in Nashville, where the minister reported that out of his 45 members, 43 were women.

10. T. F. Gailor, *Some Memories* (Kingsport, 1937), 75. In 1830 Col. Robert Alston left North Carolina with several hundred slaves "to a great plantation he had bought in West Tennessee, six miles east of Randolph." He kept open house for travellers, called his place Ravenscroft plantation, in honor of the Bishop, and had a chapel and rectory on it.

again, and trust by the help of the Lord to strengthen and confirm the members of Calvary Church . . . Mrs. Alston, at whose house I arrived yesterday, is from near Warrenton. She is a very pious woman and thinks that although she can hear of but one or two Episcopalians in the neighborhood, the Church may nevertheless be formed and a building created on her own land or at Randolph. I shall preach in the town tomorrow and here probably on Monday. There is much more intelligence throughout the district than I had anticipated. The Church, therefore, and her pure spirit-stirring liturgy are everywhere welcomed, and in almost all the towns she will ere long attain a sure footing.[11]

The newly consecrated Bishop Otey made his first visit to the West in 1834. He arrived in Memphis on December 19. In his diary he writes, "I preached to a small number collected in an upper room of the Town House; an altogether inconvenient place for services." This was especially true as the weather was inclement, and the room improperly heated. On December 21 he gave Holy Communion to forty in the Methodist Chapel, and in the afternoon confirmed three. He adds, "The want of a suitable place for worship is seriously felt by the vestry and congregation of the Church at Memphis . . . a subscription was commenced in Memphis last winter." He also mentions the fact that Mr. Wright had gone to New Orleans in search of funds, and hopes that a "temple dedicated to the service of the living God may soon arise here on the banks of the majestic Mississippi" to reach the hearts of "the thousands that are borne along almost daily upon its ample bosom." It is of interest to note that one of the most devoted members of the infant Calvary was Memphis' famous and eccentric mayor and trader, Ike Rawlings. James Davis, the first historian of the city, makes this wry comment:

> The old man was very piously inclined—a thorough Episcopalian in sentiment. Old Parson Wright preached the first Episcopalian sermon ever delivered in Memphis and established the first Episcopalian church. Isaac Rawlings took a great interest in it, contributed liberally to its support, and

---

11. *The Commercial Appeal*, May 7, 1922, carried a photographic copy of this letter and much material on Calvary.

[13]

attended divine service at his Church whenever his rheumatics would admit. His funeral sermon was preached by the Reverend Philip Alston, and this was the last of Isaac Rawlings.[12]

Unfortunately Mr. Wright contracted cholera on his fund-raising visit south, and died in Memphis April 27, 1835, very shortly after his return. The infant Church languished and nearly died during the next two years. It sent no delegates and made no report to the 1837 convention.

Bishop Otey visited Memphis again in the fall of 1836. In contrast to the optimism expressed during his visitation of 1834, this trip left him depressed at almost every stop. He was now working on his dream for a southern seminary, or college, but prospects were very discouraging. After preaching three days in Bolivar, he remarked: "We neither alarmed the careless, nor aroused the impenitent, nor broke the leaden slumber of infidelity." A few days later he was in Somerville. "Religion at this place," he wrote, "seems to burn with so feeble a flame as to be just ready to expire."

He found the road to Memphis thronged with Indians being moved to Mississippi. He spent the night of October 14th just outside of Memphis with the Sam Remberts, and received a "cordial welcome." The next day, ". . . rode to Memphis. The town was filled with Indians, and the people too busily engaged in traffic to think of their spiritual interests." In his project for raising money for a seminary the Bishop had his greatest success in Brownsville and Jackson but remarked that the majority of subscriptions "are made upon condition that the institution be placed within the limits of Madison County." Thus he, Leonidas Polk, and others planned a Madi-

---

12. J. Davis, *History of Memphis* (Memphis, 1873) 85. Rawlings was invariably called "Old Ike" though he died in his mid-fifties. In 1837 he freed his mulatto son William, who was baptized (July 1838) by the Rev. George Weller. Rawlings, who came from Calvert County, Maryland, imported his Episcopalianism from there. When Calvary Church reached a low ebb of three communicants (1837), Ike and his sister, Juliet, probably account for two of the three. I am indebted to Prof. James Roper for this note.

son College at Jackson, and even secured a charter from the state legislature, but what Otey called "the sudden and unprecedented catastrophe that came upon the commercial world" (i.e., the depression of 1837) killed the new scheme for a college. Calvary nearly expired too. In March 1838, when the Reverend George Weller came to take charge, he found but three communicants, no vestry and no regular place of worship. He stayed for only a year, but built the communicant list up to thirty. The true founder and builder of Calvary was the Reverend Philip Alston, who became its rector in 1839, when he was only twenty-six and still a deacon, but who, by his charm, intelligence, and consecration made it the second most important church in the diocese by the time of his sudden death in 1847.[13]

By 1839 Calvary had built a large frame chapel (50' x 20') two storeys high, with the upper storey as a parsonage (on Second Street north of its present location). The church, the Bishop reported, "will afford seats for about 250 persons." Within four years, in 1843, construction was begun, under the leadership of Mr. Alston, of the church at its present location (Adams and Second). This building was consecrated on Rogation Sunday, May 12, 1844. In Otey's Journal it is noted as "a large and commodious edifice, with seats to accommodate about 600," and that it had a fine organ. He concluded that "the condition and prospects of the congregation are in the highest degree encouraging."[14]

The congregation had hardly moved into its new church when it was found that the structure was unsafe for use because

---

13. Alston left an autobiographical note, in his own writing, now in the archives of Calvary. He was born in Warren County, North Carolina, attended Hillsboro Academy and the University of North Carolina (1824-30). Came to visit his uncle at Randolph in 1831, was confirmed by Otey at Ravenscroft 1834; attended several diocesan and one General Convention as a lay delegate. He studied with Otey '37-'38, was ordained deacon in 1838; put in charge of Calvary in 1839, and "ordained priest in the Methodist House, 1840."

14. *Journal of 1845.* The parish report mentions that Mr. Lawrence Lewis of Philadelphia sent an "acceptable present of communion plate." Communicants (1844) are listed as 96.

of the giving way of the roof. Fortunately, the building was saved by the construction of a new roof, described as "safe and substantial" in 1847, the year in which Philip Alston died. Calvary tower was erected in 1848, and its present chancel dates from 1881. Until then the sanctuary end was not noted for its beauty, for early descriptions tell that "the communion table was raised high on quite a wide platform. The pulpit and reading desk were odd enough to be funny; they looked like pockets on a school girl's apron, just two little balconies high up on the wall but with little doors behind. The stairway leading to these was outside, from the vestry."[15]

The Reverend David Page became the next incumbent, and Calvary continued to flourish and grow along with the town. Dr. Page began daily services, though these often had to be suspended because of "the badness of the streets." Indeed, the very rapid growth of Memphis (from 1200 in 1834, to 8,841 in 1850, to 22,623 in 1860) created such pressure on the Church that Calvary was forced to become the "mother of churches."[16] Like many other churches of the time, Calvary used the system of pew rents as its chief means of financial support, but by the '50's pews were completely taken up and rentals had risen so sharply that there was no room for newcomers. Many could not afford seats had they been available.[17]

---

15. *Journal of 1892.* An article on Calvary history by P. M. Radford, historiographer of the diocese. In 1850 it was discovered that the lot was deeded to Mr. Alston. This was remedied later in Chancery Court.

16. One of the reasons for Memphis' growth at this time (1850) was due to the fact that Memphis and its rival, South Memphis, were united December 3, 1849 (Ch. VII of Acts of 1849-50). South Memphis had been incorporated as a town in 1846 with Judge Sylvester Bailey as its first mayor. It was mainly developed and organized by the noted lawyer and land speculator, Robertson Topp. This city extended from Union to about where Crump Boulevard now runs. See *West Tennessee Historical Society Papers,* VIII, 96-97. Judge L. Bejack, "The Seven Cities Absorbed by Memphis."

17. Calvary, in its *Great Book,* has a chart of the pew sale for 1846, John P. Trezevant was Treasurer. On it are listed seven Trezevant pews. Other pew holders are: Harris, Wyat, Anderson, Park, Colston, Johnson, McMahon, Dashiel, Seawell, Hatch, Smith (3), Andrews, Woods, Lonsdale, Delafield, Hawkes, Williams, Moon, Armour, Watkins, Pearce, Smith, Shanks, Evans, Martin, Rose, Walker, Rowlett, Hovah, Chrisler, Philips, Rembert, Pope, Smithwick, Brinkley, Lamburon, Vaught, Kinney, Bray. Calvary's church history

The first indication of a mission being established by Calvary is found in the Convention *Journal of 1850,* where in its parish report Calvary lists $128.00 "to support a chapel in South Memphis." The Bishop reported in the same *Journal* (March 17): "in the afternoon preached in the Mission Church organized within the last year, and placed in charge of the Reverend Mr. Weller. This enterprise was commenced with very encouraging prospects of success. The friends of it purchased a lot having a house on it fitted up as a place of worship." He indicated that attendance was good but that Mr. Weller had returned to St. Louis and left it to Dr. Page, "who gives as much attention to its interests as the duties of his parish will permit." This first venture—the beginning of what later became Grace Church—seems to have languished. The next news of it is in March 28, 1853, when the Bishop reported that "a new congregation has been organized in Memphis under the name of Grace Church, by adopting articles of association and electing wardens and vestrymen on Easter Monday 28th of March." The new Church still did not meet in altogether suitable rooms, for shortly before (December 12, 1852) Bishop Otey noted, "I commenced celebrating the worship of God in Hightower Hall, a room over an oyster saloon, having also a dancing academy in an adjacent apartment. The hall is used as a billiard room all the week and is appropriated to divine worship on Sunday . . . the question arises, shall we worship in the 'house of Rimmon' or not at all."[18]

---

says there were 72 pews and 140 families in the mid-50's. Radford says "poor persons or even persons of moderate means were excluded." Pews brought in $3,000 a year to the church.

18. William Green, *Memoir of James Hervey Otey,* 55. Otey raised funds for a small organ for the church. There is no indication as to where the "house and lot" of 1850 were located. Hightower Hall was on the north side of Union between Main and Front. Grace's next location (1857 ff.) was in the second story of Hunt's China Shop on the west side of Main (331) between Union and Monroe (under Schetky), sometimes called the "Y.M.C.A. rooms" (see *Appeal,* March 18, 1857). The Rev. John Wheelock revived the church in 1864, and in 1867 the church moved to Hernando near Pontotoc (not far from the old second Presbyterian). It remained here until 1885. Then a site on Vance and Lauderdale was purchased, and the congregation used a small frame

The Grace Church of 1853 languished until 1856, when the Bishop said, "the congregation of Grace Church, which was organized some years ago, has during the past winter been revived." This time the congregation called the Rev. Mr. Schetky of Louisville, who took over his duties in July 1857. The parish was admitted to the convention in 1858 (the same year as St. Mary's and the Church of the Advent, Nashville) and started flourishingly under its new rector.

During the early fifties, when Grace Church was in its formative stage, as during the previous decade, many significant happenings were taking place in Memphis and the diocese which have a bearing on the story of St. Mary's. Even before the Bishop's first attempt with Madison College failed (1837), he turned his attention to female education (1835). After much labor he succeeded in getting the Columbia Female Institute in operation. This school became one of his joys and consolations. He was its visitor and part-time teacher and assisted the principal in the publication of a most unusual literary and family magazine, *The Guardian.* Often the Bishop would return to Columbia and to the school for consolation after long and harrowing trips not only through Tennessee, but through Mississippi, Arkansas, Louisiana, and even Oklahoma, until these states had bishops of their own. There is little wonder that his robust health and digestion began to fail under the constant strains, journeyings, and discouragements. Thus partly for reasons of health, partly from a desire to visit the Mother Church and take part in a centennial of the Society for the Propagation of the Gospel (S.P.G.), he made a long visit to England in 1851.[19]

church till it burned in 1893. Then a brick and stone parish house was used until an impressive Gothic structure was begun in 1906. This church was sold (to Mt. Nebo Baptist, colored), in the late 1930's, when Grace joined with St. Luke's.

19. There is a full description of this in Green's *Memoir,* 35-49, and a letter from Bishop Coxe of New York who accompanied him on part of the trip, and who adds detail of this journey, in *Ibid.,* 350-359. He sailed April 12, 1851, and returned to New York October 15.

When the Bishop returned to Columbia, refreshed in health and strength, he was crushed to discover, within a few days of his return, that a scandal involving the head of the Female Institute was endangering his beloved school. Since the principal confessed his guilt to Bishop Otey, there was no course open but to suspend and discipline the offender. Yet, as is often the case, the public, not knowing the facts, tended to sympathize with the culprit. Thus quite a party was formed in Columbia in defense of the principal, and the Bishop was criticized with undue severity. Life in the Columbia community became so unpleasant that Otey decided to heed the calls of his many Memphis friends, and remove with his family to Memphis. "I left the neighborhood of Columbia the 8th of November, and on the night of the 12th (1852) reached Memphis, where by the kindness of a few friends, I am provided with a comfortable house for my family, and where they are now living." There must have been heartaches at the move, but Otey wrote in his diary, "if I am in the path of duty, let me not give way to feelings."[20]

Shortly before Bishop Otey came to Memphis, another man with a very different background and experience had arrived, who was soon to become his disciple, friend, and ultimately his successor to the episcopate. This man was Charles Todd Quintard. He was descended from a Huguenot family which had settled in New Rochelle, New York, and which had later moved to Stamford, Connecticut. He began the study of medicine in the offices of the celebrated New York physicians, Drs. James Wood and Valentine Mott. He received his M.D. degree from the University Medical College (later NYU) in 1847. After spending a year in Bellevue Hospital, he moved to Athens, Georgia, to practice medicine and remained for four

20. Green, *Memoir,* 54. On this occasion he also wrote: "Why should I indulge in melancholy or depressing thoughts when in the exercise of my best judgment, and after counsel with friends, I am pursuing that course which promises to give me ability and opportunity to be most useful to my fellow men."

years. In 1851 he was called to Memphis to be the professor of physiology and pathological anatomy in the recently reorganized Memphis Medical College. He quickly made a reputation in Memphis. He gained the respect of his colleagues and of the students by his outstanding teaching; of the community for his work in pushing for the establishment—by lectures and by letters to the press—of a public library for the city, and he was made chairman of the committee to collect subscriptions for the library; he gained a national reputation for his advocacy of public health research and for his own work in studying the mortality rate of Memphis.[21]

Otey and Quintard soon became close friends, and under the Bishop's influence the public-minded physician began private study with the view of entering the ministry. Quintard became a candidate for Holy Orders in 1854, and was ordained deacon at Calvary on January 21, 1855. It was in this year that he resigned from the college, and in February faculty and students joined in a formal farewell ceremony. One of the students, B. F. Kink, presented Quintard with a Bible, and among other things said:

> We sincerely regret that the profession of medicine is about to lose you, one of its brightest ornaments; but the noble and glorious calling upon which you have entered is worthy of you and beyond all praise. We trust you will succeed in teaching the sacred precepts of the Holy Book with the same accuracy, clearness, and precision which have characterized your teaching of medical science; and we hope you may arrive at the same eminence in the one profession which you have attained in the other. We desire your prayers that we may all become good and useful men, that we may succeed in qualifying ourselves to alleviate the sufferings of our fellow beings.

The doctor made a reply "calculated to inspire the earnest young students who had so thoughtfully honored him."[22]

21. Keating, *Memphis* I, 329.
22. *W. T. H. S. Papers*, II, 63. S. R. Breusch, "Early medical history of Memphis." Quintard made the commencement address to the school in 1855.

In this same year the wife of Dr. Page of Calvary died of an epidemic which swept the town, and the Rector left Memphis for Kentucky. Bishop Otey and the Rev. T. F. Wardell then took charge of the Church, and the Bishop sent the newly ordained deacon to work in Tipton County (Ravenscroft, Covington, Randolph—the first two of which are now incorporated as Quintard parish). The Bishop did not intend to assume permanent control of Calvary, and in 1856 the congregation called Dr. Quintard to the rectorship.[23] He remained here little more than a year, going on to the newly formed Church of the Advent in Nashville. But this year at Calvary is extremely important for our story, since it was then that Calvary's second mission church—St. Mary's—was founded in order to reach the inhabitants of the suburbs of east Memphis (i.e., the Orleans, (Dunlap region).

5. FOUNDING OF ST. MARY'S

Since the two aspects of religion nearest Bishop Otey's heart were education and missions, it is not surprising to learn that soon after he arrived in Memphis a "Ladies Educational and Missionary Society" was organized at Calvary. Unfortunately no record survives of the membership of this organization which played so important a role in the founding of St. Mary's parish. Bishop Thomas F. Gailor says it was founded in 1853. It was certainly in existence by 1854, for Bishop Otey praised the group in the Convention of 1855, remarking that "the zeal and energy with which they prosecuted their truly laudable objects are worthy of high commendation." He explained how they had supported two young candidates for the ministry at Alexandria and Nashotah (Lacy Jones and Robert Shropshire,

23. During Quintard's rectorship $6,000 was expended on Calvary and a Gothic window placed in the chancel. Bishop Otey again took charge in 1858-59. In the fall of 1859, George White of Florence, Alabama, became Otey's assistant, and was made rector on January 18, 1860. He remained for over 20 years, till 1887, though Rev. D. Sessums became his assistant in April 1883.

both of whom unfortunately dropped out the next year) and had donated funds to missions.[24]

Official notice of the formation of St. Mary's is to be found in the *Journal of 1857,* in the Bishop's address:

> The Ladies Educational and Missionary Society at Memphis have continued to prosecute the objects of their association with praiseworthy energy. They have recently secured by donation from Col. Robert Brinkley a lot suitable for the site of a small church, and have through the assistance of some friends, made a contract for the erection of a building, the sittings in which are to be free for all who will choose to avail themselves of the opportunity thus furnished for the public worship of God. So far, their enterprise affords an encouraging example of what the devotion of a few apparently weak instruments, may by God's blessings on their persevering efforts, accomplish for the promotion of Christ's cause among us. In the midst of very much to depress and discourage, when I look at the state of the Church and of religion in this diocese, nothing has occurred for years past that has so filled me with thankfulness and hope for the future, as the inception and progress of this work.[25]

In 1934, when the Cathedral celebrated its 75th anniversary, Bishop Gailor gave an address reviewing the history of the parish. In it, he said that 1857-58 were remarkable years, for during this period Robert Brinkley gave land for the church; his own parents moved to Memphis; the city grew to a population of 13,000 (some say 20,000); it contained the only five-story building in Tennessee; the Memphis and Charleston Railroad was completed and two hogsheads of ocean water brought to Memphis to be pumped into the Mississippi; Nathan Bedford Forrest faced a mob of a thousand and averted a

24. *Journal of 1855,* entry for January 21; The Bishop reported that Tennessee was lowest in the list of all dioceses in the General Convention in contributions to the missionary funds of the Church, and said, "every parish in this diocese, except St. John's, Ashwood, has been aided by appropriations in years past from the Domestic Commission of Missions."

25. It is clear that in the mid-fifties Otey was growing discouraged over the progress the Church had made in his twenty years of service. Many quotations from his Journals would confirm this. The following is typical (January 6, 1856): "We have an exceedingly difficult and unpropitious field to cultivate. I have known for many years that an amount of prejudice, ignorance, and prepossession prevailed in this diocese respecting our communion, unequalled as far as my observation and information go, in any state of the Union."

lynching; Col. Montgomery completed the telegraph lines to Tuscumbia, Helena, and Little Rock; the Atlantic cable was completed; all the banks in town went broke (a result of the collapse of railroad speculation) ; the streets of Memphis were in a deplorable condition, a mule drowning in a mud hole at Main and Monroe, and a yoke of oxen having to be pried out of the mud at Main and Madison.[26]

Robert Campbell Brinkley, who donated the land for the church (1856), has been called "one of the little-known great men of Memphis." He and his descendants have played such prominent roles in the history and work of St. Mary's Church, from its very beginning to the present, that his memory should be held in respect. He was born in Chatham County, North Carolina. His father, an ardent Methodist, came to Madison County in 1834. Robert was educated at Bingham School, Asheville, but returned to Tennessee and studied law with Foster and Fogg, the outstanding law firm at Nashville. F. B. Fogg was a prominent churchman as well as lawyer, and a charter member of Christ Church. His influence led Brinkley to become an Episcopalian.[27] In 1841 Brinkley married Anne Overton, the daughter of Judge John Overton, one of Memphis' original proprietors, hence she inherited extensive property in the city. Fogg sent young Brinkley to Memphis on business, and he remained to become one of her most outstanding citizens and business men.[28]

---

26. *The Commercial Appeal,* January 14, 1934. It was also the year that Bishop Otey refused to consecrate a church at Riverside, because of the profusion of crosses, and candlesticks.

A reporter noted that at the anniversary meeting there were forty-nine members who had worshipped in the old wooden church (torn down in 1898), and that special honor was given the oldest members; Bishop Gailor (baptized in 1866), Mrs. Alice Trezevant Collier (baptized in 1858) ; and Mrs. Albert Forrest (baptized in 1859).

27. Mr. Fogg attended nearly all the early conventions, and was Bishop Otey's chief legal advisor. He procured the charter for the diocese and for the University of the South. He was also one of the trustees of the projected Madison College.

28. Robert Brinkley married twice. He had two children by Anne Overton, Hugh Lawson White Brinkley and Anne Brinkley, who married Col. Robert B. Snowden, who also moved to Memphis and became a leading financier, developer,

Keating, the most voluminous historian of Memphis, called Brinkley "one of the wisest, most prudent and sagacious of her citizens . . . the owner of a great estate which he managed with consummate ability, guided by a large public spirit. He was an amiable gentleman of agreeable manners, upright in all his dealings, full of enterprise, and a leader who moved toward the goal he set without faltering for a moment." Later he adds, "his private acts of charity and beneficence are worthy of his public conduct."[29]

Brinkley was also a close friend of Bishop Otey (they were both staunch Whigs), and his mansion, in which he dispensed lavish hospitality, occupied a large block at the corner of Poplar and Manassas, extending to Adams. He owned much land in this section, and was therefore happy to give this ground for the church, and later to let the Bishop have the land adjoining it for his home.

Unfortunately for the historian of the Cathedral, all vestry books of the early period of the church (1858-80) have been lost or destroyed; and since no diocesan *Journals* were published between 1860-65, information on this period is at best fragmentary and incomplete. The deed conveying the land to the church is therefore important, and worth inserting, since one of its clauses was to cause considerable trouble at a later time. It is dated May 10, 1858 (recorded May 15), i.e., after the chapel had been built, and reads as follows:

> Whereas at a meeting of the vestry of St. Mary's Church of the city of Memphis, Shelby County, Tennessee, held on the 12th day of April 1858 at the usual place of meeting, a

and benefactor of St. Mary's. Brinkley's second marriage was to Elizabeth Mhoon of Alabama. He had five children by this marriage, James, Lucile, Robert, and Bette Brinkley (who married Charles C. Currier, for so many years organist and chapter member of the cathedral) and William J. Brinkley. The descendants of the Brinkley and Snowden families are very numerous, and are interwoven with Memphis and Cathedral history. An article in the Gailor Memorial edition (1925) of the *Tennessee Churchman*, 101 ff. contains an account of the family connections.

29. Keating, *Memphis* I, 322 and III, 191-95. He developed roads, railroads, and the "finest 4-storey block of buildings in the west."

resolution was adopted to the effect that the Right Revd. James H. Otey Bishop of Tennessee be appointed trustee for the benefit and use of the members of the said St. Mary's Church, to receive and hold title to the lot on which a house known as St. Mary's Church has been erected . . . Therefore I, Robert C. Brinkley do hereby give, transfer and convey to the Right Reverend James H. Otey and his heirs forever, for the use and benefit of the members of the St. Mary's Church, to be used by them as a church lot or as a lot for a parsonage should they see fit to erect one thereon, the following described lot of land (here follows the technical description of boundaries) . . . containing 311/1000 of an acre, to have to hold the same for the purpose aforesaid, to him, the said James H. Otey and his heirs forever. And, I the said Robert C. Brinkley do covenant and bind myself, my heirs and representatives to warrant and forever defend the title to the said lot to the said James H. Otey and his heirs against the lawful claims of all persons whatever. (Book 33, page 233).

The trouble arose over the expression "his heirs forever." It would seem obvious that Mr. Brinkley's intention was to leave the land to Otey's spiritual heirs, the bishops of the diocese. But years later, in the 1870's, the lawyers of the diocese had to procure quit claims from all surviving Otey heirs to clear the title.[30]

In some of the shorter historical sketches of St. Mary's it has been erroneously stated that the land was donated for the church because it happened to be next to Bishop Otey's home. Actually the order was the reverse; the church came first, and the Bishop moved next door to it. The land for the church was promised in 1856, the little chapel erected in the summer and early fall of 1857, and the first service to which I can find reference was on November 15, though there were probably earlier ones.[31] The *Appeal* for November 22 refers first to the Church as the "Mission Church on Poplar," and in its column of announcements of various church services for that day men-

---

30. See *Book 1482,* 163 (Mar. 13, 1878), for the release. It contains the phrase "(they) have this day bargained and sold and do hereby transfer, assign and convey release and quit claim unto the said Convention of the Protestant Episcopal Church in the Diocese of Tennessee."

31. *Journal of 1858.* "Read prayers and preached in St. Mary's Church in Memphis, and same day baptized three children."

[25]

tions "the Reverend William C. Stout officiating, and in the evening the Reverend Charles T. Quintard." The notice for the Thanksgiving Day service (November 26th) shows that the service was conducted by Dr. Quintard, and it further announced that "a collection will be taken up, the proceeds to be applied to the church debt." An *Appeal* item for November 29 is particularly important since it indicates that Thanksgiving Day was the actual day of the St. Mary's organization (and possibly the day it received its name). It reads:

> The Mission Church on Poplar Street. This Church which has been erected by the pious zeal of the ladies belonging to the Episcopal Church of this city, was organized Thanksgiving Day by the election of wardens and vestrymen. The Church is called St. Mary's, and the Reverend Richard Hines has been chosen rector. Mr. Hines has arrived in the city and will preach at St. Mary's this morning. The seats are all free, the expenses of the Church are defrayed by the offering of the congregation.

The day that St. Mary's observes as its founding date is Ascension Day, May 13, 1858. This is the day the church was consecrated. A description of this in the Bishop's Journal gives us a clear and succinct picture of the ceremony:

> With the rites and solemnities prescribed, I this day set apart and consecrated to the service of Almighty God, St. Mary's Church, Memphis, according to the order and usages of the Protestant Episcopal Church in the United States. Morning Prayer was read by the Rev. Messrs. Harrison [St. Luke's, Jackson], and Schetky [Grace]; the lessons by the Rev. Dr. White [Calvary]; Ante-Communion by myself; the epistle and gospel by Rev. Mr. Wheelock [St. Mary's, Covington]; the sermon by Rev. Mr. Pickett [St. James', Bolivar], and the communion was administered by Rev. Mr. Hines and myself. Thus has a work begun by a few ladies of Calvary Church a few years ago in faith and humble reliance upon divine help, by God's blessing, been brought to a most happy and successful conclusion. The seats are all free, and the minister's support is provided out of contributions of the congregation, aided to a small extent this year by the Domestic Committee on Missions.[32]

---

32. *Journal of 1858*, 45. In 1945, the Rev. W. J. Whitfield of Holy Comforter Church of Decatur, Georgia, sent to Bishop Dandridge a copy of his grandfather's sermon preached upon this occasion. Since he mistook the date—

The *Appeal* the next day gave this brief and rather indefinite notice of the event:

> St. Mary's Church on Poplar Street yesterday was a most interesting affair. Bishop Otey, assisted by half a dozen clergymen, officiated. An admirable sermon was preached by a Reverend gentleman from Pontotoc. The Church is an edifice of unusual architectural attractions, it is Gothic.

Other Episcopal churches in Memphis, in their church notices of the day (May 13) indicated that their services would be omitted "in consequence of concurrence in the consecration of St. Mary's, where Dr. Otey desires the presence of the clergy and congregation at 10 o'clock."

St. Mary's, the twenty-fifth church established in the diocese, was admitted to the Convention of 1858, which met at LaGrange, May 26-28. The first three lay delegates, Messrs. William Armour, J. A. Anderson, and John P. Trezevant, were all in attendance. Dr. Hines appeared on the last day, and was immediately made assistant to the secretary of the convention.

Bishop Otey, since his arrival in Memphis, had been living in a suburban residence near the city. From his diary we learn that this dwelling was consumed by fire on January 20, 1858, but with no injury to his family. "This untoward event," he wrote, "has deranged all the plans I formed for the future, and led to my removal to the city of Memphis. I hope I have enough left out of the remains of my property to provide my family with a comfortable home. My present home is temporary."[33]

The home that he bought was known in future as "The

---

and thought it was written in 1885, (instead of 1858)—little attention was paid to it. The text was: "How dreadful is this place. This is none other but the House of God, and this is the Gate of Heaven." Mr. Pickett later taught at Sewanee.

33. *Journal of 1858*, entry of January 20. Green's *Memoir*, 60, mentions that he had trouble with one of the overseers of his "farm" near Memphis. This "farm" was 85 acres on the Pigeon Roost Road (Lamar). An old surveyor's book of C. C. Burke (p. 231) recently given to Southwestern, shows this plot. It was subdivided in 1866. It adjoined the Warfield subdivision and was near where the Pigeon Roost Road (Lamar) crossed the Memphis and Charleston R.R. (Southern) tracks (i.e., near where Glenview Park is today). It was four miles from the then city limits.

Bishop's House" and was on the site of the present Diocesan House, just west of the church. In his will, Otey deeded it to the Convention.[34] Again there is some doubt as to whether this home was given to the Bishop by Mr. Brinkley (or by others) or whether he bought it. The original deed (Bk. 51, 631, November 17, 1859) indicates the place was purchased for $5,010, and from Green's account of Otey's life, the home seems to have been in part, at least, a gift.

> In 1860 he was admitted to the enjoyment of the new and commodious residence which had been built for him in an eligible part of Memphis; and his remaining days would have passed in quiet and comfort, if he had not seen too plainly the dark clouds of war about to overshadow the land.

The close conjunction of the Bishop's House with the infant St. Mary's was undoubtedly to play an important role in its future conversion into the Cathedral.

---

34. Book 57, 569 (August 23, 1866) registers the transfer. William B. Miller and R. C. Brinkley as Otey's executors, "transfer and convey to the Convention . . . for the residence of the Bishop of the said Diocese (the described property) always to be the residence of the Bishop . . . and not for other purposes whatsoever."

CHAPTER II

CIVIL WAR AND RECONSTRUCTION—
DEAN HINES

WITH THE CONSECRATION of the new church, with the arrival of the first rector, and with Bishop Otey established in his new home next door to the church, it may be well to pause to consider how the subsequent history of St. Mary's may best be treated. I have thought it wise to continue with a more or less chronologically arranged narrative of the parish—the work and achievement of the various bishops, deans, Sisters of St. Mary, and other clergy connected with the Church, perhaps leaving the main narrative, at times, in order to describe building activities which have shifted and altered the structures occupying three contiguous lots on Poplar, from west to east, the Bishop's lot, the Church lot, and the Sisters' property.

Also, before embarking upon my narrative I should like to call attention to certain general factors which, it seems to me, have been influential in determining the course of St. Mary's development. In the first place the Church has, throughout its entire history, remained in the same location. Many churches have moved with the changing tides of population, but St. Mary's has "stuck it out" in the same spot and has attempted to meet the altering needs and the problems arising from the changing social and economic patterns, as these have arisen.

A second factor of considerable influence in St. Mary's development has been, paradoxically enough, its relative poverty. Professor Arnold Toynbee has pointed out in his *Study of History* that for states and civilizations (and one might add "churches") to grow and flourish, a challenge is needed. If the challenge is too severe, and the resources too weak, that civilization (or church) must fail; while on the other hand, if circumstances are too favorable, leaders will not develop the strength which comes of struggle. In more specific terms, the relative poverty of the parish has meant that funds were not available to tempt famous rectors with established reputations. The parish has, in general, called young men for its leaders. Most of these have stayed for ten years or more and have made their reputations by dint of meeting difficult situations—though it is somewhat painful to note the meagre salaries and the deprivations they have had to endure. It is remarkable that so few brief rectorships are to be noted. Another aspect of this "poverty factor" is the fact that it has called forth devoted and almost superhuman effort on the part of many chapter members and parishioners who have had the task of keeping the parish and the rector going.

A third factor, and one of great importance in our history, has been that from an early date St. Mary's was made the "Bishop's Church," or Cathedral. This has brought both tangible advantages, and some rather intangible problems. It has indeed been an asset and a blessing to have been so closely associated with the great and godly men who have been the bishops of this diocese. Then, too, there have been associated with the Cathedral certain clergy or canons—for short or long periods—who have left their mark not only on the parish but on the diocese. On the other hand, the burden of providing the building, the equipment and accoutrements which are associated with the title of "Cathedral," has to a great extent fallen upon the chapter and the parishioners of St. Mary's. And to this day the problem of what "the Cathedral Idea" is, and of what should be the relationship of the Cathedral to parish and to diocese, has never been fully solved, though much thought and many diverse ideas have been suggested at different times.

A fourth and somewhat unique factor in the life of the Cathedral has been its long association with the Sisters of St. Mary. Bishop Quintard effected this relationship about the time St. Mary's became the Cathedral, and it continued until 1912. The devoted and heroic work of the Sisters during the yellow fever epidemics, their work in the Church Home and in St. Mary's School, their life of prayer and devotion, gave to the parish a unique and lasting quality. Another feature of St. Mary's which, while not unique, has characterized its activity has been its continuing sense of missionary responsibility.

Bishop Otey made several trips to North Carolina in the mid-fifties and on one of these persuaded the Rev. Richard Hines to assume the responsibility of the newly erected chapel then on the eastern frontier of the city. Hines was only in the thirties at the time, but as he wore a full dark beard, he looked much older. It accentuated his rather gaunt, austere and prophetic look. Unfortunately, since the vestry minutes for this period are lost (except for three years, 1867-70), and since the convention printed no records (1861-65), we have to assemble what little we know of him from scant sources. Like the Bishop, he had been educated at the University of North Carolina, and had been a teacher. Bishop Otey seems to have treated him almost as a son, and he became a sort of "fidus Achates" to the Bishop. Even before the war he became secretary to the diocesan convention, was head of the Diocesan Book Society and was on other important diocesan committees. He was with Otey to the end, and preached the first "Otey Sermon" after the war. But he was, first and foremost, a great teacher. Bishop Gailor's family moved to Memphis just about the time St. Mary's was founded, and as they lived near the Church, young Thomas soon fell under the influence of Dr. Hines. In his book, *Some Memories*, Bishop Gailor gives us this informative picture of the first rector:

[31]

The outstanding personality of my early school days was that of the Reverend Richard Hines D.D. . . . . Dr. Hines was a born teacher. He had been a tutor in the University of North Carolina, and his wife, Helen Huske, was a charming lady.

After the war Dr. Hines supplemented his rectorship of St. Mary's by opening a school for boys and girls in a building on the Church's grounds, and for some years the school flourished with an attendance of more than a hundred boys and girls. It was a fine school. Every Friday we had to learn the Collect for the next Sunday, and every morning we attended a short service in the Church. There I learned my Latin grammar, and there I began to understand what the Church meant.

Dr. Hines' Sunday School was famous. He inspired young people to study. We could recite all the Collects in the Prayer Book, and many of us knew the 39 Articles by heart. Some of the boys could recite whole chapters from the Bible and even the Burial Office. There was no limit to the subjects he made us learn in Church history and the Prayer Book. After the death of his wife in 1868, he closed the school.[1]

When Dr. Quintard became bishop we often find him lavishing praise on the extraordinary performances of Dr. Hines' Sunday School pupils.

Dr. Hines faced a difficult and discouraging situation at St. Mary's, for his rectorship (1858-71) coincided with a depression, the Civil War, and the unsettled reconstruction years. Parish reports to the convention were very indefinite in those days, but from the few that remain we see that he listed 38 communicants for his parish in 1858 and a salary "entitled to receive" of $1,500, though offerings for that year were only $474.31. By 1860 the communicant list had only risen to 55; in 1868 he reported "about 90," but by the time of his departure (1870) this figure had fallen back to 68, while the report on

---

1. *Op. Cit.* 18. Bishop Gailor then recounts his own subsequent education as follows: One year under Dr. Ashbel Brown, a friend of Dr. Hines from N. C.; then one year under Mr. * * * "a stern and cruel man." From 1869-72 he studied with Capt. T. C. Anderson, principal of the High School, who let him stay and study after school hours. He finished when he was under 16. In the summer of 1873 he had yellow fever and partly for reasons of health he was sent north to study at Racine College under the famous Dr. DeKoven. In 1876 he entered General Theological Seminary, and as a seminarian assisted Mr. Harris at the Cathedral and Mr. Parsons at St. Lazarus in 1877. The Bishop told Miss Ellen Correll that making students memorize the Burial Office was the punishment Dr. Hines inflicted on students who did not know their lessons.

St. Mary's Cathedral

in Pictures

1858 — 1958

The Cathedral 1958

Interior 1958

JAMES HERVEY OTEY, The First Bishop of Tennessee

Rt. Rev. JAS HERVEY OTEY, DD. LLD.

First Bishop
of the
HOLY CATHOLIC
CHURCH
In the Diocese of
Tennessee.
CONSECRATED
Jan. 14, 1834;
Entered into rest
April 23, 1863.

Bishop Otey
and the Memorial Plaque
in the Cathedral

SISTER HUGHETTA
She served through the yellow fever
epidemic of 1878.

R. C. BRINKLEY
who donated the land on which the
Cathedral is built.

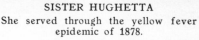

Bishop Quintard's Residence, Clergy House, the Cathedral, Sisters' Chapel and School
(1871-1898)

RICHARD HINES
First Rector 1857-1871

His finger pointed the way.

Old Bishop's House (the Otey Home), the old Cathedral, Chapel and School. (1894)

The 1894 Interior

CHARLES TODD QUINTARD
Second Bishop of Tennessee

"First Chaplain of all the Confederacy—
He served the living and the dead."

DEAN GEORGE C. HARRIS

DEAN WILLIAM KLEIN

THE CHOIR OF ST. MARY'S CATHEDRAL. C. 1875
(The first vested choir)

Left Side, reading l. to r. (seated), Frank Cruse, Rev. George C. Harris, Thomas F. Gailor, Chas. C. Currier, organist. (Standing), Herbert Dammann and James Richardson.

Right Side, reading l. to r., George Harris, Jr., Albert Thumel, George Yerger, Spence Finley and Gwyn Yerger.

THOMAS F. GAILOR
Bishop of Tennessee (1898-1935)
President of the National Council (1919-1925)

The Cathedral was completed in his honor (1926).

ST. MARY'S SCHOOL AND CHAPEL (c. 1900)

CATHEDRAL GUILD PROJECT (1906)
Standing, l. to r., Miss Prichard, Mrs. G. Cunningham, Mrs. Gwyn Yerger, Mrs. Gilfillan,
Miss Dee Coffee, Miss Carrie Wood, Mrs. Schultz
Seated, l. to r., Mrs. Morgan, Ethel Hill, unidentified.

Bond No. 1 of the issue
to build the superstructure (1906).

Cathedral construction gets under way (1906).

St. Mary's Cathedral Church School Choir
organized by Mrs. W. I. Moody

Reading down, row 1, Emmadora Willingham, Vera
Fitzpatrick and Mary Chandler; down, row 2, Lucile
Robison, Julia Moody, Lucia Burch and Celeste Glenn;
down, row 3, Mary Hunter, Frank Hoyt Gailor and Mary
Manees; down, row 4, Winifred Haines, Herbert Esch,
Sarah Berry and Louise Oliver; down, row 5, Perlie
Moody, Charles Christian and Elizabeth Thurman; down,
row 6, Caroline Davey, Lottie Rheiner, Harriet Bond and
Lottie Saugerhaus; down, row 7, Kate Davey, Louise
Glenn and Minor Martin.

BOLTON SMITH

W. I. MOODY

JACOB A. EVANS

WILLIAM KYSER

Leaders
In Completing
The Cathedral
1925

CHARLES N. BURCH

FRANK A. BAUM

A. S. CALDWELL

P. STENNING COATE

BISHOP
EDMUND PENDLETON
DANDRIDGE

BISHOP JAMES MATTHEW MAXON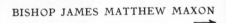

BISHOP TROY BEATTY

Len Howard, artist and designer
of the Cathedral windows.

Exterior

Completed
structure
of 1926

Interior

Bishop's House (Gailor's), Cathedral and renovated Chapel (1934).

Cathedral Junior Choir (revived by Canon James R. Sharp, 1938).

Christmas Pageants

BISHOP
THEODORE NOTT BARTH

BISHOP JOHN VANDER HORST

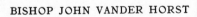

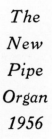

The
New
Pipe
Organ
1956

Organist
WILLIAM L. BRICE

St. Mary's Chapel
1958

The Choir
1957

Some Twentieth Century Deans

JAMES CRAIK MORRIS

ISRAEL HARDING NOE

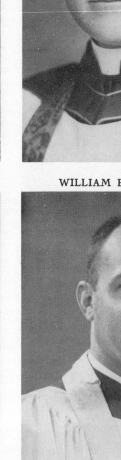

HAROLD BROWN HOAG

WILLIAM EVAN SANDERS

❧ The Chapter and Clergy of the Cathedral—1958 ❧

THE CHAPTER

Seated, left to right: W. Clark Williams, William M. Barr, Miles Nevin, William R. Hudgins, William Lea, William W. Deupree, P. C. Clarke, J. M. Patten, Sr., W. I. Moody, Russell Perry, William P. Embry, Rembert S. Donelson, John How; *Standing, left to right:* John R. McCarroll, Chris T. Ellis, Mercer E. West III, The Rev. John H. Davis, The Very Rev. William E. Sanders, The Rev. Canon Frank Q. Cayce, The Rev. Canon Robert W. Knox, The Rev. M. C. Nichols, C. Lomax Springfield, Dr. William H. Morse.

THE CLERGY

Left to right: The Rev. John H. Davis, The Rev. Canon Frank Q. Cayce, The Very Rev. William E. Sanders, The Rev. Canon Robert W. Knox, The Rev. M. C. Nichols.

← ELLEN CORRELL
Director of Religious
Education

MRS. THOMAS R.
LILL →
Librarian of the Gailor
Memorial Library

The Altar

his salary indicates it was $1,350 in arrears and the parish $3,500 in debt. It was then frequently the habit of rectors to add little personal notes to their reports. These often give clues to the local situation as well as to the personality of the rector. To his first report Hines added, "The hopes of the congregation were realized by the consecration of the Church on Ascension Day. Services are held three times on each Sunday, the night service being for the servants." His next message was, "My labors have been blessed with little fruit. I hope the past is not a criterion by which to judge the future."

Condensed summaries of our parish reports may be found in the Appendix, but I will insert here two full reports of Dr. Hines in order to show the difficulties he confronted, and to indicate that even at this early period the parish was not unmindful of others. Here is the statement for 1860:

Baptisms 12, confirmations 7, communicants 55, burials 4, Sunday School teachers 5, pupils 30.

Collections—Communion alms	$ 78.84	
Weekly offerings and other ways	$1240.38	total $1319.22

Expenses

Support of episcopate	$ 150.00	
Domestic missions	25.75	
Foreign missions	35.00	
St. Mark's Beaver Dam, Wisconsin	15.50	
Episcopal church, Fairfield, Iowa	25.00	
Society for increase of the ministry	50.00	
Poor	550.00	
Organ fund	275.00	
Other purposes	191.97	total $1319.22
Amount of salary	$1500.00	

J. P. Trezevant, Treas.

This is the report for 1869.

Baptisms 15, burials 5, marriages 6, confirmations 14, communicants—about 75, Sunday School teachers and children about 75.

Appropriations

Support of the episcopate	$ 150.00
Contingent fund	15.00
Church charity fund	150.00
Others	75.00

Rector's salary..................proceeds of offertory
Arrears of salary....................about $1,350.00
Indebtedness ....about $3,000.00

"In this church there are daily Morning and Evening Prayer throughout the year. The Holy Communion is celebrated every Sunday and on all Holy Days. For six months instruction was given twice a week to colored persons. I performed missionary duty at Ridgeway every Friday for several months.

God's loving kindness and mercy have followed me all the days of my life. To him be all honor and glory through Jesus Christ our Lord.

Richard Hines D.D. Dean[2]

As has been pointed out, hardly had St. Mary's been founded, and the Bishop retired from his rectorship of Calvary to his new home near the Church, when the clouds of war began to hover ominously on the horizon. Bishop Otey and Dr. Hines were the two clerical delegates from Tennessee to the General Convention of 1859, held in Richmond, Virginia. Since this Convention did not issue a pastoral letter, the diocesan convention requested that Bishop Otey draft one. He did so, closing with these significant words:

I cannot let this opportunity pass without calling to your notice the threatening aspect which our civil affairs have assumed, and offering a word of earnest entreaty and affectionate counsel . . . late events demonstrate most clearly how

---

2. By contrast one might compare these reports with the Calvary report of 1866, the year so many churches emerged from the war destroyed or ruined. Dr. White wrote "The report which I ought to make would embrace a period of nearly six years. I am not prepared to make an accurate report, will do so in due time. The Church of which I am Rector is in flourishing condition. Church out of debt, congregation good." He reported "communicants—over 400; salary—much too small—$3,000."

extensive and fearful the agitation, how direful the consequences which a few wicked and fanatical men under pretext
of philanthropy and religion can bring upon a whole country.

He urged his people to labor diligently by prayer, by words
and by deeds to maintain a peaceful attitude.[3]

Not even the clouds of war could deter the Bishop from
his passion for Christian education, and on the very eve of the
conflict he, along with many of the leading members of Calvary
and St. Mary's, obtained a charter from the Tennessee General
Assembly to incorporate a girl's school to be known as St.
Mary's College. Due to the coming of the war this institution
never developed, but perhaps its memory lived in the later
creation of Bishop Quintard and the Sisters.[4]

Bishop Otey and Dr. Hines were both Whigs and Union-
ists. In fact the majority of Memphians in 1859 and 1860 were
overwhelmingly Unionist in sentiment.[5] Yet even after the firing
on Fort Sumter (April 1861), the Bishop hoped for a peaceful
separation, and as late as May 10, 1861 wrote a long letter to
the Secretary of State, Seward, begging him to suspend
hostilities.[6]

---

3. The two pastoral letters he wrote, in 1860, and in 1861, bear the fol-
lowing titles: 1) *A Pastoral Letter addressed to the members of the Protestant
Episcopal Church in the Diocese of Tennessee,* by the Rt. Rev. James H. Otey
D.D., LL.D. Bishop of the Diocese. Signed Memphis, December 15, 1859
(Nashville 1860), and 2) *A Pastoral Letter to the clergy and laity of the
Protestant Episcopal Church in the Diocese of Tennessee,* by the Bishop of the
same at the request of the Convention of A. D. 1861 (Memphis 1861).

4. The act of incorporation is in twelve articles, and may be found in
Chapter 158 of the Tennessee Acts (33rd General Assembly, in 1859-60). It
was passed March 21, 1860. The list of commissioners to receive subscriptions
were: George White, Richard Hines, J. W. Rogers, J. P. Trezevant, A. O.
Harris, W. R. Taylor, Ira Hall, Frederic Smith, William B. Cook, Charles
Abercrombie, John Pope, C. J. Selden, J. C. Lanier, John W. Fowler, R. C.
Brinkley, W. B. Richmond, O. B. Parker, J. Hallum, Lewis Shanks, Shepherd
Ashe and William Rogers. I am indebted to Professor Buford Utley for a copy
of this act.

5. For example in the election of 1860, Memphis voted 2,200 for Douglas,
1300 for Bell, and only 572 for Breckenridge. The visits of Yancey and Jefferson
Davis to Memphis in 1859 had been coolly received. After the Deep South began
to secede and after Lincoln's call for volunteers sentiment shifted. Troops began
to drill, ladies began to organize societies.

6. Green, *Memoir,* 166, quotes the Bishop's diary for May 10, "write a
letter to Mr. Seward . . . read it to my friend Robert Brinkley who approves
of it highly, and asks for a copy to be sent the *Journal of Commerce* in New
York.

During the winter of 1860 and the early months of 1861, sentiment throughout the South and especially in Memphis changed rapidly. Many congregations and clergy were now unwilling to pray for the President of the United States. Though Otey had great sympathy for the southern cause, he felt—before the outbreak of hostilities—that it was not within his power to grant a dispensation from the prayer for the President in Morning Prayer. In spite of this many churches did omit the prayer, while others found a more legal solution by substituting Ante-Communion or Holy Communion for this service. This seems to have been St. Mary's action as may be seen from its advertisement in the *Appeal*.

> Holy Communion will be administered next Sunday. Morning Prayer will not be said, and thus without violation of the Constitutions Canons and Rubrics of the Church, the service will be eminently adapted to the times.

It was a trying year for the Bishop. His beloved wife died on June 4; the Church seemed about to divide; and war fever was everywhere. At the request of the diocesan convention of 1861, which met in Somerville, and whose Journal was destroyed, he issued another pastoral letter in June (the month Tennessee seceded) in which he inveighed against the evils of the abolitionists, justified the necessity of meeting force with force, and called upon all the churches to establish a weekly service, on Fridays, of fasting and prayer, and recommended the use of the Litany and of two prayers which he wrote, "In Time of War and Tumult," and "For Those in Service." In the letter were selected Psalms, and other prayers for family and camp use, and for occasions of victory or defeat. Finally at the request of convention, he permitted the substitution of "Confederate States" for "United States" in the prayer for the President.[7]

In 1861 the southern bishops, all natives of Virginia or North Carolina, confronted the issue of separation. In March,

7. Keating, *Memphis* I, 503.

Bishop Elliot of Georgia issued a call for a meeting of southern bishops and clergy in Montgomery for July 3. Fourteen clergy and eleven lay delegates attended, but little was done there and the matter was postponed to another meeting in Columbia, S. C., October 16-20. Here Bishop Polk, the old friend and collaborator of Otey, took a firm stand that the Church should follow nationality, and called for a separate Church for the Confederate States. Bishop Otey and some others did not desire to go this far. Accompanied by the faithful Hines he attended the Columbia meeting. It was while discussing the proposed constitution of the new Church that Dr. Hines made a proposal which gives us an insight into Otey's churchmanship. Hines moved that the name of the Church be "The Reformed Catholic Church." He was only supported by Bishops Otey, Green and Atkinson, and by one lay delegate. Otey's devotion to the Catholic—but not Roman—ideal is also witnessed by the fact of the inscription he composed for his tomb, "First Bishop of the Holy Catholic Church in Tennessee."[8]

In the summer of 1862, when Memphis fell to the Federal gunboats, the Bishop was in Mobile visiting his sick son. He returned in October to find the Federal troops in command, and to discover that his own home had been ransacked of most of its funiture and clothing by his departing slaves. It was a bitter blow to the lonely man: "I do not regret the departure of my servants . . . I pity them . . . I endeavored to treat them always humanely. They had as comfortable rooms as myself. If they can do better by leaving me they are free to do so."

---

8. See J. B. Chesire, *The Church in the Confederate States* (New York, 1912), 41. He maintains that Tennessee and Texas never fully adhered to the division.

Much has been written on Otey's churchmanship. It would be a mistake to classify him by the rather meaningless terms of "high" or "low." He was a follower of the 17th century Laudians, and was influenced by the writings of the Oxford Reformers, believing in the Apostolic Ministry, the sacraments, and the Catholic aspect of the Church, but he strongly disapproved of the trappings, crosses, ritualism, etc., on one occasion refusing to consecrate and over- elaborate church. But he disliked the rabid protestant wing as represented by the Evangelical Knowledge Society. He thought that under frontier conditions services should be as simple as possible.

General Sherman treated the Bishop and Dr. Hines with kindness and respect. He sometimes attended services, and did not require the loyalty oath of the Bishop. He permitted him and Hines to visit hospitals and prisoners. But the next year the Bishop's strength gave way. He was ministered to in his last days, with filial affection by his "faithful and beloved presbyter," Dr. Hines, who administered to him the Easter Communion, and a few days later, the last rites of the Church (April 23). In his address to the Convention of 1866, Dr. Quintard painted this vivid picture of Otey's last days:

> He requested that the General Confession might be repeated slowly. He clasped the cup with eager but trembling hands . . . and with eyes uplifted to heaven said, "I call upon all of you to bear witness that my only hope for salvation is in the merits of the Lord Jesus Christ." He afterwards remarked, "I never felt in all my life such readiness to depart" . . . After a few lingering days . . . in the midst of his wanderings a passage of scripture or any portion of our Church service repeated to him never failed to bring calmness to his mind and intelligence to his eyes. And even at an hour when he was supposed to be dying, and the power of articulation seemed to be gone, as his faithful presbyter was commending his soul to God in the beautiful language of the Prayer Book, there came—just audible and no more—"Our Father who art in Heaven." And so he departed.[9]

The funeral was conducted at Calvary, and the Bishop was buried in Elmwood Cemetery until after the war, when his body was removed to the churchyard of St. John's, Ashwood, where other members of his family were buried.

How Dr. Hines and St. Mary's managed their affairs during the last two years of the War, it is difficult to determine. Bishop Smith made a visit to Tennessee in 1864, and Bishop Hopkins was in Memphis in 1865. In the latter year, after the war had ended, the Standing Committee of the diocese called

---

9. *Journal of 1866*, 33-40. Green, *Memoir*, 105. The Oteys had nine children. Six survived the Bishop; two sons and four married daughters. Some writers accuse Otey of toying with spiritualism in his latter days. There was much interest in the subject in Memphis just before the war and Otey did attend some seances. He makes it clear in his own words that he did so only to investigate the phenomenon. He confessed it was amazing, but said if they were spirits, they were evil ones. Green, *Op. Cit.*, 131; Keating, *Memphis*, I, 370.

a convention in Nashville (September 6-8) for the purpose of electing a new bishop. Dr. Hines was again made secretary, and actively supported the election of Quintard, being on the committee to notify the new bishop of his election. St. Mary's sent three delegates, Peter Wager, Z. Grey and Stanley Dashiel. The convention was saddened and shocked to learn of the sudden death of Mr. Dashiel en route to Nashville. At the convention, Dr. White of Calvary brought in the first of what was to prove a long series of resolutions aimed at dividing the diocese, but no General Convention ever approved of the plan. Soon after his election the new Bishop made his way to Philadelphia for his consecration (October 11, 1865). As an ex-chaplain of the Confederacy he no doubt went with qualms about the nature of his reception, but was delighted to discover that the Church accepted the theory that the South had never in fact dropped out. He was also pleased that one of his consecrators was the Bishop of Montreal, Canada. We have met the new Bishop before, as the Memphis physician who became priest under Otey's guidance, a former rector of Calvary and of the Church of the Advent; and the ex-chaplain, doctor, and occasionally fighter in the First Tennessee Regiment. As chaplain, he baptized and confirmed several generals, and buried four after the battle of Franklin. Bishop Maxon quotes a veteran who once told him, "Wall when things was sort of quiet he preached to the boys, when thar was sick and wounded, he doctored, and when the Yanks pushed us hard, he tuk a gun and fit."

Bishop Gailor, in his *Some Memories,* gives us this picture of Quintard:

> He was a man of striking personality and unusual force, whom to see and talk with once, was to remember forever. This clean carved, positive individuality gave him great power as a preacher, but even more power in private conversation . . . His culture was so wide and varied, his humor so buoyant, his physical nature so alert, that he was a very prince of hospitality. Few men combined such gifts of mind and heart

[39]

. . . English papers described him as an American without a trace of provincialism, and so cosmopolitan that England claimed him as her own.

In another place he adds, "The first thing for which Bishop Quintard stood as Bishop of the Church, was the cause of Christian Education, the second thing for which he stood . . . was loyalty to the Church as a Divine and Catholic institution." He also says that he "overflowed with kindness," was impulsive and plain spoken, but never really unkind.

The new Bishop made his first visitation to Memphis soon after his consecration, in the fall of 1865. He remained in Memphis during the early months of 1866 also. Throughout the state the Church was in a pitiable plight; buildings were wrecked, property lost, and the infant Sewanee in ruins. In many ways, Memphis presented a contrast, for though parishes, buildings and congregations suffered, the town's early surrender, and her occupation by Federal troops, brought a specious prosperity to some. Thus the town was expanding, bustling with activity and overcrowded. There was a considerable social upheaval, for war profiteers, carpet-baggers, and ex-Federals mingled on the streets with the newly arrived hordes of freed Negroes and with the returning wounded or ruined ex-Confederates. Thus the city presented what might be called "a challenging situation." Fortunately Bishop Quintard and the Episcopal leaders of Memphis were prepared to try to meet the challenge.

This immediate post-war period (1865-71), which coincides with the last years of Dr. Hines' rectorship, is full of diverse and interlocking religious activity. To avoid the confusion of chronological treatment, I shall attempt to summarize these under the following headings: missionary activity, which includes the formation of new churches and new organizations to meet new needs; Bishop Quintard's work and his visit to England; and the parish activity of St. Mary's and the confused story of how it became the Cathedral.

During Dr. Quintard's visitation of 1865, he was usually accompanied by Mr. Hines. From his diary we learn how impressed the Bishop was with the work being done by two of Mr. Hines' young protégés, the Rev. James J. Vaulx and the Rev. John Schwrar. Vaulx was the son of a planter who lived near Jackson, Tennessee. He started the study of law at the University of Virginia, but prior to the war decided to enter the ministry, and studied at Nashotah. While still a deacon he ministered to the churches at LaGrange and Grand Junction. At LaGrange he started a school and, after becoming priest, celebrated weekly Eucharist "until the Church was taken." He came to Memphis in 1865 and under the supervision of Mr. Hines began work in the Chelsea region. This became the Church of the Good Shepherd. This is the report on the origin of the Church:

> Last autumn I began a mission in Chelsea. Mrs. Wood offered her house for me to hold service in. I began with a Sunday School of four or five pupils. At first I held service but once every Lord's Day, having an attendance of about half a dozen. In a short time with the assistance of certain devout Church folk in Memphis, we hired two small rooms where we have been holding services ever since, both morning and evening . . . To a large extent my labors have been among the strayed sheep of the fold. Many of these, English people, who have neglected the Church since coming to this country or who have been repelled from the Church by the actions of her ministers and members. Our congregation has constantly increased. We have purchased two lots for a school house, rectory and other church buildings. The school house is now being built. Our Heavenly Father has wonderfully blessed our labor of faith and love.[10]

Mr. Vaulx married one of his parishioners, Miss Margaret Garside, and Dr. Hines performed the ceremony. Not only did Vaulx create the Church of the Good Shepherd, but he was chaplain to the Canfield Orphan Asylum, and a few years later

---

10. *Journal of 1866.* He reported 40 communicants, 100 Sunday School pupils and 54 in the parish school. St. Mary's contributed $300 to the church in 1868, though the rector's salary was in arrears.

established a Refuge near the river for the broken and drifting men who passed through the city.[11]

Another young priest, John Schwrar, who studied for the ministry with Dr. Hines during the war, succeeded him as secretary of the convention. He died as one of the martyrs of yellow fever (1878). Just after the war he was given charge of a new mission near Oakville, the Otey Memorial Chapel. This is his report on it to the Convention of 1866:

> I appropriate Sunday afternoon to the colored people; have a Sunday School and service . . . My support has been derived until recently almost exclusively from E. D. Bray . . . The Chapel, situated in Shelby County about ten miles southeast of Memphis, was built with but little assistance by E. D. Bray, an earnest and liberal churchman. The windows were given by another devoted son of the Church, the late A. O. Harris. Mr. Bray has donated the chapel and ten acres of land adjacent; to the Church in this diocese . . . The people are endeavoring to repair their shattered fortunes and will, it is to be expected, be able ere long to contribute to the support of the Chapel.

From the parish reports of Dr. Hines, it would seem that he conducted a similar mission near Ridgeway.[12]

The report of the Rev. J. A. Wheelock, who took over the deserted Grace parish in 1864, shows how the war affected that Church. In his report in 1866 he says:

> The average number of communicants attending communion for the first five months was eight. There was not during that time but one man, that I am aware of, doing

---

11. In the *Journal of 1869* he reports on the Refuge. He describes it as being a refuge for the destitute and deserving poor, for the conversion of sinners, and the education of the ignorant. At first, in a small house on Main Street, he furnished straw pallets, blankets and a fire. "Nearly 150 men and boys of nearly all nations, stations of life, of all shades or religion, gladly accepted the shelter offered, and joined beautifully in a short evensong before retiring to rest." He hoped to get a larger building nearer the levee, for use as a school by day and shelter at night.

Bishop Gailor and the Good Shepherd honored Vaulx by a special service, and a memorial window in the early 1900's. He served in many other parishes after 1870, but returned to help in the yellow fever work in 1873. He finally retired to Fayetteville, Arkansas. He had twelve children, naming the youngest for Sister Hughetta.

12. Mr. Schwrar later moved to St. Thomas' in Somerville and helped rebuild it. He stayed there in spite of tempting offers elsewhere and died there during the epidemic of 1878. The convention seems to have forgotten the Otey Chapel. It was rediscovered in the present century.

business, and he was barely making expenses. Of course they could offer me no salary. The average congregation was about forty, the attendance at Sunday School forty, the average weekly offering about $4.00.

In 1865, Bishop Quintard noted that while in Memphis he had officiated in Stillman House, "where the Rev. James Rogers is starting a new church enterprise with every prospect of success." This was the beginning of St. Lazarus, which for about a decade rivalled Calvary and far surpassed St. Mary's, both in numbers and financial strength, for it was a kind of secession from Calvary. Mr. Rogers had been a priest in the diocese long before the war, but became a Confederate chaplain. He now gathered most of the unreconstructed southerners into his new sanctuary, first at Stillman House and then on Madison near Third. St. Lazarus counted among its members Jefferson Davis, Gideon Pillow, the Scales family and William Stephens, a prominent lawyer from Jackson who moved to Memphis and was long a power in the diocese. It was Stephens who persuaded the convention to waive the Canon requiring longer notice, when St. Lazarus' application for union with the convention came up (1866). The Memphis clergy—Hines, White and Wheelock— gave their consent to the formation of the new parish, as did the Bishop, though he protested the name selected "as liable to misapprehension on the part of certain well-wishers of the Church in Memphis."[13]

The Bishop became intensely concerned over the necessity for work among the needy and growing Negro population of the town. He believed in confirming both white and colored

---

13. *Journal of 1866,* 10, 90. It is perhaps unnecessary to point out that the usual interpretation of the name, St. Lazarus, was that "he was licked by the dogs (Yankees)." Some have questioned this interpretation of why the name was selected. Rogers stayed with the Church nearly a year when—I have been told—he won a large sum on a lottery and went abroad without permission. The Bishop replaced him with the venerable Dr. Wheat, whom the congregation called. Upon his return Rogers was discontented and tried to form a new congregation and eventually became a Roman Catholic. He was formally deposed in a ceremony at St. Mary's, December 8, 1868. Dr. Wheat continued as rector till 1874.

at the same altar rail, and was annoyed at the changing attitude of the Memphis press, which attacked him for his stand.[14]

In his address to the Convention of 1866 the Bishop said, "it is our duty at once to provide for the thousands of freedmen in and around Memphis," and he asked that the clergy search out colored communicants desirous of preparing for the ministry, and to provide funds for their education, and added, "We have in Memphis already established a Colored Orphan Asylum. The work was begun by Mrs. Martha Canfield . . . she earnestly desires the Church to take the Asylum under its care and control." Unfortunately, the diocese was too pressed with other obligations to do much, so for several years northern churches and charities and the Freedman's Bureau supported it. By 1869, when Mrs. Canfield had departed and left another group of trustees, these disputed the claim of the convention for control. By then the immediate need of caring for the deserted Negro children had passed, so the diocese transformed the Asylum into a school and chapel. A committee report to the Convention of 1869 indicates that Memphis churches were contributing to its support and that some members of the committee suggested a brotherhood or sisterhood be invited to take control of it. Though the property (which was on North Dunlap beyond the city limits) had substantial brick buildings, it served poorly as a Negro Church, since it was too far removed from the populous colored areas. During the next few decades repeated efforts were made to revive a school or church there, but never successfully. The Bishop mentions visiting its chapel in the late sixties and being impressed by the "very satisfactory choral

---

14. *Journal of 1868*, 38. He describes such an incident at Calvary. He was very fond of the poem, "Our mother the Church hath never a child/To honor before the rest/But she singeth the same for mighty kings/And the veriest babe at her breast/And the Bishop goes down to his narrow bed/As a ploughman's child is laid/And alike she blesseth the dark brown serf/And the chief in his robe arrayed."

During the post-war years, Memphis' colored population swelled from 3,000 to 14,000 and during certain periods controlled the vote. This created a change in the attitude of press and the whites.

service conducted by the chaplain, J. J. Vaulx." An early superintendent, L. M. Wolcott, perhaps gives us one of the best clues to the school's difficulties:

> To have anything to do with a colored orphan asylum is at best a thankless position, and especially in this community it is attended with so much odium that . . . it will be difficult to get active, working people to co-operate with you.

By 1873 its operation as a colored orphanage was temporarily suspended. It was leased to the Church Home, and enters our story again later.

Another social-work organization created in Memphis by the Church during reconstruction years did survive. This was the Church Home. The original association was known as the Church Charity Foundation (1867). It began its work at 100 Market, then moved to Shelby Street (Front). In 1869, Mrs. Speed and Mrs. Spottswood gave the Home a tract of ten acres at Buntyn, and the work was put under the control of the Bishop and a Board of Lady Managers. Work on a new building was begun on April 20, 1869, when the Bishop was present at the laying of the cornerstone. The chapel of this building was the original St. John's Church.[15] The directress of the Home in its first year at Buntyn was Sister Martha, a novice of the Community of St. Mary, who came to this work several years in advance of the Order's acceptance of the Bishop's invitation to establish a branch at the Cathedral. The Buntyn home proved to be both inaccessible and uncomfortable. It burned in 1871, so in 1873 the managers decided to remove it to the Canfield Asylum. In 1874 they purchased a home on the Raleigh Road (now Jackson) where it was under the care of the Sisters until well into the present century.[16]

---

15. It was admitted to convention in 1871, and reported 31 communicants. Peter Wager, once a parishioner of St. Mary's, was active at its start. The chapel burned a few years later and the Church became inactive. Much later, 1898, Wager revived it.

16. The *Cathedral Chimes*, Easter 1905, contains a brief history of the Home by Mrs. S. M. Benton. The Rev. R. A. Simpson was its first chaplain and he took charge of St. Mary's for several months in 1867 during an illness of Dr. Hines.

Bishop Quintard made the first of many visits to England in the summer of 1867 and remained there almost a year. He attended the first Lambeth Conference, participated in many ecclesiastical functions and organized a committee composed of eminent Englishmen, both clerical and lay, for the obtaining of support for the revival of the University of the South. When he returned to Memphis after his long absence, on June 19, 1868, he made almost a triumphal entry. After Morning Prayer at St. Mary's he addressed a large crowd, then in the afternoon all five city parishes united for a Sunday School Festival at Calvary, after which "a procession formed which moved through the principal streets of the city to a beautiful grove on the outskirts of town," where he delivered an address. A few months later he participated in the reopening of the University of the South.

Having reviewed the post-war activities of the Bishop and Church in Memphis, we shall observe the final years of Dr. Hines' rectorship. When Quintard first visited St. Mary's in 1865, he was greatly impressed by the Sunday School.

> I attended divine service at St. Mary's Church, Rev. Richard Hines rector. After the service the Rector catechized the children of his school. I never witnessed such proficiency. The children answered promptly all questions, whether in the Book of Scripture, or the Book of Common Prayer . . . the service was very gratifying to me.

When he returned, in Holy Week, 1866, he wrote, "Once more I witnessed with great delight what earnest, faithful teaching may accomplish for the lambs of Christ's flock." In this same month (April) came the sudden and unexpected death of Mrs. Hines. It was a blow from which he never fully recovered, and his health and spirits were seriously impaired. During the next year he was given an extended leave of absence (June 1867-January 1868). During this time the young chaplain of the Church Home took over. Yet even as it welcomed the Rector back, the vestry was forced to confess that they could promise no fixed salary, "in view of the pecuniary embarrassment of the time."

St. Mary's emerged from the war burdened with debt, and with the Rector's salary sadly in arrears—a condition which continued until the time of his departure. The ladies of the Church frequently gave concerts to try to alleviate the situation or to raise money for some emergency. Originally the Church had a system of "assessing different members of the congregation in proportion to their supposed means," and the vestry would send promissory notes to each member, but this never worked well even when supplemented by the "weekly offering."

A recent historian of the Episcopal Church has pointed out that within the last fifty years nearly all dioceses have adopted a cathedral system, an envelope system, the beautification of altars, and the use of vested choirs. St. Mary's began to adopt most of these features in the first decades following the Civil War. The envelope system was urged upon the vestry by Bishop Quintard in 1868, and formally accepted by it on June 11 of that year. Vestry minutes for that day give a clear picture of St. Mary's first "every member canvass," though of course it was not so called.

> The committee reported that 250 copies of an address (on the system) had been printed for distribution and that 3000 envelopes had been ordered and would be ready in a few days. After the reading of the address, it was ordered that each member of the vestry should furnish a copy to each person on his list, and that copies should also be distributed to the Sunday School children, and on the seats of the Church. The Rector was requested to read the address from the Chancel on the ensuing Sunday and to make such comments and explanations as he saw fit. Each member of the vestry was furnished with a pledge for the subscriber to sign, and was requested to call upon the persons whose names had been given them, as soon as possible.

This has a familiar ring, for all subsequent campaigns have been but variations on this theme established in the sixties. The next year the vestry cancelled their annual "Fair Concert and

Supper," so they could raise money "only in the way the Church requires it should be." Unfortunately the new system did not materially aid the financial plight of the parish, for by April, 1870, not only was the Rector's salary in arrears, but the man holding the note on the organ demanded payment or repossession. The vestry had no recourse but to request him "to take the organ as soon as possible." Mr. Trezevant, long-time treasurer of the Church and frequent lay delegate to the convention, must have advanced his own funds for St. Mary's for in June we find that the vestry appointed Mrs. Portal and Mrs. Gailor to a committee to raise $250 for a premium for life insurance on the Rector and on J. P. Trezevant, "for the amount due them by the parish so as to secure it to their families." The vestry also elected Thomas Hunt and Thomas Gailor (then but a school boy) "to get members and others disposed to give" to make regular weekly offerings by envelope. The Bishop may well have had St. Mary's in mind when in his convention address (1870) he said:

> Some object to subscriptions, some object to donations, some object to the offertory and some to pew rents, and so the matter stands. Still the poor pastor of the flock struggles on and runs in debt, and suffers in reputation, or lives on friends.

The present chairman of the "Building and Grounds Committee" should note that the first—but not the last—complaint of a leaky roof was in 1869.

The meeting in which Bishop Quintard seems to have inaugurated the plan for a Memphis Cathedral was on April 27, 1866. On that day he called together the clergy of Memphis to the vestry room of Calvary "to consult on certain measures for the better working of the Church in this city." We have another note on this meeting by the Rev. George James, a young missionary from Wisconsin whom the Bishop called to Memphis to try to revive some of the small but war-ruined churches near Memphis. His note is more specific: "Attended a meeting of the clergy of the city of Memphis at Calvary Church for the purpose of devising measures for the introduction of the Cathedral System in Memphis." He also tells how the Bishop instituted daily celebration of Holy Communion for the benefit of the clergy, "and all others who wanted to avail themselves of it," and directed him to celebrate on April 23, 26, and 27; "I administered the Holy Communion on those days at 7 A.M. in St. Mary's Church."[17]

Bishop Quintard had long hoped for a division of the diocese. He wanted a "Provincial System" for the state, with each of the grand divisions of the state having its bishop and cathedral from which to conduct mission work. He also envisioned the clergy of each cathedral city as Canons of the Cathedral, forming with the bishop a kind of "family." When this idea was rejected by the General Convention, he hoped at least to have "Rural Deans" for each division. When this idea failed, he settled for the present system of "Convocations."

It was in the diocesan Convention of 1866, when after telling of the failure of his provincial system, he informed it of his Memphis step:

> The clergy of the city of Memphis have united with me in the formation of a Cathedral Chapter. St. Mary's Church has been selected for the Cathedral Church, and the Rev. Richard Hines has been appointed Dean.

From the time of this convention until 1871, a period of confusion reigned as to whether St. Mary's was a church or a cathedral. In the convention *Journals* lay delegates are listed as from St. Mary's Church, whereas in the table of assessments and in parish reports it is usually termed "Cathedral." On some

---

17. *Journal of 1866*, 55. Mr. James gave a bleak picture of the situation in West Tennessee. He found the Covington church dilapidated; Somerville with the windows broken, though nineteen families "want a resident pastor;" LaGrange had had its windows and blinds broken and was used for storage during the war. He found that the chancel was destroyed, the church seats had been used for coffins, and the walls written over with charcoal; Ravenscroft Chapel was in ruins. The Church at Randolph burned down, Brownsville with its tower incomplete, its windows broken and plaster off. Union City had no regular communicants; Trenton, no Church property and but four communicants.

pages Mr. Hines is referred to as Reverend, but on others as Dean or the "Very Reverend." In the Convention of 1870 Mr. Stephens (of St. Lazarus) and others queried,

> 1) Whether according to the usage of the Episcopal Church in the U. S., and under the Constitutions and Canons of the General Convention, and under the Constitutions and Canons of the Diocese, there is any such office and dignity in the Diocese as that of Dean.

> 2) Whether under said usages, Constitutions, and Canons, there is any such office or dignity in the Diocese as that of Bishop's Chaplain.

This uncertainty ended when the Bishop decided to return to Memphis to live, and to take up his residence in the Bishop's House (Otey's old home). This he did in November 1870. During the several preceding years a hard struggle had been waged by Memphis Episcopalians to recover and rehabilitate Bishop Otey's old home. It had been lost after his death because of back taxes, paving assessments and other charges. On Bishop Quintard's first visit to Memphis (1865), he noted that "an enterprise was inaugurated to secure the dwelling place of our late Bishop for a permanent Episcopal Residence. By the energy of Jesse Pope, Esq., President of the Commercial Bank, warmly seconded by the Rev. Richard Hines, the property has been purchased but not paid for." From other sources it seems that the ladies of Calvary, William Stephens (the attorney for the diocese) and Harlow Dow (whom Bishop Gailor credits) were also active in the project.

When the Bishop returned (November 25, 1870) he was warmly welcomed. He noted in his diary:

> Took up my abode in the Episcopal Residence, which has at length been secured as the property of the Diocese. I was met at the station by a number of the clergy and laity, and on reaching the house found "of the faithful women not a few," who not only extended a cordial greeting, but by their words testified to their kindness and regard.

It was exactly a month after his arrival, on Christmas Eve,

1870, that the vestry of St. Mary's took the formal action giving the Church to the Bishop. This deserves to be quoted in full:

> A meeting of the vestry was held in the Bishop's study, all the members present except Dr. S. P. Green. The Bishop stated the object of meeting the vestry was to consult with them in regard to the necessity of his having a church in which he would have the sole control and management of it and to make it the Cathedral Church of the Bishops of the Diocese for all time to come, and as the Rev. Richard Hines, D.D., rector of the parish was perfectly willing to resign his charge to him, would have to have the consent of the vestry and then that of the Congregation before the same could be lawfully done. Upon asking the members their consent it was unanimously given and the necessary document signed giving St. Mary's Church to the Bishop and his successors in office as a Cathedral Church.   Peter Wager (secretary)

The next entry in the Vestry Book registers the congregation's approval:

> After service on the first Sunday after Christmas, January 1, 1871, the action of the vestry was unanimously ratified and confirmed, and the Rector in behalf of the vestry and congregation formally gave the Bishop the keys of the Church, thus closing the records of this parish as an independent organization.   Peter Wager

The picture of the transfer is completed by giving an excerpt from the Bishop's diary of January 1, 1871, which is found in the convention *Journal of 1871.*

> Feast of the Circumcision, St. Mary's Church. Morning Prayer was said by the Rev. Richard Hines, D.D., at 9 A.M. At eleven o'clock I said the Litany, the Rev. John A. Harrison of Jackson preached, after which I administered the Holy Communion assisted by Dr. Hines. After a blessing of peace had been given, the following resolution adopted by the Rector, Wardens and Vestrymen of St. Mary's Parish on Christmas Eve, was submitted for ratification:

> Resolved, by the Rector, Wardens, and Vestrymen of St. Mary's Parish, that St. Mary's Church be tendered to the Bishop of the Diocese for a Cathedral Church, and that the Bishop be requested to take such steps for the organization of the Cathedral system as he may deem necessary to carry this resolution into effect.

> Resolved, that this resolution be submitted to the congregation for ratification.

Signed by John P. Trezevant, Edward Fegan, Wardens; S. H. Lamb, Peter Wager, S. Green, Vestrymen.

This resolution was unanimously adopted by a rising vote of the congregation, after which the Rector, Warden and Vestrymen advanced to the chancel and tendered to me the keys of the Church, in the following words: "Right Reverend Father in God, in the name and behalf of the Rector, Wardens, and Vestrymen and Congregation of St. Mary's Church, we tender to you the keys of this holy house in token that henceforth this Church shall be under the sole and supreme control of yourself and your successors, as Bishops of Tennessee, for a Cathedral Church."

In accepting the keys of the Church, I said: "I Charles Todd Quintard, S.T.D., LL.D., by the Grace of God Bishop of Tennessee, do receive these keys of the House of God at your hands, as the pledge of your obedience to me as Bishop of the Diocese of Tennessee; and as your acknowledgement of my right to rule all things, temporal and spiritual, in this, my Cathedral Church; and I for my part promise to be a faithful shepherd over you, in the name of the Father, and of the Son, and of the Holy Ghost, Amen."

Various attempts have been made in Memphis to provide a Church for the Bishop of the Diocese. Calvary was offered to me in 1866. An attempt was made to unite Grace and St. Lazarus, but all have failed. Now St. Mary's is, in fact, the Bishop's Church, or Cathedral. A Cathedral is simply a Bishop's Church—a Church that belongs to the Bishop of the Diocese for his use as Bishop; a Church in which every clergyman and layman of the Diocese has, in addition to his own parish Church, an interest; a Church which is central for all common action, and in which a Bishop is the center of the visible fabric of the Church.

It is hoped in time to develop the true idea of the primitive cathedral system, which was in fact the original missionary organization of every Diocese. In the days of the Church's primeval vigor, when the spirit of the Apostles themselves yet lived and labored, and was the element of influence in the hands of their more immediate successors, every Bishop had his own Church gathered about him; his clergy were under his own eye, trained and formed under his own hand, and from his Church, as a center, went forth the clergy who supplied all the region round about the city where he dwelt, while in the precincts of his Church, and taught by his clergy, were the schools which were the seminaries of learning in all his Diocese.

From January to March (1871), the church was closed for repair and enlargement. The Bishop describes its reopening in these words:

> On Saturday, March 4, St. Mary's Church was reopened for Divine Service. There were present of the clergy, the Reverend Drs. Wheat, and Hines; the Rev. Messrs. Carmichael, Vaulx, and Wickens; the Rev. Mr. Pickett of the Diocese of Mississippi, and the Rev. Dr. Milburn, familiarly known as the blind preacher. The Rev. Mr. Pickett preached the sermon at the original consecration of St. Mary's Church thirteen years ago, and on this occasion he performed the like office most acceptably. St. Mary's has been doubled in size and all its appointments will compare favorably with any Church in the Diocese.

An epoch was drawing to a close, and another was about to begin. In 1871, the young James Vaulx left Memphis; Dr. Hines, stricken by the death of his wife, worn out by service and by lack of an adequate salary, retired from St. Mary's, but seems to have remained in Memphis for two more years, being listed in the City Directory as Principal and teacher at the Linden Street School, in which his second wife, Mrs. Mary Hines, also taught. It is unfortunate that a rift seems to have developed between him and Bishop Quintard, when for so long they had admired and loved one another.[18]

One of Dr. Hines last acts at St. Mary's was the presentation of young Charles C. Parsons for ordination to the diaconate in the newly opened Cathedral (March 5, 1871) and of Peter Wager, who had been secretary of the vestry, on April 25. It was not until 1872 that the convention recognized the Cathedral

---

18. During the Convention of 1873, which met in Memphis, Dr. Hines wrote a letter to the *Appeal* sharply criticizing the Bishop. It seemed to be a personal matter, and it is hard to determine from the letter what his grievance was. He was censured for it by the convention, although Jefferson Davis moved to table the censuring motion. In the newspaper accounts of the convention it appears that Hines was also critical of the Bishop for spending his time raising money for Sewanee. (see the *Appeal*, April 23, 24, 1873) He moved to Mississippi and died there in 1883. The convention *Journal of 1883*, 35, carried his obituary notice, and resolutions were passed praising his work (p. 74). The obituary contains these words, "He was a man of strongly marked character, and gave himself soul and body to the cause of Christ and the Church . . . his life and labors in Tennessee will always be held in loving memory by those who knew him intimately." His second wife lived until 1899.

by adding a section to its Canon on lay representation, and this clause made no real change. It reads:

> Section 4. St. Mary's Church, Memphis, having been transferred by its late Rector, Wardens and Vestry to the Bishop of the Diocese, and by the said Bishop accepted, to be known and used as his Cathedral Church, the congregation shall still be entitled to the same representation which under the Canons was allowed to when it was a Parish.[19]

---

19. This section was dropped out in the course of a general revision and rearrangement of the Canons in the early 1880's, but was later reinserted in a separate Canon, "Of St. Mary's Cathedral." Between 1900 and 1906 other sections were added specifying the organization of the Chapter. The Canon was again revised in 1936 to substantially its present form. (I am indebted to Canon Sharp for this information.)

CHAPTER III

THE YELLOW FEVER ERA — DEAN HARRIS

AFTER DR. HINES left the Cathedral, he remained in Memphis, as we have seen, as principal of the Linden Street School, before going to a pastorate in Meridian, Mississippi (1873). Bishop Quintard seems to have carried on alone for awhile, but late in 1871 he secured George C. Harris as assistant, for the 1872 parish report is signed by him as "Assistant Minister." By 1873 he is listed as Dean. In contrast to Dr. Hines, who was a gaunt, thin, austere-looking man, photographs of Harris show him with a rather full face and kindly eyes behind small steel framed glasses, and with a full drooping mustache. He was a Mississippian, and as deacon had served in Nashville with Quintard at the Church of the Advent and at Holy Trinity just before the Civil War. Like the Bishop, he had been a Confederate chaplain during the war, and had been ordained priest by Bishop Otey at a special service at St. Mary's on March 25, 1860.[1] He was only thirty-seven when he came to Memphis.

There was an aura of romance about his wife, for Mrs. Harris had been the famous Helen Johnstone, daughter of the Mississippi planter, John Johnstone, son of the Scottish Earl of Annandale, who had in the 1820's created a great plantation estate of Annandale near Madison City, Mississippi. Miss Johnstone had previously been engaged to Henry Vick of Vicksburg, who had been killed in a duel just before their marriage

---

1. *Journal of 1860*, 23. "I held a special ordination in St. Mary's Church, Memphis and admitted to the Holy Order of the priesthood the Rev. George C. Harris, of the Church of the Holy Trinity, Nashville. Morning Prayer was said by the Rev. J. T. Pickett, who also presented the candidate. The Rev. Dr. Helmuth of the Church of England and the Rev. Mr. Nash of the Diocese of Wisconsin were persent and took part in the service."

was to have taken place. Harris met her when he was minister in the beautiful Church of the Holy Cross at Annandale. Mrs. Harris was an active assistant of her husband in his church work. She visited the sick, aided the needy, helped the Sisters. She was also for several years (1878-81) President of the Board of Lady Managers of the Church Home.[2]

Let us survey for a moment the "State of the Church" in Memphis in 1871, the year Mr. Harris assumed his duties at St. Mary's. At the time there were only about 3,000 Episcopalians in the State. Judging by the parish reports given in the *Journal of 1872* (and the accuracy of such reports sometimes varies according to the degree of optimism or the pessimism of the rector), Calvary had temporarily lost its position as the largest Church. Grace Church, then under the leadership of the Rev. James Carmichael, now reported a communicant list of 260. Calvary was close behind with 250, with the venerable Dr. White as its rector. During the early seventies, Dr. White crusaded both in the state and in General Conventions against unworthy means of money raising: lotteries, dances, entertainments and the like, though he remained devoted to the method of pew rent. Calvary's strength had been cut in 1866 by the formation of St. Lazarus, whose rector was now Dr. Wheat. It reported 158 communicants and was making plans for a new church—which never materialized. Soon after the epidemic of 1873 and the resignation of Dr. Wheat (1874) St. Lazarus declined. The Rev. Charles Stewart succeeded for a time and on January 7, 1877, it chose the attractive young Charles C. Parsons as rector, and since Grace was also in decline, these two churches were united in February 1877 as St. Lazarus and Grace, with some continued protest against the name. After

---

2. See Jackson (Miss.) *State Times,* Dec. 3, 1955, for account of the Johnstones. Mrs. Johnstone built the beautiful Gothic Church of the Holy Cross at Annandale (1849-52) in memory of her husband. Mr. Harris and later Charles Carroll Parsons were married in the church. The Jackson paper says, "Legend said she (Helen Johnstone) never gave her heart to him, but remained the bride of the ghost of Henry Vick."

Parsons' heroic death in the yellow fever epidemic of 1878, St. Lazarus was dropped from the name.

St. Mary's reported 118 communicants, its largest list up to this time. The Good Shepherd had by now grown to 72, and was under the care of the ex-West Pointer, Charles Carroll Parsons, recently made deacon. The next year, on February 15, 1872, he was ordained to the priesthood at St. Mary's, being presented for ordination by Mr. Harris. A young man, Peter Wager, who had grown up in St. Mary's (he had been secretary of the vestry in Dr. Hines' day) was now a priest and both the chaplain to the Church Home and in charge of the infant St. John's Church with 31 members.

The historian of the decade of the Harris deanship is again hampered by the lack of vestry books for the period, but the two outstanding episodes of his decade, the coming of the Sisters of St. Mary and the heroic activity of the Dean and Sisters during the yellow fever epidemics, may be partially traced from other sources. The impact of the Oxford Movement on this country during the mid-nineteenth century led to the formation of several religious communities. The one which concerns our story is the Community of St. Mary, founded on the Feast of the Purification, 1865, thanks to the zeal of Sister Harriet (Harriet Starr Cannon), under the ægis and with the blessing of Bishop Horatio Potter of New York.[3]

3. For the life and activity of this remarkable woman who was the Mother Superior of the order from 1865 until her death in 1896 see *Historical Papers* No. 1 (Mount St. Gabriel Series), printed at St. Mary's Convent February 2, 1931, which contains several articles on her life and work. The five original Sisters were Harriet, Jane, Sarah, Mary, Amelia (the last being one of the group to come to Memphis). The order was an outgrowth of an earlier, less strictly organized group which conducted a House of Mercy and the Sheltering Arms in New York. After the formation of the sisterhood their activities increased. The following is a list of some of the projects they conducted during their early years:

1867-70 in charge of Barnabas House, Mulberry St., New York.
1868   opened a girls' school on East 46th St., New York.
1870   conducted a free hospital for children, 206 West 40th St.
1872   obtained property at Peekskill and opened the St. Gabriel's School; in 1876 this became their headquarters.
1873   sent the group to St. Mary's in Memphis.
1874   assisted Trinity Church, New York, in its downtown work.

Bishop Quintard was very sympathetic to the idea of religious orders, and as part of his "Cathedral Idea" conceived the plan of attaching a branch of a sisterhood to the Cathedral, especially desiring their help in the conduct of the newly created Church Home and for the establishment of a school for girls. Before coming South as a young man, he had known Miss Cannon in Connecticut, and after he became Bishop of Tennessee and she the Mother Superior, he broached the idea of establishing a group in Memphis, perhaps as early as 1869. He certainly did so in 1871, when after the General Convention in New York he visited the Convent (November 1) and celebrated the Holy Eucharist in their Chapel. Bishop Gailor, in one of his many brief sketches of St. Mary's history (1905) attributes the motivating force in bringing the order to Memphis to Sister Hughetta. This seems to be confirmed by a letter of Mrs. Charles Currier, who wrote of Sister Hughetta (1931), "Before joining the sisterhood she came to Memphis to visit. While here she told Bishop Quintard of her great desire to bring the Sisters South. He was delighted and said he would like to have them locate in Memphis." The order did not officially agree to undertake the work in Memphis until a year later at a chapter meeting held on November 1, 1872, when it gave unanimous consent. Yet we find that as early as 1870, Sister Martha, a novice who had come from the Memphis region and who had originally been directed to the order by Bishop Quintard, came to Memphis to direct the newly constructed Church Home at Buntyn. She returned to the East in 1871 to prepare for the final vows, but died there while still a novice.

The group, which came in accordance with the chapter decision of November 1872, started for the South in August 1873. They were: Sister Constance, who was to be the Superior;

In the early years the amount of prejudice displayed against the order in some quarters was almost incredible. Sister Harriet was born in South Carolina and left an orphan by yellow fever. The prologue of the *Rule* says: "Many were the graces which God shed upon our foundress, the Reverend Mother Harriet, but chief among them were cheerfulness, simplicity and mortification of self."

Sister Amelia (one of the original members of the order) who was to have general charge of the Church Home; Sister Thecla, who had been professed only the previous January and was to work in the school; and Sister Hughetta, who though only a novice at the time, was a Snowden from Memphis and naturally greatly interested in the new project. She was also to assist in the school. Two of the Sisters, Amelia and Thecla, stopped off briefly en route to visit relatives. Sisters Constance and Hughetta came directly to Memphis. The Bishop, having again decided to reside elsewhere, gave over the Bishop's House as a place of residence for the Sisters. The new arrivals were warmly welcomed by Dean and Mrs. Harris, who also assisted them in making preparation for the opening of their school, when the first of the three "great" yellow fever epidemics (1873, 1878, 1879) struck. Instead of escaping, the Sisters begged the Mother Superior for permission to remain and to nurse the sick.[4]

The Memphis to which the Sisters came was then a decidedly unhealthful region. Nearby were swampy bottom-lands annually inundated by the river. The town lacked adequate drainage or sewage systems. Its water supply consisted mainly of defective wells and cisterns. Streets, according to the *Ledger*, were "huge depots of filth," which were never greatly improved by the addition of gravel. There was no sanitary inspection of food, or milk, the latter being described as both "diluted and polluted." Even in normal times the death rate was unusually high, but major epidemics often brought in by river traffic from

---

4. I am indebted to Sister Frideswide, Mother Superior of the OSM, for letters and conversations which have given me many of the facts contained in this brief story of the Sisters' work. Since members of religious orders prefer to lose their individual and family identity, they eschew personal glorification and biographical detail. Facts on the personal history of the Sisters are therefore purposely scant. Sister Constance, a very accomplished artist and teacher, was from Boston. Sister Amelia was from Nashville and one of the five original Sisters in the order. She was trained in hospital and orphan work. Sister Thecla, also a trained teacher, was from Georgia. Sister Hughetta was a Snowden from Memphis and was instrumental in starting the school at Sewanee. She was later the Sister Superior.

New Orleans (which had acquired them from distant ports) swept the town at regular intervals. Dr. Gerald Capers in his history of Memphis gives a table of at least ten major epidemics between 1820 and 1870. These were caused by such diseases as dengue fever, cholera, dysentery, smallpox, and yellow fever. Chills and fever (malaria) was ever-present. According to this table, yellow fever had invaded Memphis three times (1828, 1855, 1867) before the three major epidemics of the 1870's.

We know now that yellow fever is caused by a filterable virus endemic in certain tropical regions of Africa and South America, which is carried by several types of mosquito, especially the *aedes aegyptus*. This mosquito was suspected as early as 1881 (by C. J. Finley) but was not definitely convicted until 1900 when investigations were made by a commission headed by Major Walter Reed. The pattern of an epidemic can now be traced. Some person (often a sailor) from the tropics would arrive in port with the virus in his blood stream. Fever-carrying mosquitos would then bite him, and after an incubating period, by their sting transmit the disease to others. The disease would run its course usually from one to five days. At first the victim suffered from headache, backache, fever and congested face; within a day or two the hemorrhaging (causing the characteristic black vomit) would begin and jaundice would occur, the sufferer would then die, or recover, though recovery seemed to offer life immunity.

In the then existing state of medical knowledge, an outbreak in a community of the dread yellowjack would cause consternation and panic. No one knew whence it came or the cause; all who could sought safety in flight, but for their own protection, many communities would stop the trains or wagons coming from infected areas.[5]

5. G. Capers, *Biography of a River Town* (Chapel Hill, 1939), Chap. VIII, from which much of this is condensed. Dr. Capers points out that these epidemics had a national significance in arousing the country to the need of better sanitation, even though at the time the secret of the plague had not been discovered.

The months preceding the arrival of the Sisters had been "calamitous ones" for Memphis. The yellow fever outbreak which greeted them in August was the last of several mishaps. In December (1872) the city "was in the throes of the 'epizootic,' an equine malady which paralyzed horse drawn traffic." Then had come a severe freeze which hampered traffic both on the river and on land for a month, and which destroyed much property. Later on there appeared a violent form of smallpox and a mild attack of cholera. Not even the first Mardi Gras parade or the visit of the Grand Duke of Russia, or the founding of the Cotton Exchange, could quite obliterate the memory of this bad year.

The epidemic of 1873 started in Memphis in early August when a steamboat from New Orleans stopped for provisions at the bluff and left two sick men who died within a few days. Fever soon broke out among the Irish settlers below the bluff in so-called Happy Hollow—a region west of Front between Poplar and Market. Then it spread to nearby Pinch, also mostly Irish. It was obvious by mid-August that a major epidemic had begun. By the end of the month fewer than half of the city's population of forty thousand remained in the stricken town. The area of contagion and the number of deaths increased through September and early October (71 deaths on October 5). Meanwhile relief work had been organized on a national scale by many creeds and denominations. Especially active were the Howards (an association something like the Red Cross) which poured in money, and sent in doctors and nurses, and helped construct hospitals.[6] Of the estimated 15,000 who

---

6. Capers, *Op. Cit.,* 193. Much was written on his epidemic. As the Roman Catholic Irish were the chief sufferers, Catholic priests and nuns did heroic work, and many died. See Dennis Quinn, *Heroes and Heroines of Memphis;* also J. P. Dromgoole, *Yellow Fever Heroes and Heroines and Horrors,* and R. Edwards, *In Memorium of the Lamented dead who fell in the Epidemic of 1873.* Some of these accounts give the impression that all protestant clergy fled. The Howards were an outgrowth of a yellow fever epidemic in New Orleans in 1853. When some clerks in the Napoleon B. Kneass drugstore, aided by some wealthy young men, distributed medicine to sufferers, they took the name of their organization from John Howard (1726-90), an English

remained in the city it is thought that at least 5,000 were stricken and that about two thousand of these died. Thus it was a trying and dangerous situation which confronted the new arrivals. Sister Constance tells how on one of her first visits to a home in Memphis she was met by a young girl weeping and in great distress, who reported that her sisters were ill, that she could find no doctor, and did not know what to do for them. Sister Constance remained with the girls and ministered to them until they recovered. This was her first yellow fever case. The Sisters began a soup kitchen, and from relief funds helped obtain nurses, medicines and delicacies for the ill. They brought words of comfort and prayer, and in some cases administered the last rites. During this epidemic they reported that they had nursed sixty cases (of whom eight died), and that Dean Harris had conducted daily Holy Communion, reserving the sacrament for the sick and dying.

In the convention *Journal of 1874* both Bishop Quintard and Dean Harris paid glowing tributes to the heroism and devotion of the Sisters. The Bishop noted in his diary:

> During the fearful epidemic of yellow fever our clergy remained faithfully at the post of duty and were conspicuous for untiring devotion to the sick and dying. They were assisted in their self-denying labors by the Rev. J. J. Vaulx and the Rev. Drs. Sanson and Lord, the latter two gentlemen presbyters of Mississippi. The Sisters of St. Mary who had gone to Memphis from New York with the view of opening a school, found themselves in the midst of the epidemic and though entirely unacclimated, devoted themselves night and day to visiting the sick and afflicted, kneeling at the bedside in prayer, ministering as nurses, braving the pestilential air, and going

philanthropist and prison reformer. The organization spread to other towns. They were men who dared to stay and face the fever. They often divided stricken towns into districts in which members would visit stricken homes. Between epidemics, membership would sometimes decrease—but money and men were always forthcoming in time of need. They were organized in Memphis in 1855. During a mild outbreak in 1867, there were 28 members. Though there were only 15 members at the beginning of the outbreak of 1878, they quickly had an organization large enough to manage a special hospital in what is now Christine School and three suburban quarantine camps. (The above is from Mr. Paul Coppock's column, "The Night Desk" in *The Commercial Appeal*.)

from house to house and from hovel to hovel serving the Lord Christ in his poor and afflicted ones.

Dean Harris added this note to his parish report:

> I feel that I should not omit to mention the work performed by the Sisters of St. Mary during the yellow fever epidemic which visited our city last fall, and yet I cannot speak of it as I would. It is so much part of their life to shrink from notoriety that I feel almost as one might in violation of a sacred confidence, to speak of them at all in this report. But the Church ought to know what it possesses in these faithful women. Coming to us just before the outbreak of this most distressing epidemic of which we have any knowledge, unused to our climate, and wholly without experience in the management and treatment of this disease, they proceeded to their work with the nerve and steadiness of veterans. That they performed it faithfully is the least that can be said. But with full knowledge that few will know how much it means.[7]

As Memphians drifted back home in November, after the frosts, the Sisters opened their new school. At first they had only four pupils; this number grew to twenty by the end of the year, and by June 1874 there were forty. By the second year they had enlarged the frame building east of the Church, and this year the school opened with eighty pupils. By the third year there were a hundred pupils, and from then on this remained the average size of the school. The Bishop praised the new school in the Convention of 1875 in these words:

> Beginning less than two years ago with four pupils, they now have nearly a hundred, while the systematic drill and training, the admirable system by which the whole is ordered and regulated, approaches nearly to perfection. The decided Christian atmosphere and churchly influence which pervades the establishment is felt by everyone who in any way comes in contact with it, and must make it very attractive to Christian parents.

---

7. Mr. Harris' report shows that the parish raised $1,942.55 for yellow fever sufferers. The Rev. P. Rath, a new rector at the Good Shepherd, seems to have died of the fever, and the Rev. G. S. Fisse, who took his place, also conducted services at the Cathedral. St. Mary's parish *Register* shows that fifteen burials were conducted from the Cathedral in September and October. Ministers conducting these services—and thus present during the epidemic—were Messrs. James Carmichael, J. B. McConnell, Henry Sanson, W. Lord, Peter Wager, George Harris.

Meanwhile Sister Amelia had her hands full at the Church Home. The Buntyn home had burned the year before, the previous matron had departed and the treasury was down to ten cents. Thus during the epidemic of 1873 the Home was moved to the Canfield Asylum buildings, and this enterprise was assisted by Mayor Johnson, a Citizens Relief Committee, and by the Howard Association. Sister Amelia took charge in October, "with many difficulties to encounter . . . assisted by a widow lady." The Bishop arrived in Memphis on November 6, and noted, "I found my hands full of work for the orphans, though Sister Amelia in charge of the orphanage has accomplished wonders." A Sister Mary, from New York, came to aid her briefly during the winter; but Sister Amelia's health failed under the strain and after a year she was recalled to the mother convent. After her retirement the Board of Managers purchased a new location, the Leath home on Jackson, and for the next two years Mrs. Randolph was its directress. It was only on January 6, 1877, that the Sisters were given full control, and in the same year Sister Frances, a recently professed member of the order, came to Memphis to assume the directions of the Home.

Meanwhile the Bishop had again turned to his project for getting a church started among the Negroes, under colored direction. It has been said that Dean Klein, in the 1880's, initiated Emmanuel Church, but in fact he simply succeeded where previous efforts had failed. As we have seen, the first move for a Negro church was made in the 1860's in connection with the Canfield Asylum, with Vaulx and other white clergy in charge. But in 1873 Dr. White of Calvary, Dean Harris, Jacob Thompson and others made a strenuous effort to recruit a suitable colored worker who could be trained for the ministry. In 1874, a Negro, George H. Jackson, was ordained deacon and given charge of what became known as Emmanuel Parish. The congregation first met in Zion Hall, and Bishop Quintard when he visited it the next year remarked, "The service was admirably rendered, the responses hearty, the singing excellent." Unfortunately the Rev. George Jackson proved derelict to his duty, and at a meeting at St. Mary's (January 15, 1878) he was deposed.[8] Thus with more yellow fever and with the pressing financial difficulties during the late seventies, the lasting construction of Emmanuel did await the coming of Father Klein.

In the early 1870's, Alfred Todhunter is listed as Superintendent of St. Mary's Sunday School. He studied for the ministry and took Holy Orders, and in 1874 returned to the Cathedral to become the first "Assistant to the Dean." He seems to have remained only for a year or two. It was also in the mid-seventies that the young English cotton merchant, Charles Currier, came to Memphis. He married Miss Bettie Brinkley, the daughter of Robert Brinkley the original donor of the cathedral property. Mr. Currier's father had been an organist and he was a trained musician. Thus began his long and unselfish service of nearly twenty-five years as St. Mary's organist and choir director as well as chapter member of the Cathedral. He brought to St. Mary's the English custom of the surpliced choir of men and boys, and is said to have been the first to introduce this custom in the South. A picture of his first choir, including Dean Harris, exists and one would like to think he was partly responsible for the enthusiastic note the Bishop made on the Easter service of 1875: "Easter in the Cathedral, services conducted by the Rev. George Harris, Dean, assisted by the Rev. Alfred Todhunter. Congregation very large and many persons were compelled to turn away for want of room. It was the best and pleasantest service I have ever known at St. Mary's. The number of communions was very large."

8. *Journal of 1878,* 22. "At 11 A.M. met the Convocation of Memphis in the vestry room of St. Mary's. At 11:30 said Litany, and pronounced sentice of deposition on Rev. G. H. Jackson (col.). Messrs. Carmichael and Parsons signed the sentence of deposition as witnesses. Another colored deacon, the Rev. Mr. McConnell was next put in charge.

Bishop Quintard went abroad from July 1875 until July 1876, again to raise money for Sewanee. While there he preached in many of the great cathedrals, attended Convocation, the Lambeth Assembly, participated in the consecration of several English bishops, and was present at the opening of Keble College whose cornerstone he had helped lay ten years before. He was everywhere made welcome. The story is told that on one occasion when the Bishop was preaching in a large cathedral on the needs and problems of the Church in Tennessee, a young man, the son of a rich grain merchant of Liverpool, remained behind, sought out Bishop Quintard and begged him to permit that he come to Tennessee to aid him. In any case William Klein did come to this country in 1876, studied at Sewanee, was ordained a deacon in 1877, and made priest on November 10, 1878. This young man became the successor of Dean Harris in 1881, and a power for good in the community.[9]

The Bishop returned from his year abroad to spend Christmas 1876 at the Cathedral. Several days later he and Mr. Harris journeyed to the Chapel of the Holy Cross, Annandale, to perform the marriage ceremony for Charles Parsons and Miss Margaret Britton. In 1877 the Cathedral was still conducting a mission at Ridgeway, originally started by Dr. Hines, but reorganized in 1875. Also in that year the Bishop began to consecrate certain "faithful women" as Associate Sisters of St. Mary. In the convention *Journals* of the next two years, St. Mary's is put at the head of the list of parishes, and the Bishop now listed the other clergy of Memphis as Canons of the Cathedral. This was another aspect of his "Cathedral Idea" that he was to be the head of a *familia* of the clergy of his cathedral city. Even though the formal listing in the *Journal* was only for a year or two, we find him many years later still appointing

_____
9. *Journal of 1876,* 79, shows that the Standing Committee recommended William Klein "a member of the Church of England" as candidate for Holy Orders. After becoming priest, he was for a while in charge of St. Paul's in the Mountain (Sewanee). The Cathedral *Register* shows that he was in Memphis helping out during the last weeks of the yellow fever epidemic of 1878.

Memphis clergy as Canons. The first to be so listed are: (1877) Charles Parsons, Chancellor; George White, Registrar; Virginius Gee, Catechist; and J. Ridley Gray, Precentor.

The ensuing years, 1878 and 1879, were critical and fateful ones both in the history of Memphis and of the Cathedral. The epidemics of these years almost ruined Memphis and changed it from "the fastest growing city in the South" to a stagnant, debt-ridden "Taxing District," for it lost its charter. It took almost twenty-five years for the city to recover. St. Mary's also suffered staggering blows, but again it was demonstrated that the blood of the martyrs became an inspiration to the church.

The city had scarcely forgotten the nightmare of 1873 when in the early summer of 1878 news of a yellow fever outbreak in the West Indies and then in New Orleans caused shudders of apprehension in the bluff city. When it arrived in Grenada, Mississippi, efforts were made to establish quarantine stations at Germantown, Whitehaven and President's Island, but already yellow fever had quietly slipped in. A few deaths occurred in early August, by mid-month the tempo increased, and the panic rush to escape the city began many days before officials pronounced an epidemic (August 23). This year approximately 35,000 inhabitants fled, leaving only an estimated 20,000 to face the plague. Of these nearly 14,000 were Negroes, and the great majority of the remaining whites were again the inhabitants of Pinch.

Let us observe the heroic efforts of the group which centered at the Cathedral. The stark reality of the situation can be appreciated clearly by observing the Cathedral *Register*. In a few weeks there were forty deaths and burials from yellow fever, and twenty-seven baptisms listed as "in extremis." Among the names of the Church Home children and Cathedral communicants were scattered the names of the priests, Sisters and visiting physicians who died during the dread days.

During this fatal summer, Sisters Constance and Thecla

had returned to New York (about August 1) for a much needed rest but Sister Hughetta and Sister Frances—the new director of the Church Home—had remained in Memphis. On August 15 news reached the vacationing Sisters that Memphis was stricken. The two immediately made preparations to return, and stopped by Trinity Infirmary in New York to arrange for money and supplies to be sent them. Here, in the chapel of the infirmary, Father G. H. Houghton commended them to a merciful God. They arrived in Memphis on August 20. There exists an anonymous pamphlet, "The Sisters of St. Mary's at Memphis, with the acts and sufferings of the priests and others who were with them during the yellow fever season of 1878," written in 1879 by someone who obviously had access to the letters and diaries of Sister Constance, and from it we can follow the work of the "noble band" almost from day to day.

Thus by August 20, there were working from the Cathedral Dean Harris, Charles Parsons (of St. Lazarus-Grace) and Sisters Constance, Thecla, Hughetta and Frances; also two associates who resided at the Home, Mrs. Bulloch and Mrs. Murdoch. By this time Parsons and Harris had appealed to Bishop Quintard (now in New York) and to the New York papers for aid. They pointed out that aid was needed so that they could (1) feed the hungry "who can earn nothing," (2) provide the barest necessities for the sick, (3) minister to the dying, (4) bury the dead, and (5) care for the orphaned children. Aid did pour into Memphis in great quantities and on a national scale. From the Bishop's diary we learn that "many clergymen volunteered their services to devote themselves to work in the plague stricken part of my diocese." He named several and added that there were twenty or thirty others who volunteered, "but the clergy in Memphis did not desire any unacclimated priests, and only two such were permitted to go. The Rev. Louis Schuyler . . . would not be dissuaded, but with sublime devotion gave himself to His work . . . On the fourth of September, I telegraphed the Rev. Dr. Dalzell of Shreveport . . . to know if he could recommend to me any acclimated priests who could go to Memphis to the assistance of Dr. Harris, Mr. Parsons and Dr. White, the two former of whom were down with yellow fever. The same day I received the Doctor's reply, 'I will leave for Memphis tomorrow.' "[10]

Thus to the original group there were added in early September the priests, Louis Schuyler and William Dalzell, and from the convent in New York the Sisters Helen and Ruth (who had been trained as nurses) and Sister Clare, an Anglican nun from St. Margaret's, East Grinstead, London, who was in Boston at the time. The Doctors, William Armstrong and Major Mickle, also resided with the Harrises. It was amidst strange sights, sounds and smells that this group lived and worked. Cannon were fired frequently in the hope of breaking up the "miasma;" the streets were white with lime except for the black and smouldering piles of burning bedding which filled the city with acrid smoke. The rumble of wagon loads of coffins was also a too familiar sound.

Shortly after her arrival Sister Constance wrote (August 25):

A strange sad Sunday. We drove in at 6 a.m. from the Church Home; two celebrations of H. C. at 7:30 and 9:30. Vespers appointed at 5:30 but no one present as even the clergy called away. Sister Thecla found three unknown persons insensible and without attendants on High Street. Dr. E. reported ill at his office . . . Dr. Armstrong reports that Sister Frances and nurse S have the fever. Went and made everything comfortable at the Infirmary. Called on the G's, very obdurate without a nurse. Applied in vain to Howard's for a nurse, but six applications by us for nurses unfilled. Sister Thecla sat up with Mrs. Harris and Mrs. Bulloch at the Church Home.

---

10. *Journal of 1879*, 16. On Sept. 4 the Bishop celebrated a special Eucharist in the Chapel of St. John the Baptist for the stricken Harris and Parsons. In his report he estimated that $500,000 was raised in the North, and $200,000 in the South for Memphis alone, plus hundreds of carloads of provisions and medicines and clothing, etc. The Howards sent in many doctors and nurses.

On August 26 Sister Hughetta was ill, but later recovered. On the twenty-seventh Sister Constance reported that she met five or six Negroes and tried to secure a nurse. They said they "were mighty jubious about this here fever and would not go." It was on this same day that the Relief Association asked the Sisters to again take over Canfield Asylum (which was on the outskirts of town and not as close to the "infected region" as the Church Home) as a place of refuge for orphans of all races and creeds. The Sisters were a little hesitant as this was supposed to be a safer job. It was this obligation that decided them to appeal to the Mother House for more help. Plague psychology, even as in the time of Thucydides, created some strange behavior, and Sister Constance experienced this when on August 28 Mr. Parsons drove her out to the Canfield Asylum. The colored caretaker of the building locked the door and gesticulated wildly for them to leave. Indeed, Mr. Parsons had to return to the city and get an official order before they were admitted. The next day a mob of men met her carriage and protested against the bringing of children "from the infested area" into their neighborhood. One man even read aloud from a paper, supposedly from the mayor, forbidding it. To this group Sister Constance calmly replied:

> Sirs is it possible that you would have us refuse these children the very protection you have obtained for your own. We do not propose to make a hospital of the Asylum. If any of the children are taken ill they shall be carried immediately to our infirmary at the Church Home.

Until September the original group, though occasionally ill from worry and overwork, had on the whole maintained their spirits and courage. They had even become hardened to the many gruesome sights indoors and to the carts with eight or nine corpses in rough boxes passing by; but on September 2 the new Sisters arrived.[11] The original group felt apprehensive

---

11. Sister Constance reports: I saw a nurse stop one (a cart) today and ask for a certain man's residence, and the Negro driver just pointed over his shoulder with a whip at the heap of coffins . . . and answered, "I've got him here in his coffin."

for them; then both Mr. Harris and Mr. Parsons, their chief moral support, fell ill. Until then they had received the comfort of the daily Eucharist, now with both ill there was none to administer it. On September 7 Charles Parsons died, the first of the band to go.[12] From then on death struck with dreadful frequency. On the day of his death the new clerical volunteers, Schuyler and Dalzell, arrived. Sisters Constance and Thecla, who had watched over Mr. Parsons and Dean Harris, were stricken on the fifth. Sister Hughetta and Mrs. Bulloch nursed them. Sisters Ruth and Helen were at the Church Home Infirmary, and Frances and Clare at Canfield. The tempo of deaths accelerated. Sister Constance died on September 9; Sister Thecla, on September 12; Dr. Armstrong on the fourteenth; Mrs. Bulloch on the sixteenth; Mr. Schuyler, the seventeenth; Sister Ruth, the eighteenth; Sister Frances, who had seemed to have recovered, on October 4. Those who were stricken, but survived were Dean and Mrs. Harris, Dr. White, and Sisters Hughetta, Clare and Helen.[13]

The Church *Register* shows that many doctors who came to assist during the epidemic died in that fatal September; among them was Dr. Paul Otey, son of the first bishop. Two other long time Cathedral members died of the fever: Mr. J. P. Trezevant, who had been senior warden and treasurer of the

---

12. He had been a Lieutenant of the 4th Artillery in 1861; won a Captain's commission and a brevet for Lieut. Colonel. In 1868 he returned to West Point as an instructor but began to study theology and took Holy Orders in 1870.

13. The above dates are from *The Sisters of St. Mary's,* and are presumably the dates of death. In the *Cathedral Register* burial dates are given. It is impressive to see whole pages where under "Causes of death" the first line will read "yellow fever" and every succeeding line will have "Do" (ditto). In 1878 the first recorded death from yellow fever was on July 27; there are single deaths on August 4 and 8. The frequent days begin on August 18. The burial dates of the "martyrs of St. Mary's" were September 7, Charles Parsons; 9, Sister Constance; 13, Sister Thecla; 18, Mr. Schuyler; 19, Sister Ruth; 23, Mrs. Scherri, "a volunteer from New York," and Dr. Heady; 25, Dr. Robert Burchard; 26, Dr. C. L. Cheirs and J. P. Trezevant, "senior warden from organization in 1857;" 29, Dr. Paul Otey; October 3, Mary Mhoon; 4, Sister Frances; November 12, Mary E. Galloway.

On January 26, 1879, an impressive memorial service for Mr. Parsons was held at Grace, attended by the Chickasaw Guards, of which he had been chaplain.

parish from the very beginning, and Mrs. Mary Galloway, for whom the Old Ladies Home is named. Robert Brinkley died that same fall at Iuka, though not of the fever.

On November 10, 1878, the young William Klein was ordained priest, and came to Memphis to assist Mr. Harris during the waning days of the epidemic. When, by the end of the year Memphis counted its stricken and dead, it found that of the 20,000 who remained, 17,600 had been infected by the fever, of whom 5,150 had died.[14]

Early in March 1879, the Bishop set to work to raise funds for an altar to commemorate the heroic work of the Sisters. The stone altar, the one now in the Cathedral sanctuary, was installed in the old wooden Cathedral in May, and was formally consecrated on Whitsunday (June 1), 1879. It was designed by the architect, Henry Congdon, and was executed by the firm of Ellis and Kitson of New York. In the pamphlet gotten out for the occasion is the following formal description of the altar by Dr. John Henry Hopkins:

> The altar rests upon a platform of dove colored marble, of three steps, with risers of Tennessee marble. On the lowest riser is the legend: † Sisters of St. Mary † September and October 1878 †. On the riser of the second step are the four names: † Constance † Thecla † Ruth † Frances †. On the upper riser these words from the Song of Solomon: † He feedeth among lilies †. These letters are cut through the polished surface and then gilded. The body of the altar and the retable are of Caen stone. The front is divided by shafts of red Lisbon marble with molded bases and *annuli,* and carved caps of natural foliage, flowers and fruits into three panels, each bearing a group of lilies in high relief. A carved band of hawthorne leaves and berries forms the cornice under the *mensa* which last is of white marble inlaid with five crosses of red marble. The altar projects two feet in width from the retable and is eight feet ten inches in length, and three feet six inches high. The retable is one foot five inches in projection, and nine feet long, with ends paneled and carved. The central

14. Capers, *Op. Cit.,* 198, says that not more than 200 of more than 7,000 whites escaped the fever and of the ill 75 per cent died. Of negroes only seven per cent died. He estimates the Catholics lost 2,000, including 13 priests and 30 nuns.

portion is of superior dignity, height and projection and out of its gabled top rises an octagonal pedestal with molded base and capital carved with morning glories, bearing the large white marble cross heretofore used as the altar cross. The projecting center is flanked by red marble shafts, with molded bases, *annuli,* and carved caps of natural foliage, carrying a trefoil arch under the crocketed gable. A band of carved passion flowers forms a cornice between the capitals and supporting tympanum of the arch above, which is of red marble this *Chi Rho* flanked by *Alpha and Omega,* incised and gilded, and with the descending dove in a panel above, in the spandril formed by the gable. Below the cornice, boldly carved in Caen stone is the device of the Sisterhood of St. Mary—the lily of the order, the ground richly diapered and gilded. The bottom shelf of the retable is carved with foliage and the risers are of Tennessee marble with the legend on the gospel side † Alleluia Osanna † and on the epistle side † Osanna Alleluia † cut into the polished stone and gilded. The risers of the upper shelves are of red Lisbon marble. They finish against two terminal octagonal pedestals, with carved capitals, and are surmounted by an ornamental carved cresting.

In the old Cathedral the chancel was more wholly devoted to the martyrs of the yellow fever than at present, for it was lighted by twelve lancet windows. The six in the sanctuary commemorated the seven clergymen who died in the South during the epidemic of 1878: Charles Parsons, Louis S. Schuyler, John M. Schwrar, Duncan Green, William Littlejohn, John L. Steele, D.D., and Otis Hackett. The six choir windows commemorated the laymen of the Church who fell in the same epidemic.

The service of consecration of the altar was, according to the press, "remarkably beautiful and inspiring." Bishop Quintard was assisted by Dean Harris, who preached the sermon, and by the Rev. George Moore of Somerville, and by the young deacon, Thomas F. Gailor, now at Pulaski. It will be unnecessary to report in full Dean Harris' sermon. His text was "He feedeth among the lilies." He elaborated upon the role of the altar in Holy Communion; he explained that the words "Alleluia Osanna" were the triumphant shout of the redeemed, but were also the last whispered words of Sister Constance. He ended with an explanation of the Tabernacle, which should be known to members of the Cathedral, and is therefore given in full:

> Beneath the cross and serving as its support is an empty tabernacle; empty, that is, on all ordinary occasions; since we do not, and under the law may not, and in my judgment ought not to reserve the Blessed Sacrament; but the time may come again, as once and once again it has come, even in my own short experience, when it not only may, but must be reserved for the sick. In the yellow fever epidemic of 1873 I came slowly and cautiously to regard it as absolutely necessary, as the only alternative to say ten, or twenty, or thirty celebrations *per diem,* which (supposing a man had strength enough to keep it up) is otherwise so full of objection that it ought not to be permitted. With this experience . . . I had no difficulty in taking my decision in the premises when again in 1878 the same question was presented in aggravated form. I give it to you as my deliberate conviction that on such occasions no priest can properly or effectively discharge the functions of his office, who, on account of strict construction of law not made for such exigencies, will refuse to reserve for the sick the Blessed Sacrament. I am not alone in this opinion among those of our clergy whose experience entitles them to know something of the difficulties of the situation. Ask any one of them so situated, and if he did not answer you that such was his practice, he will at least tell you it ought to have been. Dr. Steel of Key West was communicated in his last hour by a deacon, from the altar where he had consecrated it a week before. I remember that one morning after dear Parson's death, and before either Dr. Dalzell or Mr. Schuyler had arrived, a person not in holy orders being in my room, mentioned the illness of several others who were thought to be very near their end, and who were anxious to make communion, and I said: Go, take it reverently from the altar and communicate them. In view of it even the now empty tabernacle is itself a memorial of the epidemic. It will have no other use on any ordinary occasion than the law of the Church permits and authorizes. I have said this much in reference to it because I am conscious that it is unusual in our churches, and because there are so many unreasonable people in the world.

On the evening of the dedication there was a great Floral Festival by the Sunday School. Fifteen classes, each accompanied by its teacher, proceeded to the front of the church. At the chancel steps were three special steps inscribed "Faith, Hope,

Charity." Each class then brought forward a floral tribute in the form of a religious emblem, while a member of the class gave a brief explanation of its symbolism. "As class after class came forward, and the several sections were placed in position, from the summit of the base rose a large and beautiful Cross. The Cross completed, was then encircled upon its upper arm by a Crown; and after all was finished a pure white dove was seen to descend out of a halo of light from the corona." This pageantry was planned by Dr. S. H. Collins, and the musical parts were arranged by Mr. Currier. Miss Clara Dammann also read an original five stanza poem, "Apostrophe to the Altar."[15]

Hardly had the new altar been consecrated when the third and final scourge of yellow fever descended upon the seemingly doomed city. Fortunately the immunity built up by the exposure of the past year and the usual flight cut fatalities, though the disease raged longer, for four long months (July-October). The Sisters, mindful of the dreadful mortality among the children in 1878, removed the orphans of the Church Home to

---

15. From the pamphlet put out on the occasion I will list only the class names; the symbols each presented; and the name of the pupil explaining the symbol. For the explanation one must consult the pamphlet.
1. St. Peter's—Faith—S. L. Finley. 2. St. Paul's—Hope—Charles Bell. 3. St. John's—Charity—Mary Mhoon. 4. St. Cecilia's—the Lyre—Eloise James. 6. St. Andrew's—the Mitre—Willie Barnes. 7. St. Stephen's—the Pelican—Harry Yerger. 8. St. Hilda's—the Book—Lizzie Yates. 9. St. Luke's—the Triangle and Circle—Weakley Logwood. 10. St. Gabriel's—the Star—Mary Richardson. 11. St. Margaret's—the Font—Rudolph Belcher. 12. St. Agnes—the Lamb— Mary Burklow. 13. St. Mary's—the Crown—Annie Wainwright. 14. The Holy Spirit—the Dove—Madge Doyle. 15. (no Name)—the Holy Cross—Ella Cooper.
Miss Dammann's poem contained five stanzas: The Throne, The Memorial, The Bread of Life; The Altar Inscription; The Ascription. I shall quote only one verse, the "Altar Inscription":
Hail precious Altar of our Heavenly King!
    To thee glad lights and flowers we shall bring;
Our hearts go out to thee with throbbing joy;
    We love the words thou speakest to our soul.
"Osanna!" Be our JESU! Round His throne,
    "Alleluia, Osanna, Alleluia," roll!
"He feedeth 'mong the lilies;"—Then we read
    The names of those four virgins, true to death,
Who thirsted here for Him, but thirst no more,
Are freshened with the Spirit's living, quickening, breath.
May we cry: "GOD, Osanna!" in our dying hour!
    May we sing: "Alleluia," on that shore!
May we be 'mong the lilies where He feeds,
    And part from our Eternal Love no more, no more!

Huntsville, Alabama. The Rev. W. B. Huson, who had suffered in '78 and was therefore immune, came in August to aid Mr. Harris at the Cathedral. The *Register* shows that this year there were thirty deaths and burials from the fever, about three fourths as many as the previous year, but the total number of cases in Memphis was much smaller, only about 2,000, and deaths were estimated at 600.

The arduous labors of the Harrises during these epidemic years wore them out, and St. Mary's was so poverty stricken that it could hardly pay them a living wage. The first vestry (or chapter) book of the Cathedral begins again in 1880, and we find the chapter struggling to pay the dean "a stated amount," and the Church ridden with debt. In 1881 the Bishop sent the newly ordained young English priest, William Klein, to be Mr. Harris' assistant, with the title of Canon. Until he was made Dean (when the Harrises returned to their native Mississippi), he served both at the Cathedral and as Rector of the Church of the Good Shepherd. Dean Harris built St. Mary's from a communicant list of seventy in 1871, the year of his arrival, to 220 in 1878, before yellow fever struck, and the moving away of many Memphians reduced the number in 1880 to 160. Yet in his entire time in Memphis his salary never reached $1,000, except for one year (1873). He was a real hero, and was often welcomed back in the eighties, when the Bishop created him a Canon of the Cathedral.[16]

---

16. When St. Mary's was given a new organ in 1906, the chapter sent the old one to Mr. Harris' Church at Rolling Fork, Mississippi. He died July 2, 1911, at the age of 78, and Dean Morris held a memorial service for him in the Cathedral on July 23.

CHAPTER IV

DEAN KLEIN

THE YOUNG ENGLISHMAN, William Klein, who was to direct the destinies of the Cathedral for more than a decade (1881-1893) has become a legend at St. Mary's. Thin, tall, ascetic looking, with eager eyes, he was noted for his passionate interest in what today would be called the "underprivileged"—both white and colored. He was an earnest rather "high" churchman, and observed the English cathedral tradition of daily Morning and Evening Prayer, and of the daily Holy Eucharist. He conducted confessionals for the Sisters and others who desired it. With the aid of his English organist, Charles Currier, he beautified the services, introducing the use of chanting (there was already a vested choir) and of altar flowers. Thus he attracted many from the Memphis colony of English cotton men to the Cathedral. Even today some of our parishioners remember, as children, seeing this intense young clergyman in his broad-brimmed clerical hat, belted cassock, staff in hand stalking through the streets of the neighborhood on missions of mercy.

Mrs. Thomas Lill tells how his father, a wealthy Liverpool merchant, was greatly impressed by the fact that his son was the dean of a cathedral, visioning to himself the pomp and dignity which surrounds such officials in England but that, fortunately for his dream, though he was several times in New York, he never came to Memphis to observe the meagre reality of his son's establishment.

It was a difficult situation to which Canon Klein came. The Church, like the town, was in desperate financial straits as the

[77]

result of the yellow fever epidemics. The Bishop was still struggling to obtain a stated income from the parish for the Dean. He felt this so strongly that at a chapter meeting on February 27, 1881, he insisted that on the next Sunday, "he with the assistance of the chapter should make a thorough canvass of all present, pencil in hand, taking down the names of the people and the amount they were willing to pledge themselves to contribute . . . and that all found absent should be visited." He even announced to the chapter that he had interviewed the Ladies Aid Society, and that the ladies had expressed themselves "as quite willing to see to the collection of delinquent subscriptions" (this is the first documented evidence of organized woman's work at the Cathedral, and might prove a fertile suggestion to present chapters). Thus the first officially recorded woman's organization was the Ladies Aid, but this descended from an earlier group, organized by Dean Harris, "the Jenny Wrens," who sewed for the Church Home and engaged in other charitable activities. As Dean Klein disapproved of this name, it became the Ladies Aid, and soon the Cathedral Guild. Meanwhile the new Dean's salary ranged between $500 and $800 per annum between the years 1882 and 1885.[1]

Dr. Harris returned from Mississippi to assist, and to preach the sermon at the formal installation service for Dean Klein on March 5, 1882. After his own installation the Dean presented Mr. A. W. Pierce, son of the Bishop of Arkansas, for ordination to the diaconate.[2]

Right after his installation the question arose as to Dean Klein's living quarters. He had at first resided in the Bishop's

1. *Vestry Book* (1885), 89, indicates that the Dean was given the proceeds of the envelope contributions (subscriptions); that the loose offering on the first Sunday of each month went "to the poor"; that of the second Sunday "to missions"; the proceeds of the remaining Sundays being for Cathedral expense. The chapter usually gave Mr. Currier an annual $200, which it called "an offering of gratitude" for his work with the choir. He must have spent all this on his boys, to whom he gave small fees for attendance.
2. *Journal of 1882*, 21. Earlier in the same day, Mr. Klein had assisted Bishop Quintard in the ordination of a colored deacon, the Rev. Isaac Black, at Emmanuel.

House, which had been vacated by the Sisters after the yellow fever epidemic for a newly constructed but still incomplete home and school east of the Cathedral. Now Bishop Quintard informed him that he contemplated a return to Memphis from Sewanee where he had been residing as Vice-Chancellor. The Bishop therefore desired the chapter to raise funds for the construction of a Clergy House.

Thus in the spring of 1882 the chapter called for estimates for such a building. It is curious to note that these estimates, for a two storey house, 20 by 40 feet, ranged between $850 and $2,000. Any action on the building naturally had to await money raising activities. The summer abounded in entertainments such as concerts, strawberry festivals and even (at the instigation of Messrs. Cruse, McDowell, and Charles Coate) an amateur horse race at the Fairgrounds. Meanwhile the chapter discovered that the Sisters of St. Mary were contemplating adding to their building and so were willing to donate their original frame school house to the Cathedral. The chapter held many arguments, pro and con, as to whether this building were removable, or worth renovation, but they finally agreed to try it. Thus after almost a year, by October 1883, the structure was removed and relocated behind the Cathedral on Alabama, for a cost of $666.70. But another $150-$300 was required to make it "livable." Thus it was the spring of 1884 before the bachelor Dean could inhabit the new "Clergy House." In this same year the Bishop requested the chapter to try to get the parishes of Memphis to assist in repairing the Bishop's House in view of his contemplated return. Dean Klein was put in charge of this work and reported to the Convention of 1885 that he had spent $361 for this but that $300 more was needed.[3]

So many simultaneous activities were in operation during

---

3. *Journal of 1885*, 47. We may note here that the Cathedral paid $140 for a three year insurance premium. The building was valued at $6,500 and the altar at $1,000. The next year they changed the valuations to $5,000 on the Cathedral, $600 on the organ, $200 on the benches, $200 on the stained glass windows, and decided to drop the insurance on the altar.

the deanship of Mr. Klein that the story of them will perhaps be clearer if these are treated separately, rather than trying to trace them simultaneously or chronologically. A brief listing of the projects in which he was engaged or involved would include 1) the "Associate Mission"; 2) work with the Negroes; 3) what would today be called "neighborhood work"; 4) the activities of the Sisters of St. Mary during these years; and 5) the regular and normal parish activity. We shall also trace briefly the work of the Bishop with the parish during this period (1883-1893).

One reason for establishing a Clergy House, beside the necessity of providing a home for the Dean, was that in 1884 the Bishop reverted to one of his pet cathedral ideas, namely of making it the center of missionary activity. He therefore created at St. Mary's a "Cathedral Associate Mission" and attached to it an elderly priest, the Rev. F. A. Juny, Sr. (a one-time Roman Catholic and former professor at the University of Mississippi); and two young deacons, R. Calder Young, and F. A. Juny, Jr. At first, the elder Juny was given charge of the Church of the Good Shepherd, but after his death in 1886 the church was transferred to the Rev. R. Calder Young, who had been ordained priest that same year. Meanwhile he and the younger Juny were given an extended territory in which to do mission work. This included Brownsville, Somerville, Mason, Withe, Ripley, Covington, Ravenscroft and LaGrange. The Bishop in his diary (1884) tells of visiting these places with the young men. Actually the Bishop seems to have chosen weak instruments for this operation, for it is sad but necessary to relate that the young Juny was formally deposed from the ministry at St. Mary's on June 10, 1886 (seemingly for no moral offense, since Bishop Gailor re-installed him in 1896, and ordained him priest in 1897). The Rev. R. Calder Young was also deposed at the Cathedral on February 9, 1889, the Bishop remarking that it was good to be rid of "this wayward priest."

As early as 1884, the Dean reported to the convention that the Church had again resumed control of the Canfield (colored) Orphan Asylum, and that "this institution constituted part of St. Mary's Cathedral work." A colored deacon, the Rev. Isaac Black, was stationed there, and the chapel repaired and rechristened St. Cyprian's. The ladies of the Cathedral gave active assistance in teaching in the Sunday School. But, unfortunately, Mr. Black, like his predecessor, the Rev. George Jackson, had to be deposed. The Dean was then assisted by another Negro deacon, the Rev. Alfred Anderson, and by a lay reader, W. T. McNeal. By this time the orphans left over from the yellow fever had been found homes, so Canfield Asylum was now converted to a day school—with about ninety in attendance, as well as a Sunday School.

In February 1884 the Dean also helped negotiate the purchase of a permanent church building for Emmanuel congregation. This building was formerly a German Lutheran Church, and was located on Third Street, between Jefferson and Court. The entire diocese had been asked to contribute to the undertaking, but the Dean reported to convention (1885) that only $443.15 had been raised, and most of this from two churches. The next year Klein, assisted by the Rev. Alfred Anderson, presented five Negro candidates to the Bishop for confirmation. Two other deacons, H. R. Sargent and George Fenwick, are mentioned as working at one time or another at Canfield or Emmanuel in the late eighties. The greatest impetus to colored work came, however, around 1890 and was due to several factors: first, the Bishop arranged to have a kind of Episcopal training school for colored postulants established near Fisk University, which was called Hoffman Hall; second, he appointed an Archdeacon for Colored Work in the diocese, the first being the Ven. G. B. Perry; third, he at last found for the work at Emmanuel a seemingly consecrated and energetic Negro priest, Dr. Honesty, who had formerly been a professor at Meharry

College. Dr. Honesty changed the day school at Canfield to a preparatory school (called St. Mark's) intended to train material for Hoffman Hall. He also inspired renewed interest in Emmanuel Church, beautified its services, had an impressive vested choir and was responsible for the building of a new church for Negroes, St. Paul's, at Mason.[4]

Dean Klein wore himself out by his many activities, one of which was ministering to the poor in the neighborhood of the Cathedral. Even when he himself was hardly getting enough on which to to live, he asked the chapter to set aside the offerings of the first Sunday of each month for "work among the poor," and one of his most active organizations was "St. Mary's Mission to the Poor." One of its first activities was to start a parish day school (1885) for from twenty-five to fifty girls from the neighborhood who could not afford the tuition of St. Mary's School. In this he was usually assisted by one of the Sisters. Another important activity which he started was a gymnasium for the boys of the region. In this work he was ably supported by several men from the Cathedral, more particularly by two who were to become mainstays of the Church for many years, P. Stenning Coate and Arthur J. Warwick. Charles Coate, the elder of the Coate brothers, had come to Memphis in Dean Harris' time and was a member of the chapter. Stenning Coate came to Memphis in September, 1882. He has left this brief description of the inception of the Cathedral Gymnasium:

> In 1884 or 1885, I moved from a boarding house on Adams Street to the Clergy House, and built a gymnasium and social service building behind the Cathedral. This was the start of the Y.P.S.L. . . . Before Baden-Powell had been heard of, the Cathedral changed very tough gangs of boys into Boy Scouts, good gymnasts, and regular Saturday hikers, with a smattering of botany and woodcraft. (He then explains that in 1886 or 1887 his firm sent him to Norfolk and New Orleans, and that Mr. Warwick succeeded him as reweigher

4. Hoffman Hall at Fisk did not last very long. Later it moved to Mason and became an industrial school, and was re-named Gailor Industrial in 1936. In 1890, Bishop Quintard took an extensive trip to the East to raise money for colored work. Dr. Honesty had to be deposed in 1902.

of his cotton firm in Memphis). He (Warwick) took over
the gym work, and being an unusual athlete, inspired the boys
to build wholesome, healthy bodies.

Mr. Warwick also inspired social activities and dances,
"under the shadow of the Cathedral, a thing then unheard of,
"under the supervision of a Dean who believed it was the duty
of the Church to encourage people in their amusements." Mr.
Coate ends his note by saying that "Dean Klein was the one
who started the hospital, a free dispensary, a library, soup-
kitchen, etc. . . . the women were the big workers."

Dean Klein was worried because certain regulations relat-
ing to admission to the City Hospital barred many who were
in need. Aided by the work of "St. Mary's Mission to the Poor"
he decided, in February 1887, to establish St. Mary's Cottage
Hospital. It was first located in a private home on Bass Avenue
and could only accommodate eight, but soon on the same street
a building was constructed for the purpose. Miss Charlotte
Wells was the nurse in charge, and by 1888 the new hospital
could accommodate up to fifty.[5]

These multifarious activities of the Dean began to
endanger his health. In the summer of 1887, he was required
by his doctors to take an extended vacation, June to October.[6]
One of our long-time Cathedral members is authority for the
story that the Dean's doctor informed him that what he needed
"was a soft arm around his neck." In any case, Mr. Klein
decided to follow this prescription, for on December 26 (Feast
of St. Stephen) at seven in the morning the Bishop performed
the marriage ceremony for the Dean and Miss Charlotte Wells,
his "greylady" of the Cottage Hospital, and followed it with

---

5. Keating, *Memphis II,* 121, says the management of the hospital was
composed of Rev. William Klein, manager; Drs. E. A. Neely, W. B. Winkler,
A. G. Sinclair, physicians and surgeons. Bass Ave. was the old name for the
present Jefferson after it joins Adams.

6. *Journal of 1887.* The Dean was unable to attend this convention. The
Standing Committee, of which he was an active member, mentions his absence,
and passed resolutions of sympathy and promises to follow him with fervent
prayer for his restoration.

a nuptial Mass. Little wonder then that Mr. Klein informed the chapter the next year that he was unable to live now as a married man on his meagre salary of $1050. The chapter voted to raise this to $1,500 but it had to sacrifice the Cathedral School in order to do so.

During Mr. Klein's deanship the Sisters who survived the epidemic, conducted their projects—the School and the Church Home—efficiently and well. This was due in great part to the forceful and capable management of Sister Hughetta, who though in active control of the Memphis establishment since the death of Sister Constance, was not formally appointed Superior by the order until 1883. Thanks to the financial support of Colonel Snowden and of other supporters, the Sisters erected a portion of their new brick school building as early as 1878. This school building was completed in 1883, when, as we have seen, they donated their old frame school house to the Cathedral for use as the Clergy House. Finally, in 1888, their building program was completed by the erection of a Sisters' House and a Chapel. The latter still exists—though the other buildings have long been removed—as a constant reminder to the Cathedral of this past epoch of church history. Colonel Snowden gave the Chapel in memory of his (and Sister Hughetta's) mother, Mrs. John Bayard Snowden, who had died in 1885. The Chapel was dedicated on the Feast of the Purification (1889), by Dr. George Patterson, in the absence abroad of the Bishop. The Chapel was to the west of an imposing group of three-story brick buildings, and was entered from the east by a porch which extended in front of the Sisters' Home. Between the Chapel and the Cathedral there ran a path or short-cut to Jones Street, which eventually became so noisy that it had to be blocked off.

In 1887 Sister Hughetta purchased what was known as Hayes Farm at Sewanee. Thus by the summer of 1888, the Sisters had a place of rest and retreat for the hot months. By 1897 they established here a school for mountain girls. In 1902 Sister Hughetta moved to Sewanee to take control of this work, and after the final departure of the Sisters from Memphis this became their headquarters in Tennessee.[7]

St. Mary's School in Memphis flourished under the Sisters during the eighties and nineties, despite the competition of two famous local schools for girls, Miss Higbee's and the Clara Conway School. In her report to the convention in 1888, Sister Hughetta explained "that a certain amount of gymnastic exercise was a part of the daily routine," and that "its wholesome effects were visible." She went on to report that the school desired "to keep fully abreast of the times and to make use of all that is good in the so-called 'new education' " (their rival Clara Conway specialized in the "new-education"). She said that they had improved the Literary, Mathematical, Scientific and Classical work, and "for the ensuing year increased advantages will be secured, such as a more complete apparatus, a chemical laboratory, a valuable herbarium, and additions to the library." The enrollment at this time hovered around a hundred, of whom twenty to thirty were boarding students. These only paid $200 a year board, and tuition was "$40 upward according to the course of study or the department." At that time the Sister Superior instructed in Church History, Holy Scripture, and Illumination. The other two Sisters, Flora and Herberta, instructed history and kindergarten.[8]

From the time of their arrival, the Sisters had assumed the care of the altar and sanctuary. Many of the beautifully

---

7. Sister Frideswide said there was no school in operation at Sewanee from 1899-1902, but that it has been in continuous operation since then.

8. Other departments were under lay instructors. Those teaching in 1888 were: Susan Temple, English; Maud Stowe, Natural Science; Mary Beecher, Latin, Greek, Elocution; Carrie Keating, Piano and Voice; Professor Paul Schneider, Violin; Louis Bignon, French and German; and Miss Annie Stephenson, Art. Many of the same teachers were still instructing in the 1890's, but Natural Science was under an English lady, Katherine Vale; and elocution had been removed from the classics and given, more logically, to the physical culture instructor, Mary Farrand.

embroidered frontals and altar linens in use today are their work. The Sisters also instructed the girls and women of the altar guilds of their day. Most of the traditions of today's altar committees may be traced back to this instruction. Their devotion to the work of sacristans was so great that during the depression of the early nineties the Sisters volunteered to undertake all the expenses connected with the upkeep of the altar.

During the eighties the Bishop was in and out of Memphis at frequent intervals. In 1883 he seems to have planned to return from Sewanee to live again in the cathedral city, and so the Bishop's House was once more renovated in 1884. He did formally return in May 1885, and was greeted at a big reception held in the home of General Carroll. At this time he declared: "I have all along desired to reside in Memphis, but until the present time it has been impossible" since he had been the Vice-Chancellor of Sewanee, and since he found his salary inadequate "to reside in any city in my diocese," but he promised to try to give "one half the year to the good people of Memphis." Unfortunately soon after this the Bishop found that his health had begun to fail. In 1886 he remarked, "I fear I have been prodigal of the gift of a good constitution . . . by a needless excess of effort and labor."

He thus changed from his early idea of dividing the diocese (resolutions to this effect had been made in conventions in 1865, 1867, 1881, and 1883) to the idea of asking for an assistant (1887), but he did not bring the resolution to the General Convention for fear it would fail. When, in 1889 and 1890, he did seek an assistant, he found that the diocesan convention was somewhat hostile to the idea and instead made resolutions in favor of a divided diocese. By 1892, however, his request was so urgent and his need so obvious that the convention did agree to the selection of a coadjutor. Thus in 1893 his "spiritual son," Thomas F. Gailor, the Vice-Chancellor of

Sewanee, was nominated by Dr. F. P. Davenport of Calvary and was unanimously elected.

During the eighties Bishop Quintard made several extended trips to England, especially on the occasion of the Lambeth Conference of 1888. But he was nearly always at St. Mary's near the first of each year to announce the appointment of the new chapter.[9]

As early as March 8, 1886, the Bishop informed the chapter that "the time had come" to consider the building of a new Cathedral. This is the first reference I can find of this project. He even appointed a committee composed of Messrs. Lamb, Shuttleworth and Currier to investigate the matter. But with its poverty, and with other pressing needs, the chapter had to shelve the idea for about ten years.

In 1887 the chapter began to issue printed reports each year. These show the state of finance, and give a good indication of the various organizations which were then in existence. The first report shows that the Cathedral then had 319 communicants; a Sunday School of fourteen teachers and 145 pupils; a choir of men and boys; St. Mary's Mission to the Poor; St. Mary's Cottage Hospital; The Cathedral Guild for women (79 members); St. Mary's Guild for Women; St. Timothy's Guild for Sunday School teachers; St. Martha's Guild for girls; a Ward of the Confraternity of the Blessed Sacrament; and an Association for Intercessory Prayer. In 1888 the Cathedral Gymnasium was added. From the Vestry Book it appears that the Dean wanted to form a Guild of the Iron Cross for men, but this never seems to have developed.[10]

---

9. From the *Vestry Book,* it seems that sometimes the Bishop both nominated and appointed; sometimes the Dean nominated and he appointed the chapter members. In any case the congregation seems to have had no choice. Dr. Quintard also continued his habit of making some of the Memphis clergy Canons of the Cathedral. Those in the late eighties were George C. Harris, the former Dean; Dr. Patterson, of Grace; and the Rev. Spruille Burford of Calvary.

10. The Woman's Auxiliary was organized in 1887 by Bishop Quintard and Mrs. Shortridge of Calvary, to aid in mission work. It made its first report to the Convention in 1888. A branch was not established at the Cathedral for several years, and it was not until the present century that the Auxiliary assumed its present function of a kind of federal government over the guilds.

Various projects for raising money for special needs continued throughout this and one might add—all subsequent periods. One interesting suggestion in the eighties was to promote a lecture by Henry George, the Single Taxer, then in his prime, but this could not be arranged. Since no chapter's trials are complete without "roof trouble," we may note that in 1890 the Cathedral had to have a new tin roof, "since the present shingle roof has not been renewed since 1857."

In the early 1890's, the Cathedral Guild set for its objective the raising of funds in order to purchase a new rectory for Dean and Mrs. Klein. The financial report for 1891 shows that the guild raised $800, "with its customary energy and zeal." By the next year they had $1,500, so the chapter began the search for a suitable dwelling.[11] Negotiations began, several houses were considered, but before anything was concluded, the Dean, who on account of ill health had been given a vacation trip to England during the summer, returned in October to announce to a saddened chapter and congregation that his English physicians had told him that he could not survive another summer in Memphis. Thus he let it be known that he would retire on Easter 1893. This decided the chapter to drop for the moment the idea of buying a home, and to find a place for the Dean to rent. Several members of the Cathedral Guild rather disapproved of this method of cutting into their accumulated principal.

The Cathedral members were distressed by the news of the forthcoming departure of their heroic and active Dean. One bright note appeared, however, for in the Dean's final year Mr. Currier made what is described as "the welcome addition of some women's voices to the choir." For a year or more this innovation was so startling that it was thought best to keep

11. One of the plans involved selling 25 feet of church property east of the Cathedral to the Sisters for $2,500, while the chapter was negotiating the purchase of a lot on Washington and a loan for building, from Colonel Snowden. When the chapter decided to buy another place on Poplar, Sister Hughetta cancelled her contract to purchase the Cathedral land.

these venturesome ladies, Miss Electra Boyle, Miss Mary Rembert, Miss Blanche Steele, and Miss Matilda Reid, hidden behind curtains.

As 1893 opened the chapter turned to the necessary task of procuring a new dean. Names were suggested by the Bishop and by Dr. Gailor of Sewanee, but the chapter finally decided to call the Rev. Howard Dumbell, a young and recently ordained priest, who like his predecessor served at the Church of the Good Shepherd before coming to the Cathedral.

CHAPTER V

THE BEGINNING OF THE NEW CATHEDRAL

THE YEAR 1893 marked a turning point in the history of the Cathedral and of the diocese. In that year Bishop Quintard finally secured an assistant bishop, and thus put to rest for a while the long mooted question of whether to divide the diocese, or to provide the Bishop with a coadjutor. The election of Dr. Quintard's assistant was remarkable in that the new Vice-Chancellor of the University of the South, Thomas Gailor, was chosen unanimously on the first ballot. The new Bishop was then in the full flower of manhood and ability. He had grown up in Memphis and it was almost a foregone conclusion that he would settle there, since for many years Bishop Quintard had spent most of his time at his beloved Sewanee. Thus for a third time the old Bishop's House was renovated, and the newly elected Bishop visited Memphis in August 1893, in order to direct the project.

Another epoch in the life of St. Mary's also ended in 1893 with the resignation and retirement of Dean Klein. He and his family returned to his old home in England. His successor was quite young, the Rev. Howard Dumbell, son of the Manxman who had done so much to build up St. Paul's in Chattanooga. The younger Dumbell had only in December 18, 1890, been ordained priest at "Old Trinity," Mason, at which time Bishop Quintard noted in his journal that many attended the ceremony "for this faithful young deacon." Since his stay was so brief (slightly over a year), and since the next two deans, Turner and Green, also remained for only short periods, we shall in this chapter make a digression from the general account of the parish and concentrate on the strenuous efforts made by Bishop Gailor, the chapter, and others, to construct first the crypt, and later the beginning of the superstructure of the "New Cathedral," returning to observe internal developments in the next chapter.

In Dean Dumbell's first parish report (1894), there is this significant statement, "In November 1893, I inaugurated a movement for building a new Cathedral. This was immediately followed by a few subscriptions and an earnest effort of the Sisters of St. Mary and their Associates. The Assistant Bishop has taken the matter in hand and is pushing the work with vigor. *Laus deo.*" Mr. Dumbell can hardly claim that he "inaugurated" the matter, since, as we have seen, the chapter's minutes show that as long ago as 1886, Bishop Quintard had urged the chapter to undertake a new building. Certainly, with the arrival of Bishop Gailor and his family to Memphis on January 26, 1894, the Coadjutor became the driving force of the movement, aided by the zeal of the congregation and the Sisters. The Bishop's first year in Memphis was replete with addresses on the New Cathedral, with meetings with "persons interested," and with the organization of multifarious guilds for furthering the work of obtaining subscriptions and memorials.[1] Unfortunately, whoever conceived the idea of raising the impressive amount needed for the edifice, mainly on the basis of soliciting memorials, little foresaw the Pandora's Box of trouble which later plagued the project, the Bishop, and the Deans who were involved in the effort to construct the new building.

It is evident, from Bishop Gailor's correspondence on the subject, that even before he approached the famous New York

---

1. Here are some sample references from Gailor's diary in the *Journal of 1895:* January 2, 1894, "Met with members of St. Mary's sisterhood and their associates and conferred with them about building a new Cathedral." April 15, "Preached at St. Mary's on the subject of the new Cathedral." April 26, "Preached at a meeting of persons interested in the new Cathedral." November 1, "I preached to a goodly congregation in St. Mary's on the subject of building of the new Cathedral and took an offering for that purpose. This was the first semi-annual meeting of persons interested in the work."

architect, W. Halsey Wood, in the spring of 1895, on the matter of drawing up plans for a new cathedral, he had formulated in his own mind the general type of building he desired, and that subscription books had been distributed and Memorial Associations formed.

The letters of Mr. Wood to the Bishop, from March 1895 to March 1897 (the time of Mr. Wood's death), have been preserved. Let us observe the unfolding of the cathedral plans therefore, before returning to note the struggle on the financial front in Memphis. The Bishop seems to have been drawn to Mr. Wood because he had designed St. Paul's, Chattanooga, was one of the architects of St. John the Divine, and a man of fine character and reputation. The architect's first letter to the Bishop says, "The entire picture drawn in your letter is perfectly clear, and I thoroughly understand what you would desire in the way of a churchly building." From other remarks in this letter it is clear that Bishop Gailor had dreams of a great central tower, and Mr. Wood avers that he "will work very hard to make a success of the design." That he did so is obvious from the fact that within a month he was promising perspective drawings, and hoping that the Bishop would be able to come by to see them. Mr. Wood even swallowed hints on the "memorial idea" with seeming good grace, for on April 1, 1895, he wrote:

> Sister Hughetta has kindly enclosed a complete list of memorials together with the amount to be spent upon each. It has my entire approval, and I will proceed to place them upon the plan. And I also note what you say regarding the tablets to be placed on the walls. This feature will give a charm to the building that could scarcely be gained in any other way, and I will see that plenty of wall space is allowed for them.

One clue to the "memorial idea" is to be found in a form letter sent out by the Cathedral in 1895, under the ægis of the "Cathedral Birthday Guild." This was the approach taken in the letter:

> The Cathedral is intended to be the Westminster Abbey of this part of the world, and is to contain memorials of many

of the truest and noblest and most devout sons and daughters of the South.

The letter then went on to explain that there were to be four large marble pillars supporting the dome; in honor of Bishops Otey, Green, Polk and Quintard. The first three were to be memorials, but since Quintard was still living, the subscriptions for his pillar were to be called "offerings of affection." The price on the pillars was $2,000 each, and arches and other features of the building had their memorial price. It also proposed "that those who were confirmed by the several Bishops should contribute yearly on their birthday toward these memorials. Birthday offerings from friends everywhere are solicited. The names of all who contribute will be perpetuated . . . and deposited with the records of the Cathedral."

In the various campaigns made at this time, solicitors carried with them a personal appeal from Bishop Gailor, which read, in part:

> It is my earnest desire to build a Cathedral Church in Memphis worthy of the State of Tennessee and of this city.
>
> It is my purpose to erect the new church on the Poplar Street property at the head of Orleans, removing all existing buildings.
>
> The building is to be of Sewanee stone with a central tower that can be seen from Main Street, and which standing at the junction of four streets will command attention from every side.
>
> As this is the Bishop's Church where my work especially is to be done in the coming years, I am not only officially but personally interested and therefore venture to appeal most earnestly for your assistance.
>
> The memorial features of the building will be explained by persons who present this letter, and who alone are authorized to solicit subscriptions of money.[2]

Correspondence between the Bishop and Mr. Wood slackened off during the summer, but by December 1895 the latter

---

2. *Journal of 1896,* 42, shows that in this convention the Bishop asked permission to exchange the Bishop's lot for the Cathedral property, which indicates that at one time he must have planned reversing the positions of the two buildings. This exchange was never made.

was writing of "our cathedral," and that "the building is in my mind all the time." He stated this interesting æsthetic theory:

> The name Cathedral, for instance, suggests creamy white material, pure in architecture, and pure in color—and then inside, the glass to have certain shades of blue running through it, so that the color can be the white tones (or cream) and blue tones, and thus be a living symbol of the name it bears. I have associated it with the Early English architecture as it is pure.

Early in 1896 he added, "I intend in the exterior to keep this severely simple disposition of lines as the governing motive and I think to produce an edifice which will convey the impression of might and massiveness." Touching upon the memorial feature, he says:

> It will be very well, as you suggest, that the interior be treated in its different parts as memorials, so that the faithful departed of the diocese may still speak in the Church Militant in enduring sculpture and glowing glass and metal, making the truest and best adornment of the walls that can be imagined . . . (it) especially appeals to the human desire for an exterior present remembrance of loved ones departed, which particularly affords diocesan contributors a mode of "letting their light so shine," which is to the average humanity *(sic)* very effective.

By September, he refers to his plans as "about complete," but knows that "the matter of collection of money is a matter of considerable slowness." By early 1897, many of the drawings had been submitted to Memphis, and he is happy "they are satisfactory to you and your people." Then he turned to the making of working drawings.

Several interruptions had occurred in 1895 and in 1896 due to Mr. Wood's poor health, but while the work was under way on the final drawings, news came that Mr. Wood had died suddenly (March, 1897). This precipitated a minor crisis, for though money raising had been slow, there was a prospect of beginning immediately. Mrs. Wood first suggested that some of the office personnel, trained by her husband, finish the plans. To this the Bishop was agreeable, but as a rift soon developed in Mr. Wood's office, Bishop Gailor was advised by his legal counsel to settle with the estate, and to take delivery of the plans even though they were incomplete.[3]

These events of course necessitated the appointment of another architect. At a meeting in Memphis, September 29, 1897, a committee consisting of Messrs. Tate, Schas and Clarke was appointed to secure the services of a local architect. Accordingly, Mr. L. Weathers, of the firm of Weathers and Weathers, was put in charge; and an agreement with him was signed February 28, 1898. In April of that year the Bishop and chapter decided to lay the cornerstone during the meeting of the diocesan convention which was to be held in Memphis. This was done on May 5, before bids were let, and before any excavation or construction had begun.[4]

Meanwhile the search for funds in Memphis and the diocese was not running very smoothly. In October 1896 the harassed treasurer, Mr. George Faxon, was quite agitated. He complained to the Bishop that too many subscription books were out, that it was difficult to keep trace of them, and that much of the money reported being given for memorials "can't be used in the building."

Even national politics added to Mr. Faxon's anxiety. He wrote the Bishop in another letter:

> I think it *very* important to collect all we can of the above immediately before the election and put it in gold. If Bryan is elected the subscriptions will be cut down in value

---

3. Mr. Wood had first estimated that the building would cost about $75,000. On the basis of charging 1% for the preliminary drawings, the widow accepted $750.00 in settlement. Years later, in 1906, when she read in church papers that the Cathedral was beginning its superstructure, Mrs. Wood wrote Bishop Gailor asking for a fee. The Bishop in a very kindly letter reminded her that if she would look among her old papers, she would find that the matter had been settled. Mrs. Wood then wrote apologizing for her mistake.

4. *Journal of 1899*, Bishop Gailor's entry for May 5. "2 P.M. in the Cathedral, Memphis, I laid the cornerstone and made an address. The Rev. T. F. Martin [St. Luke's, Jackson] and the Rev. Dr. Pettis [St. Paul's, Chattanooga] assisted in the service." The stone read: "St. Mary's Cathedral projected by the Right Rev. James H. Otey D.D. 1860. Founded by the Right Rev. Charles Todd Quintard D.D. 1871. Cornerstone of this building laid by the Right Rev. Thomas F. Gailor D.D. May 5, 1898."

50%. Mr. Coate thinks that all money belonging to the fund should be put in gold.

To make matters more difficult, many givers, no matter how small the donation, were intent on having memorials, and were of course quite uninterested in the foundation and the crypt. The following letter is typical of many. A lady from New York wrote Bishop Gailor:

> . . . about a memorial I will dedicate to my beloved parents. I would like it to be some outward and visible sign, as I do not wish them to be forgotten, especially in the church they both loved so dearly. I will get you to have their names inscribed on the columns for $25.00 each . . . I cannot afford a costly gift [explaining later that she is just back from a three years' journey abroad].

In 1897 the Bishop appointed Sam Tate, T. J. Clarke, F. Schas, and A. J. Warwick to the building committee, and in 1898 added P. R. Friedel to it. After the laying of the corner-stone, it was decided to consider bids, "for as much of the foundation of the Cathedral as it was thought proper at this time to build." Among the Bishop's papers we find this statement:

> The idea in the minds of everyone then was that perhaps the foundation of the new building could be constructed around the old wooden building, and permit its continued use and occupation while the work on the superstructure of the Cathedral could be begun.

But it soon became evident that the only possible course open to the builders was to tear down the old building, "endeared by many tender memories and associations," and to excavate for the entire basement. Many parishioners were greatly grieved at the passing of the old and decaying building which had been through so many vicissitudes. Some have told me of how they wept, when during the final days the old bell in the shaky tower tolled as if for its own passing.[5]

In a chapter meeting on May 31, 1898, it was resolved

---

5. A letter from Mr. Frank Baum says that Mr. Friedel had some wooden boxes (for saving), plates and cups made from the wood of the old building and distributed to the congregation.

"that all progress be made in completing the foundation walls and the interior of the basement, rather than attempting to complete any part of the superstructure." The Bishop was lavish in his praise of "the members of the chapter who were in Memphis that summer," and named Messrs. Buckingham, Schas, Clarke, Faxon, Friedel and Baum and Dean S. H. Green as "the men who made it possible for the Cathedral to have a place of worship ready for occupation that autumn."

Two letters will illustrate 1) the disastrous effect of asking for "memorial money" when money was needed for excavating the crypt; 2) the struggle Dean Green faced during the summer of 1898; 3) the fact that he was perhaps the first to suggest the plan for incorporating and issuing bonds (the plan which was in fact later adopted when work on the superstructure was begun). The first letter is from Colonel R. B. Snowden to the Dean and is dated June 24, 1898:

> . . . You may not know that the amount which I promised to give to the cathedral is to be expended for the chancel window, which is to be a memorial window to whomsoever I may designate. This is to cost $3,000.00. I do not suppose you are ready to put this window in place. However with the understanding that such a memorial will be furnished out of the general fund, I will advance the amount of $3,000. Be kind enough to show this to the Bishop.

The next day Dean Green enclosed this letter to Bishop Gailor with one of his own requesting that he "give him a guarantee that his money will be replaced when we come to the chancel windows," and he added, "Will Brinkley promised to give something as a memorial . . . but will allow his gift for work now, provided we will place the memorial hereafter." He urged upon the Bishop the need of getting the foundation done so that these memorial subscribers "can be gathered in," and added, "Oh that some good souls would give us $10,000 to be used as *we* desire, so that this basement could be finished without touching other funds," and he mentioned that he had talked with Messrs. Schas and Buckingham about forming a "St.

Mary's Cathedral Building Company," a chartered corporation which could sue and be sued and could issue bonds.[6]

The "hole in the ground" was pushed to conclusion that heroic summer, and a big opening service was held in the crypt on November 1, 1898 (All Saints). It was to serve as the Cathedral for the next seven years, for the Bishop was prepared to "make haste slowly."[7]

During the hot summer months and early fall of 1898, while the demolition of the old church, and the excavation and construction of the crypt were in progress, the congregation met in the Hall of St. Mary's School. Two Deans, Dumbell and Turner, had come and gone during the planning and money raising stages, and Dean Green was in charge of the parish at the time of the opening of the crypt. It made a large and not entirely uncomfortable place of worship. The Bishop reported on it in his address to the Convention of 1899 in the following words:

> I am glad to report to the Convention that our Cathedral in Memphis, which existed in name for twenty-five years, is gradually approaching realization in fact. The small wooden building, fallen into sad decay, has been removed and in its place we have built the solid stately foundation of a cathedral, which while not extravagant or very pretentious in proportion to its cost, will when completed, be an honor to this diocese and the whole South. The congregation began to worship in the crypt of the new building last December, and it proved to be a not uncomfortable abiding place. I found it necessary to act on the permission granted by this Convention, to remove

---

6. Years later, in 1930, when the Currier Fund was being organized, Mrs. Charles Currier made this statement in a letter to Dean Noe in reviewing her family's connection with the Cathedral. "When Bishop Gailor tore down the old Cathedral preparatory to building the new, he went to my uncle (Col. Snowden) to get a pledge toward the new Cathedral. My uncle made a pledge . . . he told the children it was to be a memorial to grandma. Later when the Bishop decided to build the crypt . . . he got Col. Snowden to pay his pledge with the understanding that when the Cathedral was eventually built, there was to be a memorial in the building to represent the money he had given. Now these records have been lost . . . I have often heard him complain of having sunk his money in that hole in the ground."

7. *Journal of 1899,* 57. (December 25, 1898) "I congratulated the congregation of the Cathedral upon the completion of our most comfortable place of worship in the crypt, and emphasized the advantage of proceeding slowly with the building without incurring debt."

the two one storey east rooms of the Episcopal Residence, rooms which were always unsightly in appearance and after forty years of use, almost impossible to occupy. It is to be hoped that some day the diocese will be able to make the absolutely necessary improvements in the present residence, or else provide a new residence that shall be in some degree commensurate with the regard that our people feel for the dignity of the Church.[8]

The altar in the crypt was at the south end, on a raised dais, and old pictures show that the cement ceiling beams were painted with scriptural texts. A temporary wooden altar was used instead of the stone memorial altar in honor of the Sisters, which was stored in the "Mortuary Chapel," the room now taken up by the furnace, and frequently used then by Mr. Baum as the meeting place for his Bible class.

When Dean Green left Memphis in 1901, the Bishop brought to the Cathedral a young friend and protégé, the Reverend James Craik Morris. It fell to his lot to undertake the next step, the starting of the superstructure. Meanwhile the Bishop had become the Diocesan (1898) and hence a more important figure not only in the diocese, but in the religious, political and social life of Memphis. As early as the Convention of 1901, Bishop Gailor mentioned that a movement was under way among certain leaders of Memphis—prominent among whom was Albert Sloo Caldwell—for providing him with a suitable episcopal residence.[9]

The old Otey "Bishop's House" was now in bad shape. As we have seen, two rooms had been lopped off to make room for building the crypt; and the remaining part was in bad repair. Thus a new and handsome Gothic residence, the present Diocesan House, was completed in 1902 at a cost of $22,000. It was raised as a private and personal gift to Bishop Gailor, and it is an interesting commentary that when it was suggested

8. *Journal of 1899*, 73.
9. In Gailor's *Some Memories*, 148, he credits Dean Green for enlisting the interest of Mr. Caldwell. In the *Journal of 1901*, he mentions his gratitude for the "magnificent response that is being made by the citizens of Memphis to the call for a new Episcopal Residence."

that parishes in the diocese outside of Memphis furnish the new home, only about $600 was raised. Not enough to provide furniture for even one room.[10]

The Bishop and his family moved into the new home in January 1903. He called it "a beautiful and spacious residence which dignifies the Episcopal Church in Tennessee, and thus does honor to every Mission and Parish throughout the State." From this new bishop's palace, he turned again to furthering the work of the temple. Thus early in 1903 subscription books were once more put in circulation.[11]

This time, having learned a lesson from experience, the memorial aspect of subscriptions was not featured. But again there was confusion in the multiplicity of subscription books, new guilds and organizations—the despair of a careful treasurer. The chief money-raising group this time was the "Bishop's Guild" formed in April 1904, with Mr. Frank Baum as treasurer. Soon he was writing the Bishop:

> It has been about eight years since the congregation of St. Mary's has worked in one way and another raising funds for the new Cathedral . . . many guilds have been organized, some still exist, some have dropped by the wayside . . . Most humbly I venture the opinion that there is not a single person connected with St. Mary's that knows what these guilds have accomplished.

He wanted more acknowledgment made to givers, and a better check kept on the subscription books, for, he said, "it is impossible to keep alive interest in the guild if its light is hid under a bushel."

---

10. *Journal of 1903.* The Bishop noted that all the money (except from two subscribers) came from Memphis. He says the movement to get money outside Memphis "did not meet with great success," and that most of the furnishing was from the H. Wetter Co. of Memphis. *Ibid.,* 43, shows that the convention made A. S. Caldwell, Bolton Smith, R. Brinkley Snowden and P. R. Friedel, the first trustees of the Episcopal residence.

11. *Journal of 1903* (March 23). "Presided at a meeting, to hear reports of the last meeting on building the Cathedral. Committee on preparation of suitable books for recording subscriptions made a report and presented books, quite a number of which were taken . . . the style and arrangement of the book is due to Mr. Frank Baum of the Continental Savings Bank."

The chapter now resolved to adopt the plan suggested as early as 1898 by Dean Green or Mr. Schas, namely to incorporate and get a charter as "Bishop, Dean and Chapter of St. Mary's." The Bishop signed the application for such a charter on May 7, 1904. On November 25 the chapter adopted by-laws governing the new corporation and elected Frank Baum treasurer and George Faxon secretary, with Faxon also treasurer of the building fund. It was not until 1906 that the decision was made to issue bonds.

In the parish report for 1904 there is a statement that the crypt cost a total of $29,000, and was free of debt, and that there was $6,000 in the building fund. Bishop Gailor put it a little differently in his letter of appeal, issued in September 1905:

> . . . the total amount received for the building to date has been $35,401.10. Of this amount about $13,000 has been collected by the Bishop from friends outside the diocese. Less than $3,000 has been contributed by the people of Memphis outside the cathedral congregation. One large gift, $3,000, has been received from an individual [Colonel Snowden's?], about $16,000 has been raised by the communicants in small sums.

He considered that this reflected honor on the Cathedral congregation, but he thought that "$3,000 seems a paltry sum to have been contributed by the people of a city the size of Memphis" and concluded:

> We have the plans and specifications for the erection of a portion of the building adequate to our present needs, and we have a contractor's bid on the same for about $30,000. It does seem 1) that the proposed plan of the building is in no sense extravagant; and 2) that if we go to work in faith we ought to be able to begin work this spring. (1906)

Various efforts to obtain loans were made in 1905, and when these failed it was decided in a chapter meeting held on January 23, 1906 to issue the amount of $20,000 in bonds paying 5 per cent, secured by a mortgage on the Cathedral, which the Bishop negotiated on April 27.

By February 27 it was found necessary to increase the amount raised by bonds to $30,000. On May 4 the contracts were let for the building, and the bonds mostly taken up, and the indenture on the Cathedral property registered.

Once again there was architect trouble. As stated above, after the death of Mr. Wood the Cathedral employed L. M. Weathers. Since in the building of the crypt he seems to have antagonized certain members of the chapter, there was a desire among the majority to consider his employment terminated upon the completion of the crypt. He, on the other hand, contended that the contract of 1898 implied finishing the building. He stated that he had made sketches and drawn plans for that purpose, and since he had not been previously notified of any termination, he must be paid if dismissed. Bishop Gailor in a clear and impartial letter put the matter to his friend Judge Randolph for a private judgment, as he wanted to avoid litigation. The matter seems to have been amicably settled at a meeting of the chapter on April 25, at which Mr. Weathers was present, and at which he agreed that the past contract (of February 1898) had been terminated, and he was given another for the completion of the superstructure. In case of his death his plans were to become the property of the Cathedral. He, therefore, constructed the 1906 phase.

Work was begun in June 1906, and by December 23 the new Cathedral aboveground was opened, Bishop Gailor preaching to "a great congregation." The *Commercial Appeal* of December 22 contained an anticipatory account of the opening which included an historical sketch of cathedrals and bishops in general, and of St. Mary's in particular. From internal evidence this could only have been written by the Bishop himself; therefore his remarks about the building are important:

> The original drawings for the Cathedral were made by Halsey Wood of New York City, who was one of the four architects consulted by the committee on the New York Cathedral . . . The three special features in Mr. Wood's plans

were: 1) the shortening of the nave and the development of the Greek cross in the ground plan, as contrasted with the long gothic nave, and 3) the introduction of steel construction—the steel columns to be covered with hexagonal blocks of stone, in order to strengthen the building—note the vindacation of this by the San Francisco fire—to reduce the size of the supporting pillars, and thus make the altar visible from every seat in the church.

On the death of Mr. Wood in 1897, before any of his plans were completed, L. M. Weathers of Memphis was elected architect of the Cathedral and has carried on the work with admirable taste and judgment.

The parts of the superstructure now ready for use consist of the main section of the stone front, including the very handsome porch, and the complete steel construction of the floor, roof, and side walls back to the limit of the transept. While the front is marred somewhat by the absence of aisle walls, and therefore looks narrow for its height, and while the wooden covering of the steel work on the sides and chancel is puzzling to the casual observer, and unattractive, yet the actual building is very substantial and costly, and the construction of the walls and clerestory can be carried on without interrupting the use of the present auditorium which will seat 700 people.

The beautiful altar of marble and Caen stone—a memorial to the Sisters of St. Mary who died in the yellow fever in 1878, and a splendid Marshall-Bennett organ, a memorial to the late Orsmer Benton of Memphis, will add dignity and solemnity to the services, and the new carved oak pews, the tiled floor, and steam heating insure convenience and comfort.

It is not likely that many years will be permitted to elapse before this building, so creditable in every way to the people of this city and section, shall be completed in all the glory of its stately and august design.

In the same issue of the paper there is an editorial entitled "Congratulations to Bishop Gailor." It points out that there are few persons in Tennessee who do not know the Bishop in person or by reputation, and adds that this is because "his interests and sympathies are not confined to members of his own communion," that although he is loyal to his Church, "his splendid abilities have been used to further the welfare of the whole state, and especially this community." The editorial ends by saying:

The Cathedral was begun by the Bishop nine years ago, his aim being to build little by little a great church for all people, to be the center of all work carried out under his and his successors' oversight, and we congratulate him and those who have helped him upon the completion of this, the second stage of this great undertaking.

With the coming of the first World War and other interruptions, it was to be almost twenty years before the building was completed.

CHAPTER VI

THE TURN OF THE CENTURY—DEAN MORRIS

THOUGH THE DOMINANT attention of St. Mary's from 1893 to 1906 centered, as we have seen in the previous chapter, on the struggle to build first the crypt and then the nave section of the new cathedral, we must now retrace these years in order to sketch the brief deanships of the Rev. Messrs. Dumbell, Turner and Green, and to follow the work of the devoted and saintly Dean Morris. We shall also observe the general activities of the parish, of the Sisters, and of the forceful, brilliant, and determined coadjutor and bishop, the Rt. Rev. Thomas F. Gailor.

When the young Mr. Howard Dumbell, rector of the Good Shepherd, accepted the invitation to become dean of the Cathedral (April 1893) he inquired of the chapter whether he would receive moving expenses or any salary for the summer. To this the chapter cautiously replied that it could only guarantee $1,500 per year, but that it would attempt to raise a special collection for moving and might be able to induce some subscribers to pay up in advance so that he would have money during the summer. There is very little to report on his brief tenure (May 1893-February 1895). During his deanship the drive to raise money for a new cathedral officially got under way. It would also appear from parish reports that in his regime St. Faith's Guild was organized. This later became the name of the altar guild, but it originated as a guild for young women, and a very active one. In January, 1895, Mr. Dumbell tendered his resignation, "having accepted an incumbency in Brooklyn, New York."[1]

During the interim between his departure and the arrival of the next dean, C. H. B. Turner (September 1895), Bishop Gailor, aided by Dr. Tupper, had charge of the parish. Very little is known of Dean Turner. He was undoubtedly the choice of Bishop Gailor, who had earlier recommended him to the chapter when it was known that Dean Klein planned to leave Memphis. The Bishop's interest in the new incumbent is further confirmed by the fact that he went to great pains to create an impressive installation ceremony for him (there is little consistency in our history on the subject of which deans or canons are formally and ceremoniously "installed," and which are simply permitted to take over). The Bishop described the ceremony at some length in the convention *Journal of 1896*. The service was as follows: after a formal processional, the Bishop gave an address on "the history and purpose of the cathedral system"; he next installed the Dean by having him kneel while a Te Deum was sung, and the Lord's Prayer said; then the Bishop read the Office of Institution, after which the Dean made the following declaration to the congregation:

> I, Charles Turner, Dean of this Cathedral Church, do declare that I will be faithful to this Church in the Diocese of Tennessee and to the Bishop of the same. I will observe and keep all statutes, ordinances, rules and customs of the same, published or hereafter to be made and published by lawful authority; and I will cause them to be observed and kept by others. I will support the burdens of my said dignity and state; I will be at all times ready with my presence and counsel to assist the Bishop when and where he shall reasonably require this of me, and I will bear my part willingly and gladly, and will personally be forward in promoting the good works of this Church and Diocese unto holy and honorable

---

1. Howard Murray Dumbell was educated at the University of the South. He finished college 1888, seminary 1890, was ordained deacon by Bishop Welles, 1888, and priest by Bishop Quintard, 1890. He was in charge of Trinity, Mason, and St. Matthew's, Covington, 1890-91; of the Good Shepherd, Memphis, 1891-93; Dean of St. Mary's, 1893-95; rector of St. Paul's, Brooklyn, 1895-99; of St. James', Great Barrington, Mass., and of St. John's Church, Delbie, New York.

living; the extension and increase of the ministrations and teaching of the Church, the instruction as well of the young, and of persons preparing for sacred orders and offices, as of the people, in all sacred learning and good knowledge. The business of the chapter I will keep private, so long as it shall be ruled to be private, the rights of the Cathedral Church I will defend, nor will I give any assistance, advice, or encouragement to any person or persons whatsoever who shall endeavor to violate or infringe the same. I will order myself in lowliness and patience, and persuade others to walk in the same ways. Amen.

This declaration completed, the Bishop conducted the Dean to his stall; Holy Communion followed, after which the Bishop made another short address on the history of the transfer of St. Mary's to Bishop Quintard.

The same evening, in the Cathedral, the Bishop after the service of Evening Prayer, conducted by the Dean, preached a sermon to young men and admitted six to the "Bishop Otey Chapter" of the Brotherhood of St. Andrew, the beginning of this organization at the Cathedral. The next week Bishop Gailor (who soon after becoming coadjutor had reorganized the diocesan Woman's Auxiliary, appointed new officers, and persuaded the women to adopt a new constitution) called together all the church women of Memphis to the Cathedral (November 19, 1895) to address them on the subject of the missionary activity of the Church. "I told them," he noted in his diary, "that every baptized woman was a member of the Woman's Auxiliary whether she attended the formal meetings of the Auxiliary or not. That my advice was that all guilds of every parish resolve themselves once a month into the Woman's Auxiliary." This to some extent foreshadowed the future centralizing role of the Auxiliary, since from its foundation in 1887 till the time of his talk and even later, it was considered (I am told) simply as a new women's group devoted solely to missions, and one which rivalled or drew from already existing guilds.

A famous Auxiliary tradition of today was also started by

Bishop Gailor in Dean Turner's time, the "quiet day" at the Cathedral for all the Auxiliaries of the city. He began this practice in 1897 on the Feast of the Annunciation, by giving the ladies five short services and five addresses. In his diary Bishop Gailor remarked prophetically, "it was a helpful and happy day for us all, and the beginning of a long series of such days."[2]

Some of our older parishioners still retain faint recollections of Mr. Turner. From all accounts he was "quite a young firebrand," who by burning attacks on evil-doers and evil-doings in Memphis attracted many of the visiting English cotton merchants, who enjoyed hearing local conditions excoriated. The Dean, however, proved to be a rather poor money raiser at a time when money was sorely needed.[3] Thus it was not long before the Bishop and chapter seem to have lost their original zeal for the Dean, as may be seen from the chapter minutes of September 29, 1897:

> Bishop Gailor read a letter from the Very Reverend Dean Turner tendering his resignation as dean, to take effect November 1. The Bishop announced that he intended to accept the resignation and asked the members of the chapter if they agreed with him—which they did unanimously.

Soon after this Dean Turner departed to Mississippi.

On November 29, 1897, the chapter resolved to "nominate the Rev. Stephen Green as dean—if he will accept a salary of $1,800." The Bishop, assisted by a young priest, the Rev. J. P.

---

2. Dean Morris in his Service Book kept a record of leaders of quiet days during his deanship. Some of those conducting were: (1909) Rev. Stuart Tyson of Sewanee; (1910) Rev. W. Whittaker of Knoxville; (1911) Rev. H. J. Mikell of Nashville; (1915) Rev. Holly Wells of Meridian, Mississippi.

3. For example the financial report of January 1896 shows a balance on hand of 19c and liabilities of $233. The parish budgets of the 1890's usually ran from $3,500-$5,000 per annum, exclusive of special campaigns. The parish report of 1896 gave a resumé of the results of earlier attempts to get members to subscribe by envelope. These show a gradual falling off, e.g., 1892—$2,175; 1893—$1,615; 1894—$1,672; 1895—$1,685; 1896—$1,514. The treasurer added pessimistically, "At present there are only 71 subscribers in a congregation containing 300 communicants. Those who do not subscribe probably give according to their means when they come to church. But on wet Sundays and during the summer months the collections are almost nothing, while expenses at the Cathedral remain the same."

McCullough, carried on during the interim. He announced the coming of the new dean in January 1898. Mr. Green arrived to take charge in February. The day he arrived (February 15) coincided with the day on which the venerable and ailing Bishop Quintard died in Meridian, Georgia. Ever since the early nineties the Bishop had been in poor health, when, as we have seen, the convention finally agreed to provide him with an assistant. He was still hoping to attend the fourth Lambeth conference, and was distressed at not being permitted to go. Fortunately he was cheered not long before his death (December 1896) by the kindly act of the students and faculty of Sewanee. They processioned formally to his home on the mountain and Dean DuBose made a touching address of appreciation on his work for the University. Then they presented him with a beautiful cup inscribed, "The Right Reverend Charles Todd Quintard, in commemoration of the thirtieth anniversary of his consecration to the Episcopate, and in grateful recognition of his services as the second founder of the University of the South, by the faculty and students of the University. Sewanee, 1865-1895."

Bishop Quintard had done a noble work, and was mourned both at home and abroad. Like his predecessor, Bishop Otey, in his latter days he felt greatly discouraged by his seeming lack of success, for at the time of his death there were hardly 6,000 communicants in the diocese, but he influenced the lives of many. Bishop Gailor in his parting tribute said:

> For twenty-five years I enjoyed the privilege of his intimate friendship, and was blessed with the love and confidence of his great heart, which was rich beyond the measure of ordinary men in generosity and power, giving forth with abounding unselfishness and ever graceful and gracious with the love of the Lord Jesus Christ. Every important event in my life was connected with him. He confirmed me, admitted me as a candidate to the ministry, ordained me to the diaconate and priesthood, married me and consecrated me bishop.

Dean Green, who came to the Cathedral from St. Louis, had been ordained in 1873, and was a more mature and experienced man than his immediate predecessors. He was able and efficient and worked valiantly during his stay raising the final sums needed for the crypt and seeing to its construction. He corrected the communicant list, and the multifarious guilds and organizations of Dean Klein's day were now—with the exception of the money raising guilds for the cathedral construction—reduced to four: The Cathedral Guild, St. Faith's, The Woman's Auxiliary, and the Junior Auxiliary. He began the listing of chapter members in his reports to the convention, and tried to get it to take a more active interest in Sunday School work. He even got members of a former parish to contribute $300 toward the badly needed repair of the old cathedral organ.

The old Clergy House was by this time an inadequate home for a married dean, so the chapter rented a home for him on Adams near Orleans (402, in the old numbering). He soon suggested that they purchase a deanery and let him pay on the notes instead of rent. By 1900 the chapter found that it could purchase the home he was renting (for $6,350) with a down payment from a fund started by the Cathedral Guild, and that the installments on the balance would indeed be less than the rent. These arrangements had barely been concluded when the chapter received a note from the Dean asking for a leave of absence for two months in the summer. It concluded with the rather enigmatic phrase that "circumstances might arise that would prevent him from returning to Memphis as dean." The chapter divined the significance of the phrase; Mrs. Green, who came from Maine, found both the climate and the people uncongenial. The chapter therefore requested that the Dean inform it before he left, whether he planned to return or not. On June 2, the poor Dean wrote that he saw only two courses open: to leave his family in another climate for a year and remain in Memphis alone, or to resign and stay with his family. By the end of the month he let the chapter know that he had chosen the second alternative. It wrote him a sincere letter of regret. He accepted a parish in Elgin, Illinois, and the third consecutive brief deanship ended.[4]

At this point in our story, and before considering the deanship of the Rev. James Craik Morris, we shall interrupt our study of the deans in order to attempt a brief sketch of the personality and activities of Bishop Thomas F. Gailor. It is surprising that no one has done a full length biography of this remarkable man who was so long and so intimately connected with the Cathedral, which indeed, in its completed form, was erected as a memorial to him.

There are so many facets to the Bishop's long and eventful career that it is manifestly impossible to do justice to them all within the context of the "cathedral story," thus only a "sampling process" will be attempted here. Viewed chronologically, Bishop Gailor's life may be divided into the following rather clearly defined periods: first, the years from 1856-1893 might be called the "formative years," and would include his education, first ministry, and his early years at Sewanee; second, from 1893-1916, would be a time of expanding influence, when as Coadjutor and then as Diocesan (and there was little noticeable break since the illness of Bishop Quintard placed diocesan affairs in his hands virtually from the beginning) he became a prominent figure in affairs of the Cathedral and of the city of Memphis, and respected throughout the state; third, from 1916-1930 when he became a leading figure in the National Church, and known abroad; and finally, the years from 1930-1935, which form a kind of epilogue, during which he assumed the role of elder statesman and retired patriarch.

---

4. Dean Stephen Herbert Green received his theological training at Berkeley (1871), was made deacon 1871, priest 1873 (by Bishop Green). He held the following parishes: 1871-77, All Saints, Grenada, Mississippi; 1877-1882, Dean of St. Matthew's Cathedral, Dallas, Texas; 1882-83, Church of the Redeemer, Elgin, Illinois; 1883-95, St. John's, St. Louis, Missouri; 1895-96, St. Michael and All Angels, Anniston, Alabama; 1896-98, Grace Church, Kirkwood; 1898-1902, Dean of St. Mary's, Memphis; 1902-03, Church of the Redeemer, Elgin, Illinois; 1903, St. Savior's, Bar Harbour, Maine; he was rector of Caroline Church, Setauket, New York, when he died (July 25, 1919).

It is with the second of these periods (i.e., from 1893 to 1916) that we must now deal, and more specifically with those activities which do not relate to starting the Cathedral, since these have already been described. Bishop Gailor was an amazing man and his personality was so complex that it is almost impossible to capture it in a few words. Endowed with a rugged physique, a brilliant mind, a retentive memory, he possessed a natural gift of eloquence and a talent for conver- sation. He developed a characteristically forceful "style" both in writing and in speaking, and was a great raconteur of stories.[5] He had the elusive quality of leadership, an impressive manner (some even called it "dominating") which seemed to inspire respect in others. Unlike some forceful characters who prefer to surround themselves with weaker men, the Bishop seems to have preferred the company of the successful and strong. At the same time he retained the redeeming grace of a deep spir- ituality, a love for others, and for his cause, which put him at ease in any group or class. It also kept him from assuming too prelatical an air. Yet sometimes one suspects that his sheer vitality and force made things a little difficult for his subordi- nates, and may possibly account for the rapid turnover of deans which followed his arrival on the Memphis scene.

During his first decade in Memphis his work in pushing the construction of the new cathedral was but one of his many activities. He quickly made himself a place in the community, and soon became one of its leading citizens. Of necessity he was often absent on business connected with the diocese, or with

---

5. The Rev. Holly Wells wrote me this vivid sketch of Bishop Gailor's style. "There was no doubt that he was a positively gigantic preacher, and of course when he preached there was simply no other preacher in all creation. The power of his voice was only surpassed by its beauty. His oratory was a stream in flood, his rhetoric was altogether his own, and the cogency of his thought was such as to make an audience think it had really heard the last word on the subject . . . He never had any high hat manner with his clergy. We could barge in on him for dinner any time we pleased. He loved to have us. He loved company but I must say that the talk was likely to be a monologue, and that we would come away laughing at his good stories and eager to relay them to the first bunch we met."

Sewanee, and his family usually summered on the mountain. But the Cathedral could always count on his presence and leadership for certain parts of each year. At St. Mary's he developed a pattern of appearances which can be traced in outline. He tried always to be at the Cathedral for Christmas (we find the first reference to the midnight eve Christmas service soon after his coming). As early as 1897 he inaugurated during the Lenten season a continuing series of Friday evening Lenten lectures which quickly became famous. To these, in many years, he added either a Sunday or Thursday evening series of Bible study classes (sometimes held in his own home). Frequently he conducted the Monday noonday services at Calvary. The variety of topics he dealt with and the crowds he attracted to his Lenten services are astounding. In each series he presented a central theme and developed it in detail during the ensuing six weeks. A few sample selections will show the diversity of topics, and the well-knit organization he made of his material. In 1903, for example, his general topic was "the concept of immortality in various religions"; then each week he traced the idea through six major world religions. In 1907 he discoursed on six of the most famous English cathedrals. The next year his series was on "English Churchmen," and the six he portrayed were Langdon, Hooker, Laud, Butler, Wesley, and Pusey, an ecumenical lot.[6]

At first the Bishop held confirmation services on the traditional date of the early Church, Easter Even. Later he moved the service to Palm Sunday and nearly always celebrated and preached on Easter. The other season one could be sure of the Bishop's presence was on the commencement day of St. Mary's School. He began this tradition early, and always attended if it was humanly possible.

---

6. Dean Morris, in his *Service Book,* kept a record of all the Bishop's topics. Some other series dealt with The Idea of the Church, the Great Councils of the Church, the Seven Sacraments, the Christian system of Morals. The Bishop never seems to have repeated a topic.

Just as the coming to Memphis of Bishops Otey and Quintard was in each case followed by an outburst of missionary activity in the city, so soon after Bishop Gailor arrived, we detect a renewed era of church growth. In January 1894, even before he brought his family to Memphis, he drove with Dr. Davenport of Calvary to the eastern outskirts of the city (then known as the Idlewild community) to inspect and choose the site for a new mission which began construction the next year (1895). This was the origin of St. Luke's.[7]

By the spring of 1897 St. Anne's, Woodstock, was started, and flourished in 1898 under the guidance of a young priest, the Rev. J. P. M. McCullough of the Good Shepherd, who began its new building the same year.[8] By this time St. Luke's was admitted to convention as a parish; and the moribund St. John's was revived by St. Mary's early candidate for the priesthood, the Rev. Peter Wager. By 1901 a group of fourteen communicants in South Memphis, sparked by the ubiquitous Mr. Wager, and by Mr. Frank Baum, a lay-reader of the Cathedral, organized a new mission, "to be known as Holy Trinity." Services were first held in the old "Female College" on McLemore. Mr. Baum and the Dean found a promising vacant lot on Cummings "one snowy Sunday afternoon." They persuaded the Bishop to drive out, inspect and approve it. By May 1902 the church was built and was formally consecrated on April 4, 1904. Mr. Wager was replaced by the young deacon, Prentice Pugh, in October 1905.

St. Mary's, in spite of the financial burden connected with building the new cathedral, was not to be outdone in this grow-

---

7. The original church was on Union near McLean (the present site of the Helen Shop), the first rector was E. Bazett-Jones, and this church was consecrated February 22, 1903, under the Rev. F. D. DeVall, who later became Dean of St. Mary's (1916-1920). DeVall left in 1906 and was followed by the Rev. Holly Wells (1906-1912) a close friend of Dean Morris. The original church was sold in 1910, and the move made to the present location on Peabody. This church was consecrated October 20, 1912.

8. Mr. McCullough left soon for Greeneville, Tennessee. The building was completed under the Rev. T. D. Windiate, and consecrated November 12, 1906. The venerable James J. Vaulx, founder of the church, returned for the ceremony.

ing surge of missionary activity, and it undertook a new mission in "New South Memphis," at the end of the street car line on Florida, and named it St. Alban's (1903). Dean Morris with a young deacon assistant of that year, the Rev. G. R. Cadman, and with the help of Mr. Frank Baum and others, were the moving spirits in the venture. The chapel was completed in 1905.[9] In the same year Grace Church started its structure on Vance, and Calvary its new parish house.

Thus within the first few years after Bishop Gailor's coming, the number of churches and missions in the city doubled; to Calvary, Grace, St. Mary's, the Good Shepherd, and a decayed St. John's were added St. Luke's, Holy Trinity, St. Anne's-Woodstock, St. Alban's and a revived St. John's. In 1903 the Bishop organized the *Clericus*. He wanted monthly meetings of the Episcopal clergy of the city for closer fellowship, discussion of common problems, and more concerted activity. His effort the same year in the diocesan convention to get it to recommend the change in name from the Protestant Episcopal Church to the American Catholic Church was not successful, and later he abandoned the idea. It is interesting to find that as early as 1901, Bishop Gailor pointed out to convention that throughout the diocese country churches were everywhere on the decline, and that the future lay in the cities. (This was confirmed by the National Church's study of 1955).

Like his predecessors in the episcopate, Bishop Gailor was deeply interested in the problem of advancing work among the Negro people. He frequently made speeches on the subject in the East, and raised money there for the work in Tennessee. Despite this interest, however, two projects dating from the Quintard era were finally liquidated in the early 1900's. The efforts repeatedly made to breathe life into the work at the

---

9. Mr. Baum credits Mr. Smith of the Florence Pump Works as the prime mover for St. Alban's (the name was given by Dean Morris). He tells how he and the Dean would ride to the end of the car line on Sunday afternoons, and be met by Mr. Smith "in a fringe topped buggy."

Canfield Orphan Asylum were now finally abandoned, after what might be called a final blazing failure. This property, 202 by 243 feet, located at the corner of Dunlap and the Mobile and Ohio tracks had, as we have seen, passed through many vicissitudes. The ultimate, and failing, effort to make it succeed was undertaken by an English clergyman, the Rev. C. S. Bassett. He attempted to conduct an industrial and trade school for Negroes on the property. He named the school "St. Joseph's Trade School" and received the Bishop's blessing, but no funds. He placed another clergyman, the Rev. H. L. Marvin, in charge as "warden." Between them they accumulated very heavy debts for equipment, and thus brought the venture to an inglorious end. The property had to be sold to liquidate the debt, and since there were so many ties on the property (trusts, liens, etc.) further litigation was necessary before the place could be sold to the Sunshine Home for the Aged (1902).

The other failing venture was Hoffman Hall, the house which Bishop Quintard constructed near Fisk University to be a training place for Negro clergy. This was sold in 1910, and the funds devoted to the construction of a new project—which continued to recent times—the Industrial School for Negroes at Mason. It was first called Hoffman-St. Mary's after its predecessor, but later became known as the Gailor Industrial School (1936).

As early as 1896 the Bishop called attention to the need for Emmanuel to move from its downtown location (on Third, between Court and Jefferson) to the more populated Negro district in South Memphis. In 1908 he disposed of the old church (for $12,000) and with the money bought a lot on Cynthia Place ($5,000). By March 13, 1910, the new church was erected and consecrated.[10] It has grown and flourished

---

10. While this new Emmanuel was being built, the Bishop held a confirmation service for nine negroes in the Cathedral (November 1, 1908) "before a congregation of 900 negroes." He praised "the kindly acquiescence among the members of the Cathedral."

since, and has recently added a rectory, a parish hall, and a fine new building (1956). In his address to the Convention of 1907 the Bishop expressed his concern for Negro work in the diocese and sketched three possible methods for organizing it: (a) a separate convocation for colored people, (b) a suffragan Negro bishop to conduct work in several dioceses, or (c) a Negro missionary bishop for several dioceses. Originally he favored the third alternative, but changed in favor of a separate convocation. Its first meeting was in 1910.[11]

In the growing, bustling, and commercially-minded Memphis of the early 1900's there existed a kind of culture vacuum which Bishop Gailor, with his erudition, his energy and his eloquence, attempted to fill. He lectured on a most imposing and varied list of subjects before the most diverse types of audiences. Some of these addresses were public lectures given at the Lyceum Theatre with an admission charge for the benefit of the Cathedral Guild's charities. Here he lectured on such diverse personalities as "John Ruskin" and "General Nathan Bedford Forrest." He often enlightened the ladies of the new Nineteenth Century Club ("The Modern Novel," "Modern Psychology," "Municipal Government"). Strangely enough he addressed the worldly members of the Cotton Exchange on "Eternal Life," and, after a particularly daring breach of trust by a Memphis banker, lectured at a big hotel meeting of five hundred citizens on "Civic Righteousness."

He was in the forefront of a movement to procure a college for Memphis (resulting in the beginning of the Buntyn Normal School), and was active in organizing business and professional men into civic and cultural clubs. Thus in addition to such church groups as the Clericus (1903), the Churchman's

---

11. The Canon creating the Convocation of Colored People was passed in 1908, and ratified in 1909. The Bishop, though deeply interested in the Negro, was never an "integrationalist." When he proposed the alternatives of 1907, he remarked: "We respect our own race, and that is not an earth-born prejudice, but a God-given instinct. A white man who is not zealous for the purity of his blood and the supremacy of his race is a degenerate." This Canon was repealed in 1956.

Club (1905)—ancestor of the later Layman's League—he took part in the creation of the Egyptians (which still flourishes), the Idlewild Club (now defunct), and the Memphis Historical Society (now the West Tennessee Historical Society). He was actively concerned with local government with the first Chamber of commerce (which sometimes got him to represent them in national gatherings), and in the Rotary Club. In fact the Bishop virtually became the city's official "greeter," for he was generally chosen to provide the address of welcome to any distinguished visitor who might be passing through the town. Among those he welcomed were Admiral Dewey, William McKinley, Theodore Roosevelt, Woodrow Wilson, James Bryce and Admiral Schley. He also played a role in many state affairs. One he particularly enjoyed was the big Centennial celebration of the state, held in Nashville (1896). He was very active in the Memphis Day (September 14) and in the Episcopal Day (October 13) festivities. On the latter day he and Bishop Satterlee of Washington, assisted by sixteen clergy and a choir of a hundred, conducted a "great service," which the Bishop thought "did some good."

He began to journey through an ever widening radius to make college commencement addresses, or to conduct religious emphasis periods (e.g., he was twice at the University of Chicago, at Columbia, and as far away as the University of California). Even before 1900 he began to garner the usual meed of honorary degrees, but he was most happy when his beloved Sewanee made him its Chancellor (June 25, 1908).

St. Mary's viewed its Bishop's growing prestige with pride and affection, but the action he took in replacing the departing Dean Green by James Craik Morris, whom he had known and liked as a young man at Sewanee, became one of his most enduring contributions to Cathedral history.[12] When, on

12. James Craik Morris was born in Louisville, Kentucky, June 18, 1870, the son of John Hite and Frances Craik Morris. He was graduated at the University of the South, B. Litt. (1890), M.A. (1891), D.D. (1915). Studied

November 1, 1901, the Bishop announced to the chapter his appointment of Dean Morris, few could then have foreseen what a great and devoted churchman they were acquiring, or that he would be the first and only dean—within the first hundred years—to rise to the episcopate. Dean Morris was born in Louisville, Kentucky, and has been called "a complete Sewanee man."[13] He attended the Sewanee Grammar School, and lived during his Sewanee days with the family of Dr. DuBose at St. Luke's Hall. Being of a very musical nature he was organist in the college chapel during his undergraduate years, and after leaving the University was anxious to pursue music as a career. His father convinced him that music alone was an uncertain calling, and persuaded him to study law simultaneously with music. Thus he received a law degree from the Louisville Law School (1892). But by this time he had decided upon the ministry as his vocation, and began his training at the General Theological Seminary. By chance he visited Sewanee the ensuing summer and while there was offered the position of assistant to the famous English professor, William Trent, as well as that of organist in the new chapel. As this would make him financially independent, he transferred to

theology at G.T.S. and Sewanee. Married Edith Garland Tucker of Dallas, Texas, October 31, 1900. Ordained deacon by Bishop Dudley and priest by Bishop Garrett (1896). Was assistant at St. Matthew's Cathedral, Dallas, 1896-98; curate of St. James Brooklyn, 1898-1901; Dean of St. Mary's Cathedral, 1901-16; rector of Grace Church, Madison, Wisconsin 1916-20; elected missionary Bishop of the Canal Zone at General Convention 1919, consecrated (February 5, 1920) in his parish church in Madison; became fifth Bishop of Louisiana, September, 1930; retired March, 1939. He lived in Sewanee until his death on May 5, 1944. (*Living Church Annual*)

13. The Rev. Holly W. Wells, rector of St. Luke's from 1906-1912 and who knew Mr. Morris intimately, wrote this about him. "Craik Morris was not only a gentleman, but a Sewanee kind of gentleman, and because he was of this kind—'the core being sweet'—the world that knew him was a sweeter world. Then too, I think he was a Sewanee kind of Christian by which I mean that he was a typical disciple of Dr. William P. DuBose, who at that time was Dean of the School of Theology. The great Dean Sandys of Oxford called DuBose, 'the wisest Anglican on both sides of the Atlantic,' and others have said that the School of Theology at Sewanee was like the disciples band around their Master on the Mountains of Galilee. As class followed class over the years, the DuBose men came to know that they had a fellowship all their own, and Craik Morris certainly belonged to it. Indeed it was he who introduced me to the books of the great Doctor. We read and discussed them together, and I like now to think of myself as a late arrival within the fellowship."

Sewanee, and continued his theological studies with Dr. DuBose, in addition to his other duties. He was ordained deacon by Bishop Dudley in Louisville (December 1895) and left the next month for Dallas to become assistant to Dean Hudson Stuck at St. Matthew's Cathedral. After being ordained priest, he was placed in charge of a little church at Oak Cliff; he directed the Cathedral choir and acted as chaplain for St. Mary's Junior College in East Dallas. In 1897 he accepted a call to be assistant to the rector of St. James, Brooklyn, but returned to Dallas to marry Miss Edith Tucker, the daughter of Judge and Mrs. Charles Tucker (October 31, 1900). It was from Brooklyn that Bishop Gailor called him to Memphis (at a salary of $1,600) with the challenge to come and help him build the Cathedral.

Bishop Gailor presented him to the congregation on November 3, 1901. The deanery on Adams proved something of a trial to the young couple. Mrs. Morris has described it as:

> a big three story brick house with open fires in each room which made the heating of the high ceilinged rooms very difficult. (A glass of water froze solidly one night in the guest room in spite of the fact it was on the mantlepiece and a low fire kept burning all night). Ordinary curtains hung on the long French windows downstairs and looked like ballet skirts. There was no furniture in the house until some could be bought and some shipped from Dallas, so all sorts of makeshifts were in order. The Dean and I wanted to entertain at dinner each member of the chapter and his wife, but as we had only two dining room chairs, we sat on packing boxes.

The Dean and Mrs. Morris lived here two years. When this place was sold their next abode was on Washington just next to the vacant lot which is now known as Morris Park. Here they lived until the new brick deanery was built on Poplar (1910). The Washington location was hardly an improvement over the first. Mrs. Morris describes it as follows:

> a little green cottage, one of the oldest houses in Memphis, on a large plot of ground . . . it became quite uninhabitable as the roof leaked in so many places. Mr. Schas, a member of the chapter, solemnly declared that Mr. and Mrs.

Morris had to put the twins, Craik and Mary, under the bed whenever there was a rain storm. After this, the decision about a new deanery was promptly made.

The decision was not as prompt as Mrs. Morris remembers, since as early as 1905 the Dean complained to the chapter of the leaks, and that the piers under the house were giving way. Since all attention was on the new Cathedral in 1905-06, the chapter did not seriously consider a new deanery till 1909. The little green cottage had other inconveniences. One was that the stone for the new Cathedral was cut in the vacant lot next to Mrs. Morris' window. The noise and dust were almost unbearable. Another inconvenience (as Mrs. Morris remembers it) was that:

> choir practice was held every Friday night just across the hall from my bedroom, and the singing of the infant Sunday School Class which met in the Dean's study (which was also our living room). The only time I rebelled was when the parish visitor bustled in one day and announced that she had come to rub the brass altar candlesticks . . . I remember replying that I would not and could not have that evil smelling stuff in the house.

We have already noted the part Dean Morris played in helping in the erection of the nave. He spent one of his summer vacations (1905) in the task of raising funds. The duty dearest to his heart, during the construction period, was committed to him by the chapter on the day that contracts were let for the construction of the church. It was that he was empowered to plan and order an organ for the new building. Funds for this organ had accumulated from two sources. First the choir, under Mr. Currier's guidance, had been saving for this purpose for several years; then Mrs. Orsmer H. Benton donated a memorial to her husband (a little over $4,000) to be applied to the organ.[14]

---

14. According to chapter minutes the organ cost $5,241.57. Of this amount Mrs. Benton contributed $4,276.87, and the choir $964.70. Mr. Herbert Esch says that Mrs. Benton's gift was at a great sacrifice, and left her in financial straits. The old organ which survived from the wooden Cathedral and the crypt was donated to the venerable Dr. Harris, to be used in his mission at Rolling Fork, Mississippi.

The new organ was dedicated on Sunday, January 13, 1907. This description of it is found in the *Diocese of Tennessee* (February 1907):

> The organ was built by the Marshall-Bennett Company, on the "Bennett system," and contains a number of features new to this part of the country. The casual observer notices first the absence of the usual display pipes, their place being taken by fret work screens of quartered oak, facing the choir and nave. He also sees that draw stops have been discarded and that the whole action is operated by tablets and pistons placed over the keyboards and by pedal movements.
>
> The organist is attracted by the instantaneous action, by the many couplers and combination pistons all of which are adjustable, and by the complete indicator system which enables him to tell the condition of the organ at a glance. He finds the "sforzando" pedal and the "piano" pedal very useful innovations.
>
> The lover of ecclesiastical music admires this organ because it is so evidently built not for concert use, but for the services of the church. The large number of 8' foundation stops, the beautiful voicing of the pipes, and the absence of bizarre features combine to produce the full rich diapason tone so necessary for reverent playing, and so often sacrificed to mere brilliance.

On the day after dedication the famous organist, Dr. R. Jefferson Hall, gave the opening recital. "He was assisted by Miss Matilda Reid and the Cathedral choir. The program was arranged to test the capacity of the instrument in every respect, and the result was entirely satisfactory."

This is perhaps the place to point out that not the least of Mr. Morris' contributions to St. Mary's was his passionate and devoted work for and with the Cathedral choir. By the time the new superstructure was erected, the long and faithful services of Mr. Currier had come to a close. He was still on the roll as a member of the chapter, but he and his wife spent most of their time abroad. For a while there were substitute organists, but during the last ten years of Dean Morris' tenure (1906-1916) he was choir director as well as Dean. During most of this time Miss Mattie Reid was organist.

The Dean was a musician to the fingertips, and though tastes in music vary from generation to generation, and though much of the music he selected gathers dust on the shelves today, it was the best of his day, and the many parishioners who survive from his time are unanimous in their praise of the "wonderful music" of his era. The Rev. Holly Wells, who served with Dean Morris on the commission which created the *Hymnal 1940,* has written a fine account of the Dean's outlook on church music. He says that Mr. Morris realized the beauty and historical importance of plainchant, and of the German chorale, but that he felt drawn to the music of the great Victorian organists and choir directors.[15]

Again Mrs. Morris adds a "behind the scenes" touch to the Dean's work with the choir:

> It was a very loyal group of men and women who made up that volunteer choir, but it was a very uncertain quantity to count upon, as they rarely told him they wouldn't be there the following Sunday [how many organists can make this complaint!], leaving him to discover that so-and-so who had a solo part in the anthem or communion service was not

---

15. Here are excerpts from Mr. Wells' letter: "Craik was a Sewanee kind of musician. To be sure he had been a diligent student of music from boyhood, had become an accomplished organist and pianist, and no mean composer . . . He held that there were three schools of church music worthy of recognition; one of these was the Roman Catholic, found in the musical settings of the Mass . . . he thought it too florid and sensuous to be an authentic voice of the Christian religion. Roman music of the Gregorian type he could honor for its dignity, solemnity, and its historic interest . . . another worthy school was that of the German chorale . . . finally there was the English Cathedral School which he deemed best of all. Like the Book of Common Prayer itself, this music had been conceived and born in the true spirit of English devotion . . . A good example of this he found in Tours Communion Service in E flat. This particular composer, Berthold Tours, Craik regarded as probably the best representative of the English school. Other representatives would be such men as Varley Roberts, Sir Joseph Barnby, Sir John Stainer. A rather distinctive offering of this school was the development of the Anthem. Some anthems of which Craik approved were: Roberts, "Seek ye the Lord"; Tours, "Sing O Heavens," and Barnby, "There Were Shepherds"; . . . Music of this sort was used almost exclusively in St. Mary's while Craik was Dean. Mr. Wells' verdict is borne out by looking at the list of music used by the Dean, recorded in his Service Book. Besides the pieces mentioned, anthems used on several occasions were: Roberts, "Lord We Pray Thee"; Smieton, "Oh That I Had Wings Like a Dove"; and "The Roseate Hours of Early Dawn"; Sullivan, "Turn Thy Face"; Adam, "O Holy Night"; Gounod, "Jesus, Word of God Incarnate"; Stainer, "God So Loved the World." He sometimes used Handel's "Halleluia" or Mozart's "Gloria" on Easter. He used Communion Services by Custance, Tours, Eyre, Foster, Gounod, and Te Deums by Stainer, Calkin, Maunders, and Smart.

in his place in the choir. This meant sending an acolyte out to bring in and distribute another anthem or communion service. I always sat on the front row nearest the exit to the sacristy so that he could catch my eye when he discovered a certain singer was absent. Naturally all this was quite a strain, but when the music went well he felt repaid, even though tired after a service . . . I remember him taking the place at the organ on one occasion in Memphis, when dear unpredictable Mattie Reid was late for morning service. He had the gift of absolute pitch, and could hum a note and go to the piano and strike it, but he couldn't put a nail in straight.[16]

One of Dean Morris' besetting virtues was his willingness to let people unload too many burdens upon him. In addition to the conduct of the many Cathedral services and to the training and direction of the choir, he had the spiritual oversight of the Sisters and of St. Mary's School and was the chaplain of the Church Home. He was also the chief organizer and priest in charge of St. Alban's mission. The Morrises were assiduous callers and almost every afternoon the Dean, often accompanied by his wife, visited members of the congregation. Sometimes when he went alone he would on rare occasions indulge in his pet diversion, a few final innings at the Southern League ball park. Last, but by no means the least of his activities, the Dean was intensely concerned with the guidance and betterment of the children of the neighborhood. The vacant lot next to their home turned into an unofficial baseball field for the neighborhood boys. Of course they broke many of the Dean's windows, and in winter the house was sometimes threatened by the boys starting grass fires, but these events gave Mr. Morris a better opportunity to know them, and led to the formation of a Boy's Club—in which he was assisted by William Omberg, J. Axson Evans and others—which met in the crypt. Mrs. Morris tells how the boys used to congregate on her steps before 7 P.M.

16. *Chapter Minutes 1910-39*, 7. In 1911 the chapter appointed a "Committee on Improving Music." Mr. Bolton Smith requested that it "say to Miss Reid, the organist, that the services at St. Mary's would be greatly improved if she will be in her place at the organ at least 10 minutes before the hour . . . and play appropriate selections as the worshippers assemble"—and the choir to be ready to move promptly. For these services her pay was to be raised from $20 to $25 per month.

waiting for the crypt to open, and that one condition of membership was that all had to take a shower before they went home after play. Years later Bishop Morris met several of "his boys" who were soldiers in the Canal Zone.

The interest of the Dean in seeing that children had space for play resulted in his being put on the City Recreation Commission (1912), and he participated in the development of the city's playground system. Thus it is a fitting tribute that the little plot of ground opposite the Cathedral should be named Morris Park.

The chapters of the early 1900's, appointed by Bishop Gailor, varied little from year to year (see appendix E), but about the time the nave was built Mr. and Mrs. W. I. Moody transferred to the Cathedral. He was soon put on the chapter and became superintendent of the Sunday School, and Mrs. Moody's vested Sunday School choir became famous. In fact a glimpse at the picture of her choir would reveal the youthful faces of many mature members of the congregation of today. Mrs. Morris spoke of Mr. Moody as "of infinite help in many ways," a role he has continued to play in the Cathedral for over fifty years.

In a chapter meeting held on February 7, 1911, Dean Morris expressed the wish that something be done to make the men of the parish take "a more lively interest in the church." He suggested that the men of the Cathedral have a dinner in town. The first such "Men's Dinner" was held on February 28 at the Business Men's Club. At this meeting young Mr. Moody made such a "clear and lucid" presentation of the financial plight of the parish that he inspired two Cathedral traditions: First, the Men's Dinner became an annual affair for many years —though it did move back to the crypt. Second, the chapter proposed that the figures Mr. Moody had gathered be turned over to the Bishop to be incorporated and printed in an "Easter Letter" from the Bishop to all communicants, urging them to

[125]

make larger Easter offerings and bigger pledges for the next year. (The fiscal year then began on May 1.) Thus the Bishop's Easter Letter began in 1911. Bishop Gailor was frequently absent and the chapter then supplied the letters (many of them composed by Mr. Bolton Smith), in which the Easter theme was lost in the moving and almost pathetic appeals for funds, for the parish was then in great financial straits due to building the Cathedral (1906) and deanery (1910). Thus in 1914 the appeal ended: "Be True to Your Cathedral! Remove the Debt! God Bless You!" In 1915 the chapter indicated that the Cathedral might not get through the summer unless $1,500 in cash was raised and threatened to "make public" the names and amounts of subscribers. In a later letter, written the same year, they even threatened to resign, "as the only means we have at our command of arousing the congregation to the recognition of the seriousness of the situation." Yet in this same letter when the chapter mentioned that it had been suggested that they visit subscribers, they averred that "we have a delicacy in thus intruding in reference to a matter which is as much the concern of the communicants as ourselves. We had rather see the Cathedral close its doors than be kept going by donations from unwilling sources." The day of the Every Member Canvass had not yet arrived.[17]

The Dean was greatly interested in the formation of a branch of the Girls' Friendly Society, the Daughters of the King, and in the Brotherhood of Saint Andrew. In the days before the first World War, women were decided newcomers in the realm of business, and women employees in stores were objects of concern. To help provide better conditions for the "working girls" of that day the Girls' Friendly Society was organized in the 1880's. The branch at the Cathedral was

---

17. *Chapter Minutes 1910-39*, 40 (for 1914); 49 (1915). In 1910 the chapter employed Mr. D. MacGillivrey to solicit subscriptions on a percentage basis, but it did not work.

As part of the Dean's plan to interest men in the church, he brought Bishop Woodcock of Kentucky to hold a mission in the Cathedral (December 2-8, 1912).

formed on February 15, 1911. Miss Helen Turner of Knoxville seems to have been the organizer of the group and part of their charitable intention was "to provide lunches and rest rooms for girls in business." The first general council of the society in Tennessee met on April 1, 1913, at the Cathedral, and on November 3, 1914, the Central Council of the G.F.S. in America held its meeting in Memphis. In 1913 the Cathedral branch opened a "Girls' Friendly Society Inn" or club room on Second Street near Court, and the Dean was made chaplain, but the expense of this project proved too great and within a few years the "Inn" had to be removed from its downtown location to the Cathedral crypt.

It was during the Morris deanship that the Sisters of St. Mary terminated their long and valuable connection with Memphis and the Cathedral. There were several reasons for this move, though it came about rather unexpectedly. St. Mary's School seemed to be flourishing at the turn of the century. It usually had a hundred or more pupils (though most were day pupils), four departments, and twelve or more teachers. In 1899 the buildings were painted and renovated, and the Bishop in convention urged greater patronage of diocesan schools. But the Sisters themselves, ever since the creation of the Sewanee house, were becoming increasingly interested in the training school there. By 1902 Sister Hughetta left Memphis to supervise this phase of their activity. Another thing that may have hurt the school is the fact that the diocese was then supporting another girls' boarding school (St. Katharine's) in nearby Bolivar, and that popular young ladies' schools were in existence in Memphis (e.g., Miss Higbee's and Clara Conway's). The "year of the Cathedral" (1906) proved in several ways to be a critical one in the annals of the Sisters. Early in the year Sister Mary Frances died. She had been both sacristan and almoner at the Cathedral for twenty-eight years; in the former capacity she had bestowed loving care on the altar and trained many generations of altar guild workers. As almoner she was untiring in her visitations, and to many of the neighborhood families was "their best earthly friend." St. Winfred's guild gave a credence table in her memory, and other guilds donated the brass alms basin.[18]

The same year Sister Mary Maude, who had been the Superior since the departure of Sister Hughetta, was recalled to Mt. St. Gabriel and became the Mother Superior of the order. On November 15, 1906, in a solemn ceremony in the Chapel, Bishop Gailor set apart a new Southern Province of the order. Sister Anne Christine was made Sister Superior of the new province with Sister Herberta mistress of novices, and the Rev. S. C. Hughson the chaplain. In his address on this occasion, Bishop Gailor called it "an epoch in the history of the diocese." Alas, it proved to be the beginning of the end. Few women of the region felt the call to the monastic life, and the central chapter began to realize that fewer houses, with larger numbers of sisters in each, was desirable. About this same time they consolidated their school in New York City with the school at Mt. St. Gabriel. Sister Anne Christine had for over twenty years been the efficient director of the Church Home and she preferred this work to the supervision of the new province or the conduct of the school. By November 1909 she stepped down from the headship and she and Sister Susan returned to the Church Home, Sister Ella becoming the new Superior of the province. It was about this time that the order felt it had over-extended, and by May 1910 the Sisters indicated to the Bishop that they were giving up the school and the province in Memphis. Sister Herberta and Sister Hannah went to Sewanee, and Sister Phoebe to Peekskill. Three events developed quickly: (1) the school was continued, under the ægis of the Bishop,

---

18. This 'Credence' was of wood, and is at present used for the alms basins. The present marble credence in the reredos was given by Mrs. James Prewitt in honor of a devoted altar guild worker, Miss Lillian Smith. It was designed by Canon James R. Sharp.

and entrusted to the direction of the two most important lay teachers, Miss Helen Loomis and Miss Mary Paoli.[19] In the June commencement address of the year (1910), the Bishop "spoke gratefully of the work done by the sisterhood . . . expressed regret at their withdrawal . . . and offered a few words of encouragement to the new management." (2) Before the end of 1911 the Bishop announced that "by the generosity of the people of Memphis I have been able to buy the property of St. Mary's School." In 1912 the Sisters' House and Chapel were deeded by the sisterhood to the diocese as a gift. (3) Just about the time that the Bishop announced the purchase of the school property he was in a position to announce that Sister Anne Christine had been released from her vows to the Order of St. Mary (9 a.m. September 30, 1911). He established her the head of a new order, the Community of the Holy Spirit, and at his invitation she continued in charge of the Church Home. Sister Anne Christine was the only member of her new community but remained for fifteen more years the head of her beloved Church Home. She has been described as possessing "a truly masculine executive ability." She worked wonders at the Home, and provided the children, among other things, with a summer home in the Arkansas mountains near Hardy.

By 1909 the chapter finally realized that it was absolutely necessary to provide a new deanery for the Morrises. The search began for funds and for a suitable lot. At last one was found immediately across the street from the Cathedral (this was in the early days of automobiles when rectors were expected to live near the church). The Curriers wrote from Europe offering part of the old Brinkley place further east on Poplar, but as it was located next to a smelly dye plant, the offer was graciously declined. The chapter tried to trim the estimates of the archi-

19. *Journal of 1911* (May 28). "I agreed to take the school under my official supervision provided it was put on the same basis as our diocesan schools with the Bishop as ex-officio chairman of the Board of Visitors, and a clergyman of the church made chaplain and responsible for religious instruction."

tect, Mr. Cairns, from $7,500 to nearer $6,000 but the work was begun and completed in the early fall of 1911 at the original figure. On October 30 a reception was held by the Morrises for the whole parish, so that they could inspect the new deanery.

Few physical changes were made in the Cathedral structure from its erection in 1906 until its completion in the 1920's. The Bishop donated a screen for the rear of the nave in 1909 and in the same year Mr. Schas had the walls and ceiling tinted, and a scripture text ("The Lord is in His Holy Temple") painted on the archway which then divided the nave from the Chancel. Shortly before the Dean left, the chapter had a cement floor laid in part of the crypt, though the portion used as a Sunday School room remained wooden, to the distress of later Church School superintendents.

During the years shortly before the first World War, Bishop Gailor took the first of his many trips to England. He seems to have made this journey in 1906, while the Cathedral was abuilding. In 1908 he attended the fifth Lambeth Conference, preached in many famous English churches, and visited the continent. He noted in his diary that he was greatly pleased at preaching to two thousand in Westminster Abbey; "the Dean was very kind in his praise of my sermon." In 1914 he took his family on an extended trip to Europe, primarily to visit his son, Frank Hoyt, then a Rhodes Scholar at Oxford. Unfortunately, he was in Paris when the war broke out, and as his hotel was closed, he and his family took refuge with Dr. Watson of the American Church in Paris—where the Bishop preached for two weeks. By August 18 the family got safely away to England—where they stayed until they were able to find passage on a boat for America on October 31.

The early war years, though watched with a mixture of curiosity and anxiety by the American people, had no immediate impact on their activities except perhaps to create a war prosperity and to tempt some venturesome youths to seek enlistment in the Entente armies. It was, therefore, not war work, but the multifarious church and community activities and the strain of Cathedral finances which began to wear the Dean's health down. He was ill most of the summer of 1915. The next year he decided to heed a pressing call from Grace Church, Madison, Wisconsin. From here he later went on to become the first Missionary Bishop of the Canal Zone (1919) and Bishop of Louisiana (1930). It was a great loss to the parish and to the city. In the Bishop's diary for November 6, he noted that he was "distressed to have to acquiesce in the decision of the Rev. James Craik Morris to resign his position as Dean of the Cathedral, and accept a call to Madison, Wisconsin. His reasons for taking the step were so cogent and convincing that, as a loving friend, I could not say 'no' to him." He concluded with this statement: "I am free to say that the break-off of the happy relationship of fifteen years service together is the hardest trial I have had since I was made Bishop. In many ways the loss to the City of Memphis and to the Diocese of Tennessee is irreparable. Dr. Morris leaves with the fervent love and prayers of all who know him."[20]

20. *Journal of 1916.* One of the last of Dean Morris' activities was to procure the services of James P. Krantz to take on "the special needs of the neighborhood," and to organize a "Social Service Department" of the Cathedral. Unfortunately Mr. Krantz left the next year to assume control of the Anti-Tuberculosis work in Nashville.

CHAPTER VII

COMPLETING THE CATHEDRAL

IT WAS A HARD TASK to replace Dean Morris, for as someone remarked, "When he smiled at you he made you think that this was a good world." Bishop Gailor carried on for awhile, assisted by the Rev. Dr. Arthur Howard Noll.[1] In January 1917, the Bishop suggested several names of possible successors to the chapter and it appointed a committee (C. N. Burch and J. A. Evans) to act with the Bishop in the matter of selecting a new dean. Several prospects were viewed, but by March the chapter decided to invite the Rev. Frederick DuMontier DeVall. He came to the Cathedral from the Church of the Ascension in Montgomery, Alabama, and was formally installed on May 6, 1917.[2]

The new Dean was no newcomer to Memphis. Many remembered him as the efficient young rector of St. Luke's during its formative years (1902-1906). Unfortunately he was a doomed man when he came to the Cathedral, for he was already ill with the disease that carried him off in four years

---

1. Arthur Howard Noll was ordained deacon in 1887, priest in 1888. His early ministry was in Texas. He became rector of Mount Olivet Church, New Orleans, 1892-95. He then came to Tennessee and was in many mission stations (South Pittsburg, Somerville, Monterey). In 1899, he was made secretary of the diocese, a post he retained for 28 years. In 1918 he was made Canon of St. Mary's in charge of the Good Shepherd, Holy Trinity, and neighboring missions. He was a learned scholar and produced *The History of the Church in the Diocese of Tennessee* and other works of history, especially on Mexico. He edited Bishop Quintard's *Memoirs of the War,* and was famed for his beautiful penmanship. He illuminated the Cathedral's *Memorial Book.*

2. Dean DeVall received his theological training at General Theological Seminary (1899). He was ordained deacon in 1899 and priest the following year. He had served in Trinity Church, New Orleans; at St. Luke's, Memphis; St. Andrew's, Chicago, and at the Church of the Ascension, Montgomery, before coming to the Cathedral.

(the only rector of the parish to die in office). His task was not made easier by the fact that within a month of his coming, the country was at war, and then the influenza wave struck. Many Cathedral members went into the service and others were busy with "war work." The national flag was added to the Cathedral processions. Whereas Dean Morris was loved and adored, but overworked because he was willing to undertake too many tasks, Dean DeVall was a man of decided executive ability, and a man of ideas—many of them ahead of his time. The diocesan convention recognized this trait and within a brief time he headed the Committee on Religious Education. In this capacity he did much to improve the Church School work of the diocese; he instituted a system of teacher training, a method of organized grading, the better keeping of records, and the use of lists of recommended readings. His efficient collaborator at the Cathedral and on the diocesan committee, Mrs. William Omberg, put many of the above-named reforms into effect at St. Mary's, and began the sending of teachers to Sewanee for summer training. In the diocesan reports on Church School activities during the years of Dean DeVall's tenure, St. Mary's school invariably carried off the prizes—the gold banners and gold crowns—offered in those days for the best school. References in the Bishop's diary to the Sunday School pageants of the day invariably speak of the crowds as "taxing the capacity of the Cathedral."[3]

Dean DeVall made other innovations at the Cathedral. He was, perhaps, the first dean to realize that the appointed chapter of the past was too small a group for the obtaining of full congregational support. At first neither he nor the chapter was quite ready to suggest the addition of elected members, so he

3. *Journal of 1920*, 147, says, "The banner school in point of organization, departmental system, and grading, is the Cathedral Church School of Memphis. It is interesting to note that this church school has a woman for its superintendent (Mrs. Omberg), a member of this committee." Mrs. Omberg also aided the National Department in its development of the "Christian Nurture Series" and used it in the Church School.

requested the Bishop to retire some of the older members as honorary members so that new blood could be brought in. But by December 1920 (shortly before his death) the chapter did authorize an election which would be held on January 16, 1921, "at which time those members of the congregation selected by general vote could be proposed by the Dean as those who would have the Bishop's appointment." But this plan missed fire. At a meeting held on January 12, Mr. Coate objected to such a plan; while Mr. J. A. Evans and Mr. Bolton Smith defended it "as a means of stimulating greater interest among the congregation members." It was, however, decided to postpone the plan in order to consult the Bishop and "the rules, regulations and usages of the Church." This meant that the election of members was postponed for over ten years.

Taking advantage of war-time enthusiasm, the Dean instituted a big Cathedral registration "for service to the Church and to God." According to the *Commercial Appeal,* he enrolled 117, who signed cards "which will be turned over to a war council of seven men who will classify and call on individuals when they are needed for any special work." The article went on to point out that the Dean was following the pattern of President Wilson in selecting a national army, but that only those "willing to fight in the great battle for righteousness are asked to sign the cards." It was to be a volunteer movement and not a draft. Dean DeVall was also anxious to publish a Year Book of Cathedral activities, but it could never be financed; and he planned a Forum to discuss topics of the day, especially the League of Nations, but it was never launched. He did institute a Service League for young people—ancestor of the Y.P.S.L.—and organized the women's guilds into a United Guild, with Mrs. Irby Bennett as president, thus anticipating the later unifying role of the Woman's Auxiliary.[4]

4. The following were the organizations (and presidents) listed in the annual parish report for 1920: United Guild, Mrs. Irby Bennett; Sunday School, Mrs. William Omberg; Men's Bible class, Mr. Shubael Beasley; Woman's

The Dean also imported from his old parish in Montgomery an able, devoted, and trained kindergarten teacher, Mrs. Judith Dennis, who started a day kindergarten primarily for the neighborhood children.[5] She began her duties as teacher and parish worker on September 1, 1917, and continued this school for over ten years. Some of the chapter wanted her to act as an assistant to the secretary and treasurer of the chapter (P. C. Clarke), but they finally agreed that she was "more needful in assisting the Dean," and the post of assistant treasurer, "without compensation," was entrusted to Mr. Herbert Esch (1918-1923).

One "historic institution" passed during Dean DeVall's time. Miss Matilda Reid, the organist during most of Dean Morris's era, retired (though in the future she substituted on occasion) and was replaced first by Mr. J. L. Norton, who combined the post of organist and choir director (1917-1918), and then after an interval—during which time Mr. Herbert Esch or Mr. Sam Loring took the console—by Mr. Arthur Bower as director and his wife, Birdie Chamberlain Bower, as organist. They began the system of using paid soloists in the choir.

But, as we have noted, the Dean was a sick man. Before he had been at the Cathedral a year he was sent by his doctors to Biloxi for rest, and then advised to give only "limited talks" in his sermons. On February 8, 1921 the chapter, the congregation, and the diocese were shocked to learn of his sudden death. The next day (Ash Wednesday) before a packed congregation at the Cathedral the new Bishop Coadjutor, the Rt. Rev. Troy

---

Auxiliary, Mrs. C. J. Barnett; St. Faith's Guild, Mrs. Guion Armstrong; Cathedral Guild, Mrs. G. Friedel; Girls' Friendly Society, Mrs. W. Chandler; King's Daughters, Mrs. Throckmorton; Boy Scout Leader, Mr. F. Deupree; Service League, William Deupree.

5. Mrs. Dennis was started with a very low salary, and had a serious illness in the 20's. She finally made $80 a month. Soon after the Cathedral was completed (1928) the chapter decided to abandon the school and Mrs. Dennis joined the staff of Miss Hutchinson's School. She died a few years later (1935). She left $100 to the Church School.

Beatty, assisted by the Memphis clergy, conducted the funeral service. A beautiful telegram of appreciation from Bishop Gailor was read and the following passage by the Bishop might serve as the Dean's epitaph:

> Dean DeVall was a devoted priest of the Church, intelligently loyal to her traditions and history; with an unusual ability for organization. He was in poor health for a number of years before he died, and showed wonderful courage and self-control in carrying on his work despite almost constant physical pain and weakness.[6]

By 1918 Dr. Gailor had been bishop for over twenty-five years and the need for a coadjutor became pressing. The convention, as usual, reopened the issue of the division of the diocese, and was itself divided as to whether to give the Bishop a coadjutor or a suffragan. In 1919 it finally decided on the former, and in a special election in May, after twenty-two ballots, chose the Rev. Troy Beatty, who only recently had come to Memphis as the rector of Grace Church (November 1916), though he had been originally ordained in Tennessee years before by Bishop Quintard.[7] This election of a coadjutor was most timely for within a month of Bishop Beatty's consecration (September 18 at Grace Church), Bishop Gailor emerged from the General Convention held in Detroit as the leading figure in the American Church.

A short digression is necessary at this point to explain the

---

6. The chapter's resolutions included these words: "The chapter knew his intense desire to extend the influence of St. Mary's . . . to increase its membership and to make it a great force for good in the community. He gave special attention to the Church School and under his guidance the school increased in numbers and is conducted with such skill and ability as to cause it to be considered a model for other schools."

The Dean was buried in New Orleans, and a fund was raised for funeral expenses and for Mrs. DeVall.

7. Bishop Beatty played a minor role in the history of the Cathedral. He was ordained deacon in 1891, priest 1892, and held parishes in Georgia before coming to Grace (1916). As Coadjutor he resided in Chattanooga and was an assiduous visitor of the diocese. In 1921 the Church of the Advent tendered itself to him as a "pro-cathedral," but he gracefully declined saying that he had no right to a cathedral, and that what he needed was a portable one. He was an ardent Knight Templar and a high dignitary in the order. His funeral was also from Grace. Incidentally it was Bishop Beatty who nominated Mr. Morris for Bishop of the Canal Zone.

significance of this convention which practically revolutionized the central government of the Church. There had been need of this for many years, since the National Church had been little more than a body of autonomous dioceses loosely held together by a Presiding Bishop chosen on the basis of seniority of consecration. His chief and almost only duty was to preside at meetings of the House of Bishops and at conventions. He continued to reside in and manage his own diocese. About the only other unifying force in the Church was the Board of Missions. Such presiding bishops were—in the words of one church historian—"nearly always on the point of decrepitude, if not indeed over the edge."

The work of the 1919 Convention was first to pass an amendment providing that in future the Presiding Bishop was to be elected by the House of Bishops and confirmed by the House of Deputies for a six year period (to take effect after the death of the then Presiding Bishop Daniel S. Tuttle, many of whose duties were entrusted to Bishop Gailor). Second, a new canon provided for a "Presiding Bishop and Council" (later changed to the "National Council of the Protestant Episcopal Church in the United States of America"). Bishop Gailor, though not presiding bishop, was made the first president of this Council. It consisted of twenty-four members: bishops, presbyters, and laymen, some elected by the General Convention and some by Provincial Synods, and its general function was "to administer and carry on the missionary, educational, and social work of the Church." Bishop Gailor described his own duties in these words: "I had the responsibility of organizing the Council and of making it known to the Church." Its first meeting was held in Washington on November 25, 1919, at which time the group was given a reception at the White House by the President. In the next General Convention (1922), Bishop Gailor was re-elected, and later remarked, "For six years I had the responsibility of explaining the new organization to the clergy and people of the Church. I visited nearly every diocese and spoke at public gatherings in 94 towns and cities."[8]

The new National Council created five departments: 1) Missions and Church Extension, 2) Religious Education, 3) Christian Social Service, 4) Finance, and 5) Publicity. These were not the only dramatic changes to issue from the 1919 Convention, for the women's work was reorganized and changed from the "Woman's Auxiliary to the Board of Missions," to its present title of Auxiliary "to the National Council." A Church Service League was instituted, and a Nationwide Campaign for funds was launched.

The Bishop's new responsibilities made it imperative that he reside away from the state, and travel the length and breadth of the land. Thus diocesan work was immediately transferred to Bishop Beatty. We cannot follow in detail Bishop Gailor's peregrinations nor all his activities during these crowded years (1919-1925), but perhaps his proudest moment came when he attended the great Lambeth Conference in 1920. Here he spoke for the American Church; he introduced his fellow American bishops to the King and Queen at their garden party, and he had an interesting personal interview with King George V. He was also made an honorary Doctor of Divinity at Oxford University in their colorful degree-granting cere-mony. He preached the closing sermon of the Conference in St. Paul's. As an aftermath of the great Japanese earthquake, Bishop Gailor made an extended tour of Japan and China in 1923.

---

8. Gailor, *Some Memories*, 221. For the changes in the Church see *Journal of the General Convention 1919*, also DeMille, G., *The Episcopal Church since 1900* (New York 1955) from which the above is taken. Bishop Tuttle died in 1923 and until the election of Bishop Murray (1925) Bishop Gailor acted as the Presiding Bishop. The six year rule was found to involve difficul-ties, and this was changed in 1937, when no time limit was set but the P. B. was to retire at 68. In 1943 this was further amended to provide that he resign his original see, and be a Bishop without jurisdiction over any particular diocese. Some wanted to create a primatal see for the Bishop.

Meanwhile in Memphis the deaths of Dean DeVall (1921) and then of Bishop Beatty (1922) brought new men into the life of the Cathedral. Another important change wrought in the diocese during these years was that the diocesan Convention of 1921 reorganized itself on the model of the National Church, and created a "Bishop and Council" with five departments (now six, with the addition of the department of college work) similar to those of the parent body. Fortunately, in the organizational meeting held in Christ Church parish house January 28, 1921, the recently ordained James R. Sharp was chosen executive secretary. This marked the beginning of his long and invaluable services to the diocese, to the bishops, and to the Cathedral.

The chapter met shortly after Dean DeVall's death and dispatched a wire to Bishop Gailor asking that as soon as possible he send someone to take the Dean's place temporarily; "that you appoint a permanent Dean as soon as you find one who will be thoroughly satisfactory"; and that "you preach for us on Easter Sunday." As temporary supply, the Bishop again turned to Canon Noll, who was assisted for a while by the Rev. A. C. Killefer of Monterey, and when he left, by the Rev. C. P. Parker of Fayetteville, Arkansas.[9]

This interim lasted from February to September 1921. Several prospects were considered, but on June 15 the chapter authorized Mr. Sam Loring to write a letter to the Rev. Israel H. Noe of the Church of the Incarnation in Atlanta, presenting a formal call. This letter was answered in the affirmative on July 14, and the new dean began his work in September. He was a recent Sewanee graduate, a native of North Carolina, and though he had had only five years experience in the ministry, both bishops recognized him as a man of such outstanding

---

9. Mr. Killefer had an interesting career. Born in Pennsylvania in 1856, he lived to be nearly a hundred. In the 1890's he held missions in East Tennessee. He was in Florida 1908-1914, but returned to St. Paul's, Franklin. He then became head of a boys school, St. Raphael's House, Monterey. It was from here he came to assist the Cathedral during the summer.

personality and force that they felt he was the "man for the job." Both the chapter and congregation quickly concurred.[10] Mr. Noe arrived in Memphis in September 1921, one might almost say to the sound of trumpet and drum, for his first service in the Cathedral (September 11) was with the assistance of the Shrine band and the Knights Templar. Mr. Herbert Esch enthusiastically reported to the chapter meeting of September 21—the first full meeting since Dean DeVall's death— that "the Dean responded to the hearty welcome with a wonderful sermon, and the service was one of the most inspiring services that had ever been held in the Cathedral." Meanwhile the Dean had been welcomed at a Clericus breakfast (September 19) and Bishop Beatty who attended noted in his diary, "He and his family have been very cordially welcomed to Memphis, not merely by the Cathedral congregation, but by the entire city, and I trust he is at the beginning of a very happy and fruitful ministry." At this same September chapter meeting the Dean displayed boldness in innovation: he presented the Chapter with a new *Church Bulletin,* which would appear weekly and contain events and happenings of interest to the congregation; he wanted a Men's Club which would meet each month and which would start with dinner and proceed to an open debate (It was decided to call this the "Cathedral Open Forum"); and he asked for regular monthly meetings of the chapter. These ideas started bravely, but the Forum died (to be replaced later by the Men's Council); while in those days of small chapters and no regular meeting place, it proved impossible to secure regular chapter meetings. Within a brief time other "new departures" were under way, including a regular Every Member Canvass, and a bold venture by the women to

10. The Rev. Israel Harding Noe was born in Beaufort, N. C., December 20, 1891, the youngest of four sons of a Confederate veteran, all of whom entered the ministry. He attended the University of the South, 1910-1917, and received the B.A. and B.D. degrees. He was ordained deacon June, 1916, and priest 1917. He married Ellen Morris Camblos June 14, 1910. He served at St. Thomas Church, Windsor, N. C.; St. James, Macon, Georgia; and at the Church of the Incarnation, Atlanta, before coming to the Cathedral.

start a restaurant, The Kopper Kettle, in downtown Memphis.[11] But before undertaking a description of the many parish activities of the new era, we must pause to consider the "great undertaking" which strained the energy and occupied the attention of the Dean and congregation during the next four years (1922-26), namely, the completion of the Cathedral building.

It has often been assumed that the instigation of the idea to complete the cathedral came with the new regime—and undoubtedly the drive, the campaigns, and the idea of making it a living memorial to Bishop Gailor did come then, but "to complete the building" had been in the air and in the thoughts of the chapter and members of the congregation virtually since the completion of the nave (1906). A chapter meeting of November 1913 first seriously discussed the proposition of adding another portion. This was at the very time when St. Mary's was struggling with a high debt and low income; but that year the women held an unusually successful bazaar which netted them $500, so Mr. Moody suggested that this be put aside in a fund toward "the new building" (since this would draw 6 per cent interest) instead of paying it on a debt which only required 5 per cent. This is the first reference in the chapter minutes to a "new building fund." By April 1917, Mr. Moody reported that this fund had reached $5,500. During Dean DeVall's time hopes rose higher and in 1919 when the war was over, the cathedral stationery carried a picture of a completed cathedral with the motto: "Eventually—Let's Begin."

---

11. In a letter of Dean Noe's in *The Mirror*, there is this statement on the Kopper Kettle: "Last year the Church Service League took a most progressive step at the suggestion of Mrs. William T. Braun and Mrs. Barton McGee of the Woman's Auxiliary and with the assistance of Mrs. Jacob A. Evans, and opened up the Kopper Kettle Lunch Room in the heart of the city. The organization pledged $10,000 to the fund for the completion of the Cathedral, and up to the present time have paid in $5,000 in cash, and now have $1,000 in the treasury. In addition to this all the material equipment has been paid for and the lunch room has been a success from the start." He thanked the "faithful band of unselfish women who have served in season and out as hostesses, cashiers, workers . . . the present head of the Church Service League is Mrs. W. H. Chandler."

By next year enough progress had been made for the chapter to ask an architect, C. O. Pheil, to sketch a proposed building and the Bishop suggested the name of a prominent New York Architect, Mr. Upjohn, with whom he wanted Mr. Albert Caldwell to consult. These preliminaries were shelved following the death of Dean DeVall.

It would seem that during the summer of 1922 Dean Noe and Mr. Caldwell were in conference on the "new cathedral," and that by the time of the chapter meeting of October 3 they were ready to confront the chapter with their plans, for on that date the Dean informed them "that the principal order of business was the formulation of plans to finish the Cathedral."[12]

At that meeting Mr. Caldwell reported that he had already been working with the architect, Mr. Bayard Cairns, and that they had found no "working plans" in existence for completing the Cathedral. He said that Mr. Cairns thought that the elimination of the triforium gallery (originally planned by Mr. Wood) would not only enhance the beauty of the building but save $10,000 and that eliminating the carved stonework on the tower would save another $25,000. Mr. Cairns estimated then that the structure would cost about $175,000 but that heating would add $10,000; pews $4,000; organ additions, $15,000; architects fees $10,000 (of which he would donate half), thus making an estimated total of $210,000. Mr. Cairns further promised "that if an earnest effort was made to try to raise the necessary funds to finish the cathedral, he would draw working plans free of charge, this entailing about a month's work in the office."

After Mr. Caldwell's talk a motion was made and passed that a Building Committee be appointed, and Mr. Caldwell

---

12. *Chapter Minutes* 1910-38. In the *Tennessee Churchman* (1925), the Gailor Memorial Edition, there is a statement by the Dean that "in the summer of 1921 the Dean wrote him (Caldwell) asking him to undertake the tremendous task, as a living memorial to Bishop Gailor." Either the Dean meant 1922, or else he wrote Mr. Caldwell before he came to Memphis, which was not until September 1921.

was made its chairman with power to enlarge at will. This same meeting discussed the idea of changing the name of St. Mary's to "Gailor Memorial Cathedral." The movement came clearly into the open the following Sunday (October 8), for the Bishop noted in his diary, "In the Cathedral, Dean Noe read Morning Prayer and I preached. I gave my consent to the movement inaugurated for the completion of the building of the Cathedral." Unlike the previous struggles which had been mainly led by the Bishop, this final drive was made in his absence; and since it was to be done in his honor, he could not gracefully have participated in it.

Mr. Caldwell and his collaborators planned the first big Citizens Drive.[13] It was designed not only to appeal to the cathedral members, to Memphis Episcopalians, to the Church throughout the diocese, but to Memphians of all faiths. Mr. Caldwell also enlisted the support of the new coadjutor, Bishop James M. Maxon, former rector of Christ Church, Nashville, who had been elected during the summer to fill the vacancy left by the death of Bishop Beatty, and who had just been consecrated on October 18. Bishop Maxon visited Memphis in December, sat in (December 12) at a dinner attended by representatives of all faiths and "formally launched the project."

The committee was most anxious to bring the subject to the attention of the diocesan convention. On January 4 Bishop Maxon conferred with Messrs. Bolton Smith and George

13. Unfortunately I am unable to discover the list of the many Memphians of all faiths who volunteered to serve in the two Citizens Drives to solicit funds for the building to honor Bishop Gailor. The *Tennessee Churchman* (Gailor Memorial edition) contains pictures of the leaders of the two campaigns (December 1922, and spring 1923), with the following captions: "Albert S. Caldwell, originator of the 'Gailor Memorial' to honor our beloved Bishop and Chairman of the First Citizens Campaign and of the Cathedral Building Fund; Joseph Newberger, Chairman of the Second Citizens Campaign for Cathedral Fund; Frank Hayden, Treasurer Second Citizens Campaign for Cathedral Fund; Homer K. Jones, Asst. Treasurer Second Citizens Campaign for Cathedral Fund." From the same source we learn that George H. Patten was Diocesan Chairman of the Building Fund, and that the Chapter's Building Committee was composed of W. I. Moody, chairman, Bolton Smith, Jacob A. Evans, P. Stenning Coate, and Charles N. Burch.

Darrow (Mr. Caldwell's chief assistants in presenting the project throughout the state) and they decided to have a slightly premature celebration of Bishop Gailor's thirtieth anniversary as bishop in Nashville on January 17, 1923. Here they would present him with a present (a gold watch), so that Mr. Caldwell would have an opportunity to explain the cathedral project before the convention opened.

The easiest way to follow the vicissitudes of the great money raising efforts of December 1922-February 1923, which consisted of behind-the-scenes solicitation by Mr. Caldwell and his committee, and a more open and publicized "Citizens Drive" led mainly by civic leaders and non-Episcopalians, is to scrutinize the clear reports made by Mr. Caldwell at regular intervals to the chapter. The first such report was made on February 6, 1923, and reveals both the modification of cathedral plans and the fluctuating hopes and disappointments of the drive. At that meeting Mr. Caldwell explained that they had begun with estimates of $190,000 (this would only have provided for plain glass windows, simple electrical fixtures, more pews and removing the organ), yet when plans for this work were submitted to two contractors both bids were above $225,000. After changing the specifications from Bowling Green stone to Bedford stone, a third contractor had submitted a $200,000 estimate. (These were the days of rising prices.)

He reported that when the Citizens Drive started in December 1922, he and his friends had already raised $120,410 at the trivial expense of $453.58, whereas the first Citizens Drive only netted $27,972 in subscriptions at a cost of $1,573.67. "Since this drive ended," he reported, "$3,236 has been obtained, three fourths of which the Dean got." By this time total subscriptions (less cost of the campaign) netted $149,591. He explained that he had tried to enlist some of the business leaders for a second solicitation of Memphis, "but in a quieter and what was hoped would be a more effective way." But of the seventy men he

[144]

hoped would take cards, only seventeen took any and little had been heard from them; "there is no disguising the fact that the start is poor." He mentioned that his visit to Knoxville "produced no enthusiasm" and he "hoped for no substantial aid from that quarter." Of Chattanooga he was at first hopeful. He also described the tactics (mentioned above) of the Gailor Anniversary Dinner. "There were present at the dinner 290 people, and it was a great success as far as honoring the Bishop went. Every speaker referred to the completion of the Cathedral and heartily endorsed the movement. I, at Bishop Maxon's request, spoke on that subject solely. But nearly three weeks have elapsed, and the dinner has not yet helped the Cathedral either in Nashville or in the state." Although the Convention of 1923 did pass a strong resolution urging every parish to complete its subscription by March 1, Mr. Caldwell found nothing but discouragement from the diocese from which he hoped to secure at least $25,000.[14] "I have written three letters to the ministers and some laymen of each parish in the diocese; the first early in October enclosing pictures of the completed Cathedral and some literature, and received never an answer." Again in November he sent them all a resolution of the Convention of 1921 which had declared the completion of the Cathedral "to be a diocesan work" and a facsimile of Bishop Gailor's letter to the chapter. Again he received only a few non-committal answers. Finally, in December he sent the parishes a third letter "urging them to do something, even if not much," and enclosed subscription blanks showing that the payments were easy and told them of the renewed Memphis drive in January. "I received only two answers, one refusing to contribute anything; the other sending $12.50, and stating that was all I need expect from that parish." He had little hope from the parishes "unless

14. In the Convention of 1924, in the absence of Bishop Gailor, Bishop Maxon made the address. He urged members of the diocese to contribute, and to assume $25,000 of the projected $225,000 cost. He appointed collectors for each parish. In the *Tennessee Churchman* (1925), 75, there is a copy of this message and a list of the committees and collectors he appointed.

Bishop Maxon makes good his promises in regard to them." He was also disappointed in the Memphis parishes, whose total subscription came to $17,560. "There ought," he said, "to be some way to touch the hearts of our fellow churchmen in Memphis, but I confess I don't know how." Though $70,000 short of his goal, he was still hopeful that the second Citizens Drive might succeed or that Bishop Maxon might wake up the diocese. They still had until November 1924 to make good, but he admitted he was reaching the limit of his endurance. He promised to work on until the next chapter meeting; if success seemed near he felt he and others might raise their pledges to complete the drive but, he added, "If complete failure faces us, then I am willing to work till November 1, but only when I am convinced I shall have active and earnest co-workers, men who will go out and beg just as I have done."

Mr. Caldwell's March report passed from the mild disappointment of his previous report to deep discouragement, and in view of ill health he asked to be relieved from active work, though consenting to remain in charge of the Building Committee until his final report and resignation on July of the next year (1924), when Mr. W. I. Moody stepped into the breach. Not a great deal had transpired between the February and March reports. However, since he gave a new breakdown on gifts and other topics it will merit a brief summary. The financial section showed:

Subscriptions from Episcopalians

St. Mary's	$90,055	
Calvary	21,525	
Grace	9,155	
St. Luke	790	
Holy Trinity	130	
St. John's (then a mission)	70	$121,725
Non-Episcopal pledges prior to the Citizens Drive	18,550	

Non-Episcopal pledges from the
December drive 20,507   39,057

Total	160,782
Less Expenses	2,127
	158,655
Second Citizens Drive..	9,064
Total Pledged	$167,719

Other items of his report were as follows:

1) January, Second Citizens Drive: Fifty men promised to take names and only 19 have taken them, and nothing heard from them. The promised leaders had not been heard from or were absent from the city.

2) Knoxville—"no great amount will be forthcoming from Knoxville."

3) Nashville—"nothing since last report, the dinner stirred up enthusiasm but nothing came of it, and Bishop Maxon has been absent."

4) Chattanooga—"nothing heard from it, but still hopeful."

5) Other parishes—"Bishop Maxon promised to help in them, but evidently has not yet been able to do so."

6) The future—He thought the cathedral could be completed for $210,000 and that three-fourths was raised. They still have till November 1924 before subscriptions lapse, and is still hopeful.

7) Suggestions: a) that the Dean and two members of the chapter who are willing to work should take over. These should:

b) get Mr. Salisbury to push through the (Citizens) drive before April.

c) get Bishop Maxon to work harder on the diocese.

d) get the chapter to work on the other Memphis parishes.

e) enlist Bishop Gailor's aid; "We told him we would not ask him to solicit subscriptions and we will not," but he thought he might openly and heartily advocate "the completion of his own Cathedral despite the proposed change of name. If he would do so failure would be impossible."

f) He was willing to remain chairman, but wanted relief from work the next two months.

The active driving period was now over, and it remained to be seen whether the remaining $50,000 would be raised during the following year. In October 1923 Bishop Gailor returned for a chapter meeting. He had already engineered the removal of St. Mary's School—which had been under the direction of Miss Helen Loomis since the departure of the Sisters—from the old location next to the Cathedral to a new location on Poplar (now occupied by the Shriners).[15] He now announced that he wanted to turn the old school property over to the chapter, mentioning that there was a $2,300 mortgage on the property which he expected the chapter to assume. He sketched his plan for the future use of these buildings: a place for the Sunday School, for office purposes, "or perhaps as a dormitory where certain church officials might be housed, and where a place might be afforded for the visiting clergy to stay while stopping over in Memphis." According to the minutes, the chapter members "listened with interest" and decided to wait the return of Mr. J. Axson Evans before actually making the transfer. This was done by April 1924.

By spring 1924 there was some difference of opinion within the chapter over whether the whole amount should be in hand before starting, or whether if within reach of the goal, the prospect of building operations might not stir up subscribers, and assist in collecting pledges. It was decided to wait, as no one wanted to increase the bonded indebtedness. By July 9, 1924, Mr. Caldwell, now in poor health (and spirits), made his final accounting and retired completely from the committee. Laudatory resolutions on his work were passed, and he was given thanks by the Dean, Bishop, Chapter and congregation. As in previous reports, his final one contains so many interesting details that some of it should be indicated.

---

15. Bishop Gailor continued to oversee the School and to appoint trustees, but the diocese and Cathedral assumed no financial responsibility for it. Mr. Binswanger, Mr. Stansbury and Mr. R. L. Taylor applied to the State for the charter. Management remained with Miss Helen Loomis and Miss Katherine Neeley until they retired in 1949.

Again it begins with a financial statement:

Cash and securities with J. A. Evans (treas.)	$123,419.49
Cash and securities with Frank Hayden (citizens)	19,721.21
Regular subscriptions past due	16,430.75
Regular subscriptions due December 1	13,778.75
Miscellaneous subscriptions—good and bad	21,772.00
Total	$195,122.20
Uncollectible	10,000.00
Balance	$185,122.20

This amount was clearly short of the goal, for it contained too many dubious pledges. Mr. Caldwell's hopes of both Nashville and Chattanooga had now dimmed, and on June 20, 1924, Mr. Cairns had gotten seven bids, the lowest of which was $235,263. He concluded sadly, "it is apparent no contract can now be let," and bemoaned the fact that the movement had not been started in 1921 instead of 1922. He was still not without hope, and realizing that the suggested new name for the Cathedral embarrassed some he made the suggestion (which was ultimately followed) that the old name, "St. Mary's," be retained, but that on the cornerstone an inscription be added, "This Cathedral completed in ...., as a memorial to Bishop Gailor." "I believe," he said, "all subscribers would be satisfied."[16]

The final paragraph of Mr. Caldwell's report has a certain pathos: "I have given nearly two years of my time and mind to this work, inspired not only by the desire that a beautiful edifice should be provided as our Bishop's Church, but by admiration and affection for that Bishop who was my college mate." He was mortified by his failure, and insisted that new

16. The cornerstone of the completed Cathedral actually read: "This Cathedral was completed January 19, 1926 as a testimonial to Bishop Thomas F. Gailor in commemoration of his service as Bishop of Tennessee for thirty-two years and for six years organizing President of the National Council of the Episcopal Church."

blood and new methods were needed, "defaulting subscribers even avoid me for fear I will dun them," he added, and tendered his resignation.

As in the past, and again frequently in the future, when St. Mary's faced a crisis, it turned to Mr. W. I. Moody. The same meeting which accepted Mr. Caldwell's resignation unanimously elected Mr. Moody as the new chairman of the Building Committee, and, said the secretary, "He gave the chapter a very hopeful view of the building situation." There was no wonder working in tapping new financial resources or in gaining diocesan support, but by January 1925 Mr. Moody reported to the chapter that by altering the plans—more specifically by leaving off a proposed chapel and vestry room—they could tailor the church to fit the sum in hand. The next day he attended the diocesan convention which met in St. Luke's, Memphis, and reported to it that St. Mary's had $165,000 in hand and that bids would be let in February.

On February 8, he reported to the chapter that eight bids had been received, and that the following contractors gave the lowest estimates:

H. J. Gilbertson Construction Co. (general construction)	$161,000
Dawkins Electric Co. (wiring)	2,300
Fischer Heating Co. (heating)	3,900
Prichard Brothers (plumbing)	387
Total	$167,587
Architect and incidental	11,000
	$178.587

This was about $13,000 over what was on hand, but it was voted to take the plunge, and the Building Committee signed contracts on February 16, 1925. Dean Noe had to remind Mr. Esch, of the Building and Grounds Committee, that since work would soon begin it would be necessary to find a "suitable place" for worship. Within a few days the Scottish Rite Masons offered their Cathedral on Union, and here St. Mary's held its services for the next ten months. The old brick school buildings of St. Mary's School, recently acquired from the Bishop, were slightly renovated for the Church School. The Dean felt that this period of temporary quarters would involve some strain on congregational loyalty, so he made the suggestion that "district committees" be set up throughout the city to serve as foci of interest in the various neighborhoods. The Kopper Kettle finally closed its doors in the summer of 1925, and its equipment was moved to the crypt as the basis of the Cathedral kitchen. By November, the Building Committee was ready to announce that January 19, 1926, would be the date for the opening and that Bishop Maxon would be in charge of arrangements. The grand opening was to precede by a day the meeting of the diocesan convention in the new Cathedral. The new District Chairmen were assigned the task of finding housing for the expected throng of visitors. Thus as 1925 drew to a close, and a scaffolding gradually disappeared, and as final interior work was being hastily completed, the fever of interest in the new Cathedral mounted. All Memphis awaited the great day with excitement.

Early in January notices began to appear in the press directing attention to the opening: the Bishop wrote one of his brief historical sketches for the *Commercial Appeal* under the headline, "St. Mary's Cathedral has Romantic Colorful History —Church was admitted into the Union *(sic)* May 26, 1858— Was Religious Center of City during Civil War Days and Yellow Fever Epidemic." The final words of the Bishop's article should be noted:

> The Very Reverend Israel H. Noe became dean in September 1921 and under his vigorous and devoted leadership the Cathedral building has been brought to completion.
>
> Where all have done nobly and unselfishly in this last effort to finish the work, and where nothing could have been

accomplished without the magnificent co-operation of our women, it would seem almost invidious to make special mention of any names. And yet this sketch would not do justice if the names of Mr. Albert S. Caldwell, Mr. Jacob A. Evans, Mr. W. I. Moody, Mr. Bolton Smith, Mr. Charles N. Burch, Mr. P. Stenning Coate and Mr. W. D. Kyser were not placed on the roll of honor.

Other articles called attention to the distinguished clerical visitors who were expected, gave invitations to all to attend, and sketched the opening program.[17] Perhaps the best way to recapture the spirit of the day is to reproduce—with some abbreviation—the very fine account which Mr. Jack Carley, then a young editor with the *Commercial Appeal,* gave of the event.

Fulfillment of a vision of more than half a century ago, erected to the glory of God as a church for all people and all creeds, St. Mary's Episcopal Cathedral was formally opened yesterday morning as a living memorial to the Rt. Rev. Thomas F. Gailor, Bishop of Tennessee, poet of the church and first citizen of Memphis.

The history of Memphis churches . . . is replete with deeds of courage and self sacrifice . . . but nothing could be more inspiring than the service by which the new Cathedral was opened.

And Memphis church history from now on will date from that opening, for there can be but one Episcopal Cathedral in the state, and the building of a Cathedral is a matter of centuries rather than that of a lifetime.

And St. Mary's is builded well. Its wall will defy the ravages of time and the stone of its foundation should last long, but it is built on even more than stone. It is built on love and hope and faith, a tribute from the citizens of Memphis and members of the diocese to one they have learned to revere and respect.

A church for all people and all creeds. That is Bishop Gailor's wish and yesterday morning creed and color, race and prejudice were forgotten when two thousand Memphians and visitors, some of them from far distant cities, entered

17. *The Commercial Appeal,* especially for January 8 and 16. The celebration was to begin on Monday, January 18, with a meeting of the Daughters of the King; Tuesday there were two celebrations of the H. C., 7 and 8 a.m. The big opening service was at 11. There was to be a Woman's Auxiliary meeting that afternoon, a reception for the Bishop, and a big dinner at the Gayoso in the evening. Wednesday and Thursday were the days of the convention.

the doors of the beautiful Gothic structure . . . to do honor to Bishop Gailor—and to worship the God of their fathers.

It was beautiful. Again—it was inspiring, and coming in a generation when superficially there appears a trend of drifting away from worship that has been the corner stone of civilization, it was significant.

Certainly Memphis has never before witnessed such a colorful ceremony. Eight bishops of the church, fifty priests from distant dioceses, the governor of the state, the mayor of the city and his official family, and the vestries of all Episcopal churches in the city took part in the service.

Resounding throughout the Cathedral were the Alleluias of a choir of 100, echoing again and again were two thousand voices saying, "I believe." There was not standing room even when the head of the procession entered the door, with a crucifer carrying the cross of the risen Christ. The sound of "Onward Christian Soldiers" burst through the Cathedral. The two thousand voices took up the refrain. Marching behind the crucifer were the combined choirs of the Memphis Episcopal churches. The solemn cathedral purple of their cassocks was broken then by the first bright colors—the standard bearer carrying the national colors . . . The Crucifer had reached the chancel. The end of the procession was still a block away outside. Behind the colors marched Governor Peay and his staff and Mayor Paine and the city commissioners. They represented all the people who could not come . . . Still the hymn went on . . . More crucifers, more flags, the procession seemed unending. Then came the priests of the church, from little mountain missions in East Tennessee to the wealthy, larger parishes of the cities; some were greyed by their years of service, others were young and vigorous, but all marched with that steady even tread, their eyes alight with the faith that is theirs and with the happiness they were sharing with their Bishop. Still that grand old hymn . . . and then came bishops, eight of them. First the youngest of them all, Robert Campbell, Bishop of the missionary diocese of Liberia . . . a former member of the Order of the Holy Cross. Then the others in turn, Henry J. Mikell, Bishop of Atlanta; William Mercer Green, Bishop Coadjutor of Mississippi; James R. Winchester, Bishop of Arkansas and former rector of Calvary Church; Lewis W. Burton, Bishop of Lexington; Edward Demby, Suffragan Bishop of Arkansas, and one of the two negro bishops of the church . . . James M. Maxon, Bishop Coadjutor of Tennessee, and then Bishop Gailor who took his seat on the throne near the altar.

Preceding the Bishops was the Dean of the Cathedral, the Very Rev. Israel H. Noe, who in the four years of his

[153]

service at St. Mary's, accomplished the work that had been projected by Bishop Otey . . .

The Rev. Arthur H. Noll was master of ceremonies.

The usual order of service for the morning followed; Bishop Green read the two lessons. Bishop Mikell read the prayers, and Bishop Winchester the closing prayers, after the sermon . . . The service was simple, with all the dignity of the old Church of England. It was the occasion that made it memorable . . . During the service the first memorial window to be placed in the Cathedral was dedicated by Bishop Gailor. It is in memory of William D. Kyser, Jr., and was presented by Mr. George Darrow.

Bishop Gailor is noted as an orator, but it is doubtful if ever before he preached as he did yesterday. Imposing in appearance yet simple in demeanor, he talked in a heart-to-heart manner rather than preached, and as always his diction was flawless.

He is more than a prelate. He is a writer, he has composed hymns, and for six years as organizing president of the National Council he showed his ability as an executive.

The service had begun at 11 o'clock. It was 1 P.M. before the recessional began with the choir singing "O Heavenly Jerusalem." It was over. St. Mary's after almost a year in course of construction was at last opened. It has yet to be dedicated and consecrated.

(Then follows a list of the clerical visitors and of other events on the program. The whole of Bishop Gailor's sermon on the text "Wist ye not that I must be in My Father's House" followed Mr. Carley's article.)

The day ended with a reception in the afternoon, and in the evening a dinner at the Gayoso in the Bishop's honor. "It was," said the *Commercial Appeal* in reporting it,

an expression of the joy of his people in welcoming him back home, in pledging their loyalty, their devotion, their love.

For two hours the prelate sat and listened to words of praise and affection from the lips of his fellow Bishops, priests and laymen of the diocese. Perhaps no living Memphian has been so lauded as Bishop Gailor was last night.

And he took it all as became the man to whom it was offered. His response was characteristic. Whatever measure of success he had attained, he said, he owed to God, his sincere belief in the efficacy of prayer, his mother and Mrs. Gailor.

The completion of the new structure raised the old problem—What is a Cathedral? and what is to be its function in the diocese? Again, as in the past, ambiguous answers were given. The handsome Gailor Memorial Edition of the *Tennessee Churchman* which appeared shortly before the opening of the Cathedral gives some indication of the thinking of the time. This brochure contained four articles (and four pictures) on Cathedrals; the first was an historical account of the building of some great Cathedrals of the past; the second, by Bishop Gailor, was a brief historical sketch of St. Mary's; the third, written by the Dean of the new Washington Cathedral, traced his views on the general role of the Cathedral in the American Church.[18] The remaining article, entitled, "The Cathedral Idea," came nearest to indicating contemporary plans for St. Mary's. It is obviously based on a letter by the Bishop in the same booklet and its most significant paragraph reads as follows:

> For years St. Mary's Cathedral has functioned merely as a parish church. The present time presents a wonderful opportunity for the establishment of St. Mary's as a Diocesan Cathedral in fact as well as name. The Cathedral has been completed, and plans must be outlined for future progress. A diocesan consciousness needs to be developed, and what could better symbolize the unity of the diocese than the Diocesan Cathedral as the center of missionary activity. St. Mary's is rapidly ceasing to be a mere parish church. It is the Bishop's seat. The movement to endow it has begun, and when the endowment is complete, it will cease to have a communicant list. The Chapter will be composed of the officers of the diocese, and other diocesan representatives. The Canons will be the active heads of the various departments of the Bishop and Council, so that from the Cathedral will radiate all the activities of the diocese. A new Cathedral House is contemplated, one floor of which will be used as living quarters for mission priests engaged in diocesan mission work.

This, then, may be called the "Cathedral Dream" of the

---

18. This was, according to him, to be: 1) a center of missionary and church extension work; 2) a center of education; 3) a place in which the worship of Almighty God shall be carried on in the most fitting and dignified manner possible and 4) a center of social service activity.

twenties, though at the time it was vaguely mixed with a slogan developed during the fund raising campaign: that the Cathedral was to be "A House of Prayer for All People." This latter idea, though well meant, was obviously impossible to implement. The former idea—seemingly Bishop Gailor's—of a Cathedral divorced from a parish; of a Chapter composed of diocesan representatives; of Canons who were to be the heads of depart- ments of the Bishop and Council, of course never materialized. The idea of a "Cathedral House" was kept alive for a while, but since this house started out in the decrepit and impractical old St. Mary's School building, even this idea had to be modi- fied. The "role of the cathedral" continued to challenge the bishops and deans of the future.

CHAPTER VIII

DEAN NOE

BY ALMOST SUPERHUMAN effort the cathedral structure was completed and opened, with great pomp and circumstance, on January 19, 1926. But we must realize that the interior of the newly opened building presented, once the colorful throng had departed, a decidedly bleak appearance. Most of the organ apertures were empty, temporary chairs filled both the nave and the choir, a dossal hung behind the altar, and brass rails separated the chancel and sanctuary from the main body of the church. On the outside was a vacant gap immediately to the east, then came the brick chapel and the old three storey school building of the Sisters, both in a sad state of repair.

Before undertaking the narrative of the parish activities during the deanship of Mr. Noe (1921-1938) and before considering the "Cathedral plans" developed by Bishop Maxon as diocesan, let us observe briefly the main changes made in the cathedral fabric during Dean Noe's tenure. By August, new pews were installed and this improved the general appearance of the interior, but it was obvious from the very first that the acoustics were faulty. This problem was of immediate concern, yet it was four years before it was solved. These were the pioneer days of the radio, and the Dean, as Memphis' first radio preacher, looked naturally for an electronic solution. He suggested this as early as April and by May the committee studying the problem recommended that this remedy be tried. A loudspeaker system was therefore installed that summer at a cost of $1,500. But it became evident even before the end of the summer that this solution was a failure. Then various sounding boards were placed above the pulpit. These improved the effect somewhat, but failed to solve the problem, for when the Bishop visited the Cathedral in 1927 he complained bitterly of the acoustics, and the Dean affirmed that St. Mary's "was losing hundreds of new members every year"; and that it was almost impossible to have preaching missions, or to invite other ministers to speak, with things as they were. Experts were consulted, various suggestions made, and finally the problem was solved when Mr. Coate reported to the chapter (January 1930) that Mr. R. L. Taylor of the Federal Compress Company had volunteered to pay the cost of acoustical board for the entire interior ($7,500). By April this work was completed. Everyone rejoiced and the Dean declared (in the *Chimes*), that "the difficulties and handicaps under which we have worshipped during the past two years have been good for our spiritual development. God has enabled us to make brick without straw."

It was also obvious from the day of opening that the old Benton organ, already damaged by a storm, was inadequate for the new building. The search for a donor for a new organ was entrusted to the Dean who announced to the congregation on Sunday, May 13, 1927, that Mrs. Blanche Steele Coate was giving the new organ. In making the announcement he said: "The whole city and not St. Mary's alone will be the beneficiaries of Mrs. Coate's generosity in making a gift that would redound to the glory of God, and whose melodious chords will find responsive echoes in the reverent hearts of grateful worshippers." In a chapter meeting on May 27, Mr. Stenning Coate confirmed the donation and brought to the meeting Mr. Adolph Steuterman and Mr. M. V. Mullette of the Kilgen organ company to explain its specifications, and how he would incorporate some of the old organ. "Briefly, the new organ would have three manuals, 43 stops, harp, chimes and many other up-to-date devices that are found on fine organs." It was explained that the new organ would be one of the finest instruments in the city. This news was "gratefully accepted" by the chapter, and at the next meeting Mr. Coate announced his intention to add an echo organ in the west end of the nave. Work began almost at once in removing the old organ and by September 1927 the new instrument was ready for use.

The departure of the old organ marked also the departure of the former choir director and the organist, Mr. Arthur Bower and his wife, Birdie Chamberlin Bower. They had served faithfully and well since 1919. The new organist, chosen by Mr. Coate (and paid for by him, for his first year) was Mr. Arthur Davis from Christ Church, St. Louis, purportedly the best in the region. The press announced that he "came to Memphis because he believes there is a great opportunity for building up a great music center, both from a religious and civic standpoint." The dedication and opening recital on the new organ was on October 27. Press reports were ecstatic:

> He revealed the tonal quality of all stops, especially the vox humana and the chimes installed in the echo organ . . . He used rare judgement in the selection of several numbers with striking orchestral effects, simulating performances of a symphony of which Memphis is unfortunately devoid . . . Tears were seen in many eyes in the opening Hymn to Glory, Pietro Yon's tribute to the soldiery, and dedicated to the American Legion. Virile spontaneity and freshness marked the opening salute . . . Spectacular effects were produced from the echo, wild cries of the Valkyries . . . mighty shrieks, almost discordant, crashed into pæans of victory as souls were welcomed into Valhalla, etc., etc.[1]

Bishop Gailor, who gave an address at the dedication, announced that organ recitals would be given on each Sunday evening during the winter, beginning the next week. Due either

---

1. *The Commercial Appeal*, October 28, 1927. The following were the pieces played at the opening: *Hymn to Victory*, Yon; *The Bells of St. Anne de Beaupre*, Russell; *Romance sans paroles* and *Elves*, Bonnet; *Toccata and Fugue in D Minor*, Bach; *Largo* from the New World Symphony, Dvorak; *Carillon Sortie*, Mulet; *Moonlight*, Kinder; *Minuet Antique*, Watling; *Echo*, Yon; and four Wagner transcriptions.

Mr. Davis certainly tried the popular approach typical of his day, transcribing many piano and orchestral pieces. After one program which contained McDowell's "To a Wild Rose" and Schubert's "Serenade" the papers announced "Organist Davis promises a program of selections of a lighter sort next week."

to Memphis' indifference to organ music or to the nature of the programs, Mr. Davis gave up these recitals after the first year and disappointed the hope expressed by the chapter that he "should endeavor to make the Cathedral a center of musical life for the city." He resigned after his second year and was succeeded after a short interval by Mr. Lawrence Meteyarde, who came in September 1930 and remained as organist for eleven years. Mr. Meteyarde had been an Associate of the Royal College of Music, the winner of many prizes in English and Welsh music festivals and had directed several famous Welsh choirs. He came to Memphis from the Ensley (Ala.) Academy of Music. Frequently he wrote short religious poems which were published in the *Chimes*.

There is no space here to list the full complement of memorial gifts: windows, architectural features, plaques, etc., which were donated to the Cathedral. But little by little the building began to attain a more livable and less barren appearance. As early as 1927, after a memorial service for Sister Hughetta on the Feast of the Purification, the alumnæ of St. Mary's School and the Associates of the Sisters, under the leadership of Miss Matilda Reid and a committee, undertook the tremendous task of raising the approximately $10,000 needed for a marble reredos.[2] This beautiful work, designed in its symbolism and details to match the altar, was completed and installed in December 1931 and formally dedicated on February 2, 1932.

It was at this time that the inscription on the top riser of the altar steps was changed from † He feedeth among lilies † to † Sister Hughetta † February † 1926 †. It should be remem-

---

2. Sister Hughetta died February 1, 1926, at the Convent in Peekskill. A few months later (May 18) Bishop Gailor proposed to the alumnæ at a meeting at the School that they raise funds for a memorial reredos. The original committee was composed of Miss Matilda Reid, chairman, and Miss Mary Love, Miss Elizabeth Mosby, Miss Geraldine Jones, and Miss Elizabeth Cairns. Some money remained and the committee purchased a window, installed to the memory of all the Sisters of St. Mary's. It was designed by Mr. Howard from an embroidery by Sister Hughetta which formerly hung in the Chapel. (The window on the Gospel Side next the transept.)

bered that the original dove on the altar was a "descending dove." When the altar was moved to its present position in 1925, the dove was broken and a substitute ordered from Italy. This proved to be a "cemetery dove" flying forward. Bishop Gailor strongly disapproved of the new one, saying that it looked like a hatrack.

Meanwhile the seven windows representing the Ascension of Christ surrounded by the Apostles were placed in the apse (October, 1930) and other nave and transept windows were designed and completed by the great artist in stained glass, Mr. Len Howard. His windows are not only beautiful works of art, but in a sense unique in that he designed, executed, and installed every window, from the very first (1925) to the final clerestory windows in 1956. The blues, reds, gold and greens from these windows added a dimmer and more subdued light to the interior. The present stone altar rail replaced the former brass one (brought from the old building), in 1930, though the marble parapet rail and chancel steps were not completed until 1936-37.

Bishop Gailor, even on his journeyings, remembered "his cathedral" and when he returned from his Palestine trip (July 1928) he brought home a stone from the balustrade of the pool of Bethesda which was placed in a niche in the north transept wall. Again, after a visit to England (in 1930), he brought home a portion of a stone column (now in the south transept) from legendary Glastonbury.[3] The above mentioned changes and additions along with a new litany desk, hymn boards, and a stone book stand for the Memorial Book, and the alteration of the doors to open outward instead of inward,

_____

3. The inscription below the Glastonbury stone reads, "This is part of one of the columns of the ancient abbey of Glastonbury, England, the Avalon of Tennyson's *Idylls of the King,* the place where Joseph of Arimathea preached the first Christian sermon in England." Bishop Dandridge, who realized—as all historians do—that the story of Joseph's visit was purely legendary, never passed this inscription without remarking that it should be changed, at least to "reputed to have preached."

constitute the physical improvements made in the interior during the period 1926 to 1938.[4]

The other big building problem of the time was what to do about the old St. Mary's School, now called the Parish House. The ravages of time, of its long period of service as a school and of disuse after the school moved away, had left it in bad shape. A committee was appointed in 1925 to improve it as a place for the Church School, but little was done. Meanwhile the Church School, first under Mrs. Leroy Taylor and Miss Ellen Correll and, after 1925, under Mr. Joseph Patten, began to expand rapidly. The crypt was overflowing, and the Parish House was inadequate, so something had to be done. Mr. Shubael Beasley and Mr. Patten (both appointed chapter members in 1928) led a determined movement to replace the old school buildings by a new structure.[5] In April 1929 Mr. Patten brought to the chapter a strongly worded resolution from the executive board of the Church School (drawn up March 6) asking that "the Parish House and the Chapel be torn down and that the chapter be requested to use the money in the Parish House Building Fund." The resolution further stressed the "urgent need" of a Church School building, and asked the chapter's approval for proceeding immediately with a new building project. The May chapter meeting approved of these ideas; Messrs. Coate, Moody and Clarke were appointed a Ways and Means Committee, and Messrs. Patten, Kyser and Beasley a Committee on Building. Meanwhile the women's

---

4. The donors of some of the above listed items (see Appendix for fuller listing) were: chancel windows, Whitfield King; altar rail, Dr. and Mrs. A. R. Bliss; parapet rail, Mrs. W. D. Kyser; litany desk, F. H. Carlyle; credence table, Mrs. J. A. Prewitt; Hymn boards, in memory of Mrs. Anna B. Maas. The bell from the old cathedral was first kept in a small tower between the Chapel and the Cathedral; then shifted to the tower of the Chapel and when this was removed in 1941 to the Cathedral tower, where it was silent until an electric ringing system was installed.

Bishop Gailor asked the diocese for memorial windows for Bishops Otey, Quintard, and Beatty but never got them.

5. *Chapter Minutes (1910-1938)*, 152. "Mr. Beasley asked the chapter to allow the church school to go ahead with plans for a one floor church school building on the site of the old St. Mary's School next to the Cathedral."

organizations of the church began to urge the enlargement of the plans so that the new building would include an auditorium, cooking arrangements and space for community and diocesan activities. They also wanted the chapter's assurance that the new plans would be in keeping with the cathedral architecture. However, they were willing, they said, "should funds be limited," to agree to begin with Sunday School rooms.[6]

The resulting enlargement of plans, from a simple Sunday School addition to a grandiose "Clergy House"—pictures of which began to appear in church publications—involved much more than the original movers contemplated. It thus comes as something of a surprise to find that the plans (drawn by the architect, E. L. Harrison) submitted for the new building were on October 29, 1929, "rejected as unsuitable" on the motion of Mr. Patten.

By April 6, 1930, it would appear from *Cathedral Chimes* that three plans were still under consideration: 1) To erect a two storey brick building, using materials from the old school building. This was estimated at $31,000 with an additional $10,000 if "architectural readjustments and housing the Boy Scouts were contemplated"; 2) To cut the old structure from three and a half storeys to two—but this would only last ten years or so; 3) To erect a permanent new Parish House (of four storeys) with adequate facilities for the Church School, Cathedral organizations, neighborhood work, and a diocesan center—at the cost of $100,000. The last plan was in essence the one discarded, but it was still considered "as a grand memorial" for some possible donor.

During the discussions the old school buildings were razed. Fortunately, the architect of the Cathedral, Mr. Bayard Cairns, undertook, at his own expense, to save and repair the brick

---

6. *Chapter Minutes (1910-1938),* 159. The signers of this petition were: Alice Collier Neely (St. Faith's); Loretta Bliss (Dean's Guild); Grace Braun (Head of dinners); Pearl Throckmorton (Daughters of the King); Knoxie Chandler (Cathedral Guild); Louise Clark (Woman's Auxiliary).

Sisters' Chapel built by Colonel Snowden in 1887. When finished it was covered in stone to match the Cathedral with which it was connected by a stone cloister and a Cathedral garth. Work on it was completed in 1931, and on May 19, 1932, it was formally dedicated to the memory of Aspasia Seraphina Bogardus Snowden (Mrs. John B.) and Mary Jay Snowden Cairns (Mrs. Fred), the grandmother and mother of Mr. Cairns.

Mr. Moody, now chairman of the Parish House Committee, again snatched a measure of victory (though in the end it seemed a rather dubious one) from seeming defeat. He got Mr. Cairns to plan a concrete building containing one big room on Alabama. In December 1930 it was voted in chapter meeting that work should be begun immediately. The new building was publicly announced in March 1931 and was then designated as "the first unit of a building for the use of our Church School," and the congregation was informed that it would cost $11,000, of which $4,500 had already been promised "by certain friends and members of the parish," the remaining $6,500 to be raised by a summer drive.

Thus, in May, contracts were let for four important items: the Church School building ($11,500); the Chapel ($15,000); the reredos ($10,000—also designed by Mr. Cairns and executed in Italy for the Gorham Co.); and the two large west windows ($5,000), given by Mr. and Mrs. J. A. Evans.

Unfortunately the architect in designing this underground room (now the gymnasium of the present Parish House) did not foresee the hidden springs, leaks, and seepages which began to plague the "new crypt" almost from the moment of its completion (June 1931). Valiant, repeated, and futile efforts were made during the entire thirties to prevent this constant leakage. Before the end of the decade these efforts were abandoned, and all that remained of the brave dream of a new Parish House building and clergy home was an unsightly projection covered with a tarpaper roof, which rose about six feet above the ground level through whose windows (on Alabama) could be seen a pool of dirty water with debris floating on the surface. During the period of construction of this room, several Church School classes met in the Art Academy on Adams.

In describing the activities of the parish during the period of Mr. Noe's deanship—other than the building activities which have already been sketched—we may use the expression of an old communicant who remarked that "the unexpected was always to be expected." When the young, energetic and dynamic Mr. Noe arrived, he soon captured the attention of the congregation, the entire community, and of the newspaper reporters. With his energy and imagination he quickly became not only "newsworthy" (to borrow *Time's* expression) but an important Memphis personality.

His very first *Church Bulletin* (itself an innovation) carried a fervent plea by the new Dean for everyone "to be a booster," to try to bring in a hundred new members, and to join some Cathedral organization. His energies were far from exhausted by the drive to finish the building. He was the first Memphis clergyman to foresee the possibilities of the new medium of the radio, and he began to broadcast regularly (over WMC) from 1923. His sermons, always with striking titles, dealt with the latest books, plays, and articles, and with the manifold moral problems of the jazz age, and of the prohibition era. He was everywhere in demand as a speaker; at ladies clubs, at men's luncheon clubs, and at all types of public gatherings. As one introducer said (1925): "In a comparatively short time Dean Noe has become an inseparable part of Memphis and a recognized factor in all civic, economic and æsthetic movements which tend to uphold the life and morals of the community in which we live."

In a period when youth was being damned, the Dean voiced faith in the young; in the year of the famous Scopes trial (1925) he wholeheartedly championed the cause of evolution. The town and press followed avidly the many challenges he made to the fundamentalist position. He saw the movement as "part of a national conspiracy" and in one sermon remarked, "In the beginning God said, 'Let there be light, and there was light.' In the twentieth century Mr. Bryan said, 'Let there be darkness,' and the Tennessee legislators said it was good, and it was so." Inspired by his crusade, the Cathedral Y.P.S.L. composed a song which went like this (author unknown):

> We're monkeys, we're monkeys, Oh here comes our band;
> On the right side of evolution we now take our stand.
> We're all for Dean Noe and for Mr. Scopes,
> And we think the Tennessee legislature is one great big joke.
> Down with the fundamentalists!
> Ah, William Jennings, Ah, Mr. Bryan.

The Dean fought his first rounds against local upholders of the Tennessee position (the Rev. Willis Furr of Central Baptist, and the Rev. Charles Malloch of the Cumberland Presbyterian Church). But when, according to the papers, the fundamentalists declared war on modernists in Memphis, some big guns were imported to Memphis to blast opponents. The Rev. W. R. Riley of Minneapolis came to the First Methodist to join the Rev. J. Frank Norris, who was already in town. These champions of Special Creation challenged one and all to debate them in the new municipal auditorium. The Dean accepted the challenge, and all looked eagerly for the fray. But differences soon developed. Was the debate to be on "fact" or on "theory"; was the decision to rest on an impartially picked panel (the Dean's proposal), or on an audience decision (his opponent's stand)? The Dean realized that an audience decision would be fatal to his side, since the Baptist Bible Union was then in convention in Memphis. After some weeks of haggling, the big debate was finally cancelled, and the May 8 headlines read: "Evolution Debate Off—Or Rather Noe and Riley Stage It in the Papers." That summer Bishop Gailor preached a sermon on "religion and love," from the text, "Whoever shall say to his brother, 'Thou fool,' shall be in danger of Hell fire," and the evolution name-calling calmed down a bit in Memphis.

During the construction of the Cathedral the National Church was conducting its "Nationwide Campaign," and the Dean visited many cities speaking in its behalf, both within and without the diocese. This campaign for funds was quickly followed by a nationwide evangelistic effort called the "Bishops' Crusade," or as one of the local papers expressed it, "what would be termed a national revival by any other Protestant organization." Again the Dean's talents were enlisted in other pastures, and St. Mary's itself held two great missions, following the completion of the building. The first (1926) was conducted by the Rev. J. A. Schaad and the second by Bishop Shayler of Nebraska and the Rev. E. W. Mellichampe of Sewanee. Yet even before these missions were held the Cathedral membership had boomed. The Dean presented a confirmation class of 89 to the Bishop when the congregation was still meeting in the Scottish Rite Cathedral, and the first Palm Sunday class in the Cathedral contained a hundred members. The Sunday School was also growing, and again winning diocesan banners and gold crowns. About the same time the Dean organized an Order of Sir Galahad for boys, which met in the sepulchral gloom of the old school building, and The Brotherhood of St. Andrew was revived.[7]

The clerical staff, which in 1926 included, in addition to the Dean, the Rev. Stanley Young (St. Mary's first perpetual deacon, ordained in 1923); the venerable Canon Noll; another Canon, the Rev. Charles S. Ware; as well as the Archdeacon B. F. Root; was enlarged by the addition of a new and energetic young Canon Missioner, the Rev. Alfred Loaring-Clark,

---

7. Mr. S. C. Hodges was "King" of the Sir Galahads, which started in October, 1925. The Brotherhood of St. Andrew was revived by Mr. C. D. Montgomery. The Junior Guild was formed by Miss Kathleen Fleming, and Acolytes were organized into St. Vincent's Guild. The Church School Service League, led by Miss Louise Fleece and Sara Sadler, won prizes at the Fair for paper work and basket weaving.

or the "flying parson" as he was dubbed by the press (since he had been a wartime aviator). Mr. Loaring-Clark took over some of the missions from Canon Noll and Mr. Young, especially St. Alban's, the mission in Covington, St. Anne's, Woodstock, and St. John's, Buntyn. His work in the last named was so successful that by February 1928 he had organized it into a parish which was admitted to the diocese in 1929, and he was called as its rector. (This was the third time that someone from St. Mary's had revived the Buntyn mission.) After Mr. Loaring-Clark's departure, Bishop Maxon appointed the Rev. Hiram Douglass as a diocesan canon (1928-1937).

These are but a few of the many activities of the 1920's. As has been mentioned, while the congregation was worshipping at the Scottish Rite Temple, the Dean developed the idea of keeping congregational activity alive by the creation of "District Chairmen." He divided Memphis into seventeen regions (later reduced to ten) with a chairman for each (something like our present "groups"). The list of the 10 original chairmen may be found in the Cathedral's first and only printed *Year Book and Directory,* which the Dean brought out in 1926.[8]

The chapter soon realized the possibilities of this district organization and used it in Every Member Canvasses, drives, and for other purposes. Beginning in 1929 and continuing into the early thirties, it became an indirect means for enlarging the chapter, for district chairmen, under the name of Cathedral

---

8. The Directory itself was an interesting venture. It seems to have been planned for use as a form of pressure on members to subscribe ("even if only one cent") by marking contributors' names with an asterisk, but this plan was abandoned. The *Directory* contained a foreword by the Bishop; pictures of the Bishop, Dean and Cathedral; a condensed history of St. Mary's, and lists of the services, officials, and church organizations and members. The following organizations and their presidents (for 1926) were listed: The Cathedral Guild (Mrs. R. L. Taylor); St. Faith's (Mrs. Alice C. Neely); Daughters of the King (Mrs. R. N. Throckmorton); The Woman's Auxiliary (Mrs. W. B. Rogers); the Junior Guild (Mrs. Walter Ford); the Church School (Miss Ellen Correll); YPSL (James Napier); St. Vincent's Acolyte Guild (Nils Florentz). The ten district Chairmen were: 1) Jesse Edgington, 2) Mrs. Chester Allen, 3) Toy Percer, 4) H. O. Gardiner, 5) Frank Strayton, 6) W. J. Gilfillan, 7) Arnold Armstrong, 8) Finley Faxon, 9) Frank Baum, 10) Mrs. W. P. Martin. The Chairman of Chairmen was Mr. W. D. Kyser.

Council, were invited to sit in chapter meetings and, though not permitted to vote on all subjects, acted as a kind of parish vestry (or lower house) in combined session with the chapter (or upper house) in the years before Bishop Maxon enlarged the chapter by the addition of elected members.

From the beginning the Dean had urged the organization of a Men's Club. One was launched in 1927 with a big dinner at which Mayor Rowlett Paine (then recently confirmed) spoke. This group soon changed its name to the Men's Council, and it long continued to have charge of laymen's activities, ushering on Sunday, Every Member Campaigns, and the monthly men's dinner. The Dean also had a flair for pageantry, and not long after the new Cathedral was built, he devised an Epiphany pageant (now called "Feast of Lights"). This feast later expanded both in its features and in the participation in it by the clergy of other Memphis churches. Thus it soon became a "tradition," which many people today consider an ancient service of the Church.

During the late twenties and early thirties, the women of the Church were extremely active. They seemed, however, to have made considerable experimentation with names. After calling their organizations "Circles," and then "Chapters" (of the Auxiliary), the women finally returned to the time-honored designation of "Guilds." The year 1931 was a great year for Guilds (or "Chapters" as they were then called). At that time there existed only the "historic" three; the Cathedral, St. Faith's, and St. Mary's, plus the group called the Junior Guild (transmogrified to the Dean's Guild in 1929); but in February 1931 there is mention of two newly formed "Circles," the Bishop's (later Gailor) and St. Anne's (which went into decline later). In March (the month "Chapter" was adopted) the Auxiliary reported that "four new chapters were being organized" by Mrs. S. K. Jones, Mrs. J. H. Johnson, Mrs. Cliff Mabie and Mrs. A. R. Bliss. Within the year three of the four, at least, took form and name: St Hilda's, St. Katharine's (later, Catherine) and St. Dacus (later, Dorcas).[9]

The Dean's "middle period" coincided with the coming of the great depression. Both Church and country began to feel its heavy pressure. Before, however, its full implications were evident, the congregation held a big Tenth Anniversary Celebration for the Dean at Hotel Peabody. He was showered with appreciation and praise for having increased the membership of St. Mary's from 300 to 900, and for having raised the budget from $7,000 to $25,000. Unfortunately, as the depression deepened, both membership and budget declined. It was soon after this that observers began to note a subtle change in the Dean. Perhaps no one, not even the Dean himself, will ever fully understand what brought about this change, but whereas he had once been forthright and clear in his statements and sermons, he now became increasingly obscure; whereas he was once famed for the tremendous range of his interests and of his sermon topics, he gradually—no matter what the text—began to return to a single theme: the struggle between the inner, spiritual self ("the Christ within us") and the outer material self (the body). And he continually urged "living on the higher plane." No layman, or historian, should attempt to interpret mystic utterances and the Dean's messages were becoming increasingly mystical, symbolical, and allegorical. The Dean still continued to be active in parish work and in pursuing the tasks for which he was especially gifted; visiting the sick and afflicted, and consoling the bereaved. He also continued, on

---

9. After the departure of the Sisters the care of the altar—the linens, vestments, memorials, etc.—has been the work of the devoted volunteers (from all guilds) of St. Faith's (sometimes called a "guild," sometimes "altar committee"). The following have directed, or have take a long and active interest in this work: Miss Lillian Smith, Mrs. Alice Collier Neely, Mrs. Hugh Edgington, Mrs. Thomas Lill, Mrs. William Omberg, Mrs. Charles Roe and Mrs. Lanier Perkins.

Bishop Maxon reorganized the work of the Cathedral acolytes (St. Vincent's Guild). I have found no record of its officers or membership. Some of the men who have directed this important work are: Frank Baum, Nils Florentz, Bartlett Hanson, Clyde Washburn.

occasion, to challenge his fellow ministers on certain trends of the times.[10] He now began to expend much time and energy in explaining to his devoted followers, in classes held in the Cathedral and at Hotel Peabody, his elaborate system of symbolism and numerology. This was an era when many distressed people were looking for some new Moses to lead them to a promised land; so many were enthralled by the Dean's obscure messages even when they could not understand them. In fact possibly because they could not understand them.

In the early thirties, as the Dean was leading the congregation to a new plane of living, Bishop Gailor, full of years and of honors, returned to Memphis. His period of greatest prominence (1919-1925), had been followed by a period of extensive travel (1925-1930), and he now came home to a well-earned rest. He was warmly welcomed by Cathedral members at a banquet in honor of his seventy-fourth birthday and his fiftieth year in the priesthood. But troubles soon began to afflict him. He had a slight stroke, he had to have cataracts removed from his eyes, and on October 8, 1931, he lost his beloved wife. The venerable prelate survived her four years. Fortunately, he lived to receive the homage of the President of the United States, the Governor of the State, the members of the diocese, and of his beloved university at a tremendous celebration in honor of his fortieth anniversary as bishop, at Sewanee on St. James' Day, 1933. The Presiding Bishop characterized it "as being one that would go down in history as one of the greatest in all the life of the American Church."[11]

10. Two examples of this in the thirties were 1) when he attributed the depression to the moral decay of Memphis and the nation. The press reported the sermon under the headline, "Is Memphis Going to The Religious Bow-Wows," and ran several columns of rebuttal to the Dean by other clergymen and laymen. 2) He was also opposed to the growing trends toward pacificism and neutrality, and quit the Memphis Pastors Association after refusing to participate in their big Mass Meeting for Peace at the Auditorium. He explained that "Peace must come through individual regeneration, not through legislation."
11. *Journal of 1934*, 22-24. The ceremony featured 1) a message from President Franklin D. Roosevelt delivered by his personal representative, Admiral Grayson and an official escort from Ft. Oglethorpe; 2) Resolutions by the two houses of the Tennessee legislature, presented in an address by

Bishop Gailor also lived to participate in the Seventy-Fifth Anniversary Celebration of the Cathedral on January 16, 1934, which was held in the crypt with many clergy of other denominations and with representatives of the city government in attendance.

The passing of Bishop Gailor (October 3, 1935)—who had maintained such a long and intimate connection with St. Mary's—brought about the elevation of the coadjutor, the Right Reverend James M. Maxon, as the new diocesan.[12] Before his accession the chapter and congregation had been somewhat apprehensive regarding the new Bishop's "Cathedral Policy." For he had long lived at the opposite end of the state, rarely visited Memphis, and rumors were rife that he was a strong advocate of dividing the diocese. In fact, as late as 1930 he had been made the head of a diocesan committee to study this matter, and the report brought in by the Bishop and Council in that year found that it was advisable to form a new diocese for fast growing East Tennessee and concluded "that though the time had not yet come . . . it is to be expected in the near future." Fortunately for St. Mary's, during the early thirties a

Governor McAlister; 3) letters from over a hundred American bishops and from leading bishops from England, Scotland, Ireland, and Canada (bound in a sumptuous volume); 4) a companion volume of addresses from the parishes of the diocese (signed by 6,000).

The procession to the chapel was: 1) choir, diocesan officials and honorary committee; 2) Admiral Grayson and escort; 3) Governor McAlister and staff; 4) Representatives of educational institutions; 5) Clergy; 6) Bishops; and 7) Bishop Gailor attended by two personal friends, Charles Martin and George M. Darrow.

12. After the death of Bishop Beatty, Bishop Gailor called a special convention (June 22, 1922) to elect a new coadjutor. The rector of Christ Church, James M. Maxon, was elected. He was consecrated on October 18. He was born in Bay City, Michigan, and married Miss Blanche Morris of the same place. He was in business before entering the ministry; graduated from G.T.S. in 1906; was ordained deacon and priest in 1907. He was first at Grace Church, Galesburg, Ill., then president of Margaret Hall and rector of St. John's, Versailles, Ky. (1910-17), before coming to Christ Church, Nashville. In Nashville he was very active in both church and community work, improved the church school, held mid-week Bible classes, organized a boys' Club for paper boys, and did much for the rehabilitation of ex-convicts. He improved his own parish finance, and helped organize the Community Fund. He was also responsible for starting Camp Gailor-Maxon (1929). One of his first official acts as Bishop was to make his long-time chaplain, the Rev. James R. Sharp, Canon to the Ordinary.

Nashville benefactress, Mrs. Delia Robinson, left a large sum for the use of the diocese, and as the time drew near when Bishop Maxon would become diocesan, he began to see less merit in division and more in preserving the unity of the diocese.

A great Memorial Service was held for Bishop Gailor in the Cathedral on All Saint's (November 1, 1935). Two days later Bishop Maxon was formally and ceremoniously installed at St. Mary's, the first official installation in Cathedral history.[13] Shortly after these services, the new Bishop met with the chapter (December 8). He gave it sound advice on financial matters (recommending a "Loyalty Sunday") and then turned to the topic which was occupying the thoughts of most chapter members, his plans for reorganizing the Cathedral and for regulating the relationships between the bishop, the diocese, the dean and the chapter. Thus he discussed his proposed amendments for Canon XII (the one defining Cathedral organization). The chapter meeting had been preceded by a parish dinner welcoming the Bishop to St. Mary's. Here, too, he touched on his plans. As reported in the *Press-Scimitar* the following day, he declared that he intended to make St. Mary's an exemplar of what the Church in Tennessee should be, "a great Mother Church in which every communicant in the diocese will have a real sense of proprietorship." "I do not," he said, "intend to come to the Cathedral and shine awhile and then go elsewhere . . . A Cathedral is not a place to exalt the ego, to win a front seat in heaven. It must be a great spiritual center reaching out with vision, to the people everywhere." He wanted the Cathedral to

---

13. The service for Bishop Gailor is described in the *Journal of 1936*. Addresses were made by Judge Burch (for the laity), the Rev. Prentice Pugh (for the clergy), and by Bishop Maxon (for the diocese). At the service it was announced that the colored school at Mason, formerly called "Hoffman—St. Mary's," would be changed to "Gailor Industrial School."

At the installation service for Bishop Maxon, Dean Noe read the "call to the congregation," the Bishop's letter of consecration was read by Chancellor Bartow Strang. Dr. Blaisdell of Calvary "read the words of intention for the Bishop who responded . . . The Dean and Chancellor then conducted him to his chair repeating the words of installation. The joint choirs rendered beautiful music . . . There were children present who will long remember this service."

undertake work of a city-wide nature, to point the way "in the evangelism of music," and for these ends he planned to begin the custom of Evensong every Sunday at 5 P.M. (for all Memphis parishes) at the Cathedral. (This was later limited to the Sundays in Lent). He also wanted the Dean to visit around, and in turn to invite others into his pulpit. He realized that widening the scope of the Cathedral would mean greater expense, and he wanted others to share this.

Many members of the chapter found these plans a little vague, and when they realized that he had made no reference of any intention of remaining in Memphis, and when they found that Chancellor Strang was investigating the title of the Bishop's House, they remained apprehensive. Thus early in the next year (January 1936) several members wrote the Bishop a letter. They pointed out that there was a feeling "that this Cathedral is only a local parish church. To change this condition we earnestly request that you now take over and occupy these buildings, making them a diocesan center—a center for your missionary clergy, a center for your Forward Movement, a center for every movement which has to do with the general work of the diocese. If this Cathedral is allowed to develop into a parish center, or even into a Church which is only nominally the Bishop's *Cathedral,* the purpose of the donors in subscribing for these buildings has been frustrated. . . ."[14]

The Bishop referred this note to a special convention committee, "On the Development of the Cathedral," and in his own address made it clear that he planned a larger use of the Cathedral. The committee (composed of the Rev. Prentice Pugh, J. M. Patten, and J. K. Craig) made a strong recommendation that the Cathedral be made more than a parish church, yet at the same time they "wanted the members of the congregation to have their rightful share in the control of the policy

---

14. *Chapter Minutes (1910-1938),* 186. The signers of this letter were: F. W. Faxon, Herbert Esch, P. Stenning Coate, P. C. Clarke, W. I. Moody, and J. M. Patten.

and government of the Cathedral work." It then made the usual suggestions of making it a center of missionary work, religious education, Christian social service, and evangelism. It ended with a recommendation that Canon XII be changed. Dr. Blaisdell brought in the proposed changes which were adopted by the convention. In effect these enlarged and remodelled the chapter. They are the basis of the present Cathedral organization. Briefly, Section 1 retained the old statement that the congregation "shall still be entitled to the same representation (i.e., in convention) which . . . was allowed to it as a Parish." Section 2 incorporated the new definition of the Chapter, "which shall be composed of the Bishop of the Diocese, the Bishop Coadjutor if there be one, the Chancellor of the Diocese, the Dean of the Cathedral, all *ex officio;* and of not less than nine or more than 21 other members . . . of whom three shall be appointed annually by the Bishop, three shall be elected annually by the Convention, and the remainder shall be elected annually by the congregation of the Cathedral parish . . ." Section 3 defines the presiding officer; Section 4 states that "The principal Minister . . . shall be known as the Dean of the Cathedral, and he shall be appointed, as shall any assistant Ministers of the Cathedral, by the Bishop with the concurrence of the Chapter." Section 5 created new names for the Wardens, "The Bishop shall designate annually one member of the Chapter to be known as the Bishop's Warden, and the Chapter shall designate one member of the Chapter to be known as the Chapter's Warden . . ." The final Section (6) makes any by-laws "subject to the approval of the Bishop."[15]

---

15. *Journal of 1936,* or more conveniently in *Journal of 1956,* 21, for the Canon XII. Mr. Patten made the suggestion that the three chapter members elected by convention be chosen from the three convocations, but this idea was never adopted.

Bishop Maxon during the remainder of his episcopate gave considerable thought to the relationship of the Cathedral to the diocese. He strongly desired that it cease to be primarily a parish church. He wrote at least six long letters to the chapter elaborating his ideas. The first is quoted below. The others, which may be found in the chapter minutes, were written on February 12, 1940, February 10, 1941, November 13, 1943, October 9, 1946, and finally when he made Mr. Sanders acting dean on December 23, 1946.

Thus the chief observable results of the agitation to improve the Cathedral's status were: full control by the bishop in the appointment or dismissal of the dean; a new chapter organization with elected members and new names for the wardens; a convention committee which rarely if ever met; an additional report (begun in 1941) in the *Journal* by the dean of any activities of "a Cathedral nature," i.e., of services like the Lenten evensongs (inaugurated and continued during Bishop Maxon's period) or The Feast of Lights, in which the clergy from other parishes participated. Two important changes did transpire the next year (1937). In January, just before convention, Bishop Maxon met with the chapter and announced that he intended in the course of the year to come to Memphis to reside. This piece of news was met with rejoicing and with a rising vote of thanks by the members of the chapter, the the secretary recording that "the chapter receives with gratitude and thanksgiving the news of the Bishop's decision to make Memphis his home and headquarters." The Bishop's second item of news was that since the old Bishop's House was too large for him, he had decided to turn it into a Diocesan House, "which would include the Bishop's offices, offices for members of the diocesan staff, headquarters for the publication of the diocesan paper, and a diocesan library with an official custodian, and a 'prophet's chamber' or rooms for visiting clergy and probably the residence of the city missioner," and offices for the dean and cathedral staff. The Bishop soon made the Rev. Sterling Tracy, an ex-newspaper man who had been ordained deacon only a few days before, his first custodian of the library, editor of *Forward in Tennessee,* and occupant of the prophet's chamber.

With his decision to "go west," the Bishop felt that a coadjutor was required for East Tennessee. In a special conven-

---

After 12 years it was found that the larger elected chapters became almost as "permanent" as the earlier appointed ones. Therefore in 1949 it was decided to elect only five new members each year for three years, one-third retiring each year.

tion (May 18, 1937) Dr. Oliver Hart was elected, but declined. He later became Bishop of Pennsylvania. The election of a new coadjutor was thus postponed for almost a year (April 20, 1938) when the Rev. Edmund P. Dandridge, also like Bishop Maxon, from Christ Church, Nashville, was elected. Shortly before this special convention, Bishop Maxon again met with the chapter and read it a long ten page carefully prepared letter on his concept of the role of the Cathedral. He said that he could not, even after diligent search, find any clear definition, or even partial determination of what was involved in the diocese by the word "Cathedral." All that he did find was that in usage it "had been a Bishop's church," open to him at all times, over which he had absolute control both as to the appointment of the chapter, the dean, or other clergy. "In other words, it might be defined as a sort of private chapel for the Bishop." He felt that only confusion could follow such a lack of clarity. "We can," he said, "return to the status of a parish church . . . or we can go on to perfect a Cathedral organization." He opposed the idea of a pro-cathedral, and felt that neither American nor English usage gave any help, since they differed in organization and function. He added, "the Cathedral must not and cannot be supported by a local congregation . . . yet it has hitherto been supported by one congregation. The diocese has never been asked to contribute to the support of the Cathedral, and I don't know at present whether it would be willing . . . if it were able to do so." He thought that the diocese needed education in a "Cathedral Idea" and that it would be many years before it would accept the principle of any obligation to support the Cathedral. Thus he only looked for two sources of supply—first, the continuation of support by the Cathedral congregation; and secondly, the building up of an endowment, "bit by bit."

He announced that he was asking for a coadjutor for East Tennessee, and explained his plans for the Diocesan House more fully, concluding: "We simply must have some place which the whole diocese will recognize and accept as a center and base for operations." He thought it providential that the Bishop's House was available for the purpose, hoping that it would be ready within a month for these new uses.

Mr. Stenning Coate, the chapter member perhaps most interested in the "Cathedral aspect" of St. Mary's, wrote the Bishop a warm letter of thanks, and asked that he have this paper mimeographed and given each member of the chapter. He praised the Bishop for pointing out that there was no record of previous bishops' hopes, and added, "Fifty years from now your plans may seem crude, but you have written down definite plans to help the present and future generations." He also thanked him for pointing out the need for better finance, "for the chapter realizes it cannot interest the diocese in taking up even a small part of the present building expenses." Mr. Coate's great interest in the "Cathedral Idea" was later reflected in his munificent gift to the Cathedral; Bishop Maxon's, by at least four more long letters to the chapter on the subject during the 1940's.

On June 9, 1937, the Bishop moved into his new Episcopal Residence in Memphis (2791 Central Avenue), and in the same month the chapter held its first meeting in the "chapter room" of the new Diocesan House, though it was not formally opened until October.

As these new relationships between bishop and chapter were being worked out, the congregation—or portions of it— were becoming increasingly alarmed at the direction in which the Dean's "new philosophy" seemed to be leading him. He was by now (1937) letting it be known that since December 1936 he had been gradually restricting his diet (the things of the body) in preparation for his demonstration that man could "here and now put on immortality" and rise above the material needs of life, living "in spiritual relation to God." The proof of his theory (and the Dean was undoubtedly sincere) was to begin on January 2, 1938. The great fast (undertaken in the glare of newspaper publicity) continued for three hectic and harrowing weeks—till January 24—when, according to the press, "the quest for immortality was frustrated" and the Dean fell into a coma and was rushed to the hospital.[16]

As fate would have it, the Bishop was away from Memphis most of the fall. Returning in December, he was stricken with an illness so serious that he was not allowed to have visitors or to learn of the fast which was exciting Church, town and even the nation. The chapter seemed stunned into inactivity.[17]

About January 18, or six days before the tragic end of the fast, the Bishop was finally informed of events. "Once I was informed of the Dean's vagary," he told Mr. Carley of the *Commercial Appeal,* "there was but one thing for me to do— remove him . . . There will certainly be a place for him in my diocese, a place where his vast spirituality and great talent can do further good when he gives up his vagary." On January 19 Bishop Maxon wrote this letter, at once kindly and firm, to the Dean:

January 19, 1938

Very Rev. Israel H. Noe
Dean of St. Mary's Cathedral
Memphis, Tennessee
My dear Dean:

For the first time I am today well enough, though still confined to my bed, to be advised of what has transpired during the past two weeks.

At the outset I wish to say that I am writing this letter in all kindness and love.

---

16. The Dean was taken to the Baptist Hospital and remained there several weeks. His friends, Judge C. N. Burch and Mr. Walter Armstrong, persuaded him to take further treatment at Johns Hopkins. Later he visited his family. In the Bishop's letter to the Dean on February 9, before he left for Baltimore, the Bishop ended, "I assure you of my unswerving concern and devotion to you. Never once have I failed you, nor will I do so now."

17. As the press pointed out, the congregation was divided between those who hoped the Dean would end his fast, and those who believed in the Dean and thought history was being made. The Dean's brother, the Rev. Alexander Noe, begged him "to come down off the Mount of Transfiguration."

I regret to advise that it is convincingly evident to me that it is necessary that you be removed as Dean of St. Mary's Cathedral. This removal will take place at once. However, your stipend will continue for the next six months and you will be permitted to occupy the Deanery for that period.

St. Mary's Cathedral does not represent any particular individual or any particular group but is the church of the whole Diocese. Hence the manner of living and the religious activities of the Dean naturally carry the connotation of representing the whole membership of the Diocese. Feeling, therefore, that your present manner of living and expressions of religious convictions are foreign to the view of the great majority of the membership of our Church and to its history and traditions, I am constrained to take the step above indicated. I do not think that you are at present your normal self and I wish to give you an opportunity to return to your normal self when you will be able to exercise the abilities and spirituality which you so abundantly possess in the spread of Christ's Kingdom.

I am taking this occasion also to urge and beseech you to discontinue the fast you are now undergoing, and under medical advice to take the nourishment which you should have.

I am therefore writing this letter, not doubting your sincerity, but as your Bishop and your friend, who is deeply interested in you and yours.

This is a painful letter to write but it is written in all Christian fellowship and in obedience to duty, after prayerful consideration.

Affectionately,

(signed) JAMES M. MAXON

On January 21 a chapter meeting was called by the Bishop (though he was unable to be present because of his illness) to consider the following items which he presented to it:

1. Reading and filing his letter of January 20 to Dean Noe and its approval or disapproval by the chapter.

2. To consider extending the Rev. Israel H. Noe such adequate support as the chapter might deem necessary.

3. To consider and approve or disapprove the Bishop's nomination of the Rev. Canon James R. Sharp to be the Acting Dean, and of Dr. Sterling Tracy to be his assistant.

4. To consider and approve or disapprove the Bishop's nomination of a committee to make such inquiry and

investigation as might be necessary to suggest a suitable person to be Dean of the Cathedral.

The chapter approved of all the proposals, and recommended that the Dean's salary continue "until further action by the chapter."

An exciting period in St. Mary's history had ended.

CHAPTER IX

ANOTHER WORLD WAR — DEAN HOAG

BISHOP MAXON, in entrusting the shepherdless congregation to the care of Canon James R. Sharp (January 20, 1938), made an extremely fortunate and wise decision. Perhaps no one within or without the diocese was so fitted by temperament or by the respect in which he was held, to conduct St. Mary's through the difficult period following the removal of Dean Noe. As the Bishop's chaplain, as Canon to the Ordinary, as executive secretary of the Bishop and Council, and secretary of the Convention, he was trusted by the Bishop, the Diocese, and the Cathedral congregation.

At the direction of Bishop Maxon and with the expense underwritten by the Woman's Auxiliary, the *Cathedral Chimes* was revived. Thus Canon Sharp could reach by mail members of the congregation, many of whom had ceased to attend services regularly.[1]

In the first number he greeted the congregation as follows:

Dear Friends of the Cathedral Parish:

My first word must be one of grateful appreciation of the kindly and cordial welcome you have given me as I begin the task so suddenly and sadly laid upon me, of the temporary supervision of the worship and work of this great parish. I

---

1. The *Chimes* is an invaluable source for recent Cathedral activities. The title seems to have originated in the early 1900's when the Sunday School brought out a small annual magazine by that name (1905, 1906). This contained some historical articles, and some which explained current projects. Another *Cathedral Chimes* (Vol. I, No. 1) reappeared on February 28, 1926. Dean Noe from his coming to the Cathedral had issued a church bulletin containing announcements and a personal message, and after the Cathedral was completed he adopted the title of *Chimes.* This only lasted during Lent of 1926, and contained from 4-10 pages, many of which were devoted to National Church news, missionary news, or to meditations taken from church papers. The *Chimes* was again revived (Vol. I, No. 1) more or less in its present form

ask your prayer and cooperation as we, together, strive to set forward the work and to carry on the splendid tradition of loyalty and service built up in the years that are past.

He then informed readers of his plan for reviving the *Chimes;* of continuing during Lent "the great Sunday evening services sponsored by our Bishop and the Clericus, in which all our congregations in the city take part;" of his plan, with the help of Mr. Meteyarde, of developing a Junior Choir (for whom he ordered "Mary blue" vestments). This, he said, would enable him to attempt another innovation, "a choral Eucharist for the very first service of Easter day." He also asked the congregation's help in "rounding up" a confirmation class; "Dr. Tracy and I with Miss Correll's assistance as heretofore, will see that they are prepared if you will tell us who they are."

As this letter shows, the Canon was at first assisted in his work by the Rev. Dr. Sterling Tracy (recently brought into the ministry by Dean Noe), who remained at the Cathedral until fall, when he departed for work in Cambridge, Mass. The Rev. Guy Usher, ordained deacon on February 27, was also assigned by Bishop Maxon to the Cathedral on March 1, though by the end of April he was transferred to Calvary. The Bishop then brought in the Rev. T. Porter Simpson, "a Canon, a member of the Cathedral staff, but not of the Parish organization," whose chief duty was to work in the mission field and to serve at the Church Home, which had recently moved to new quarters at Oakville.[2] Canon Simpson remained a little over a year.

In the month of Canon Simpson's arrival (May 1938), a long time member of St. Mary's staff, the Rev. Stanley Young,

---

with Cathedral news on its outer pages, on November 17, 1929. This continued uninterrupted, except for summer months, until July 2, 1933—which was Volume IV (and the depression). Canon Sharp's revival, called Volume V, Number 1, was on February 20, 1938. It has continued unbroken, mainly under the editorship of Miss Ellen Correll.

2. Mr. W. I. Moody, long a member of the board of trustees of the Church Home, was responsible for the sale of the old property on Jackson Street (for $80,000) and the purchase in 1938 of the new and more commodious quarters at Oakville (for $32,500). The Sisters of St. Anne gave up control of the Home in 1936.

died. He had been a lay reader since 1908, and had in 1923 been ordained as the first "perpetual deacon" in St. Mary's history. During the years of clerical shortages he was very active in keeping alive many of the old churches and missions in West Tennessee. As Bishop Maxon remarked to the chapter, "he served many ways, for many years;" a brief and splendid epitaph. Meanwhile the new staff was busy. In February Dr. Tracy organized the younger children (age 10-14) into a group called Crusaders of the Cross. Intended originally as a Lenten study group, it continued to flourish for several years as a feeder to the Young People's Service League. This latter organization, which had been allowed to lapse during the final year of Dean Noe's tenure, was revived in March by the Rev. Guy Usher.

On April 20, 1938, the special convention, called for by Bishop Maxon in January, met and elected another rector of Christ Church, Nashville, the Rev. Edmund Pendleton Dandridge, as the Bishop's coadjutor, for since the death of Bishop Gailor (1935) Bishop Maxon had carried on alone. The new coadjutor (consecrated September 20, in Christ Church) continued to reside in Nashville and was assigned— as was now traditional—the missionary work of the diocese.[3]

By now the Bishop and chapter were deliberating on the selection of a permanent dean. In March Bishop Maxon informed the chapter: "I am proceeding carefully in the selection of a Dean. Leading laymen in the diocese have urged upon me that the man selected shall be outstanding." And the clergy had urged him, he said, to get "a real leader. I shall work in closest harmony with the chapter and congregation in this matter," he told them, but he urged patience since "good men

---

3. Bishop Dandridge was born in Flushing, New York, September 5, 1881. Studied at Woodbury Forest School, the University of Virginia (B.A., 1902, M.A., 1903); Oxford, England (B.A., 1908); Virginia Theological Seminary (B.D., 1906, D.D., 1921). He was ordained deacon in June 1906, priest in December 1908. Married Miss Mary Robertson Lloyd (October 6, 1909). He served in Greenbrier Parish, Virginia, 1908-11, St. Paul's Church, Petersburg, Va., 1911-23, and Christ Church, Nashville, 1923-28.

are very hard to secure." At this same meeting he informed the chapter that the House of Bishops would meet in Memphis in November, and warned them to expect a great meeting. By May the Bishop's choice rested on a priest he had known for many years, the Rev. Harold Brown Hoag. The Bishop invited him and his wife to visit Memphis, on May 25 and 26, to meet the chapter. The entry in his diary for May 26 shows what happened:

> At noon had a luncheon meeting with the chapter com mittee, when we met the Rev. Mr. Hoag and discussed matters pertaining to the deanship. At a subsequent meeting of the committee the recommendation was made that I appoint the Rev. Harold Brown Hoag dean. I wrote him a letter outlining the work of the deanship and tendered him the post of Dean of St. Mary's Cathedral, effective August 1.[4]

In the June 2 meeting of the chapter, the Bishop read the following letter:

> My dear Brethren: I hereby nominate as Dean of St. Mary's Cathedral, in accordance with the provisions of Canon XII, Sec. 4 the Rev. Harold Brown Hoag, at present Rector of Christ Church, Burlington, Iowa, and ask your concurrence therein.
>
> I make this nomination with the distinct understanding that should the services of the Dean be such that in my judgment there should be a change in the said deanship, I reserve the right in accordance with the provisions of Canon XII, Sec. 4, to remove the said Dean. I suggest that the new Dean come into residence by August 1 or as soon thereafter as possible.

The chapter unanimously concurred in the Bishop's nomination, and the appointment was announced in the *Chimes* on June 12. *The Commercial Appeal* (June 3, 1938) pointed out that Mr. Hoag was forty years old at the time, and that he had started a career in engineering before deciding to enter the

---

4. *Journal of 1939.* In this same year Mr. William Gehri came to Grace, Father Vernon Lane to the Good Shepherd, and the Bishop inspected the site for the new location of St. John's.

ministry. "He is a strong man, especially in his work with children, young people, and young married couples," it reported.[5]

Soon after this the Bishop left for his usual summer vacation on St. Joseph's Island, Canada, and Canon Sharp carried on throughout July, "with Morning Prayer, without sermon," but with a series of informal conferences on the history and use of the Prayer Book (attendance optional). He also instituted a question box and permitted the summer congregation to share in the selection of hymns.

The new Dean, his wife and daughter, arrived in August, and the Bishop (from Canada) welcomed them in a letter in the *Chimes.* The Hoags decided not to reside in the old deanery as it had not been renovated since the departure of the Noes in July. They were furnished a home on Stonewall, and the old deanery was soon transformed into a religious education building, a somewhat inconvenient arrangement since even in those days it was a serious problem to get the children across the Poplar Street traffic.

Dean Hoag's first message to the congregation (in the *Chimes*) was dated September 1:

> My dear people [this became his standard salutation in his weekly messages] "Lord, what will thou have me do?" with these words it was my privilege to begin my first sermon in the Cathedral on August 7. That question is ever uppermost in my heart at all times . . . This grand Cathedral parish has many devoted and active workers in its ranks . . . who are assuming positions of responsibility and leadership. However, there should be more who are actively engaged in the work of the Church . . . This parish is tremendous in size.

He called for volunteers and for information on the sick and distressed and promised to keep a daily office hour (10-11:30 A.M.), "Remember I am at your service twenty-four hours a day."

---

5. Dean Hoag was born in Chicago December 23, 1897. He attended High School in LaGrange, Illinois; attended Cornell, The University of Wisconsin and General Theological Seminary. He was ordained deacon May 1923 and priest the following year. He married Miss Eunice Seitz. He had been assistant rector of St. Luke's Church, Racine, Wisconsin, and rector of Christ Church, Burlington, Iowa before coming to St. Mary's.

On September 18 the Dean and Canon Simpson were formally installed and a reception for the new Dean and his family was held in the Diocesan House. Two days before the installation, the Bishop furnished the Dean with a "young curate," the Rev. David S. Rose (recently ordained deacon at Christ Church), who remained throughout the winter as the Dean's assistant in young people's work and in the Germantown, Collierville, and Woodstock missions. With the help of a young Southwestern professor, Mr. C. P. Lee, he staged a Nativity Play (from the York Mystery Cycle) on December 23. As the Memphis climate proved too severe for Mr. Rose he departed for Florida in April 1939. In November Canon Simpson left. Dean Hoag now worked alone.

The new Dean's first year was in many respects a trying one for him and for the congregation. The former Dean returned to the city in the summer, restored in health and strength, and during the fall of 1938 was often in attendance at St. Mary's services. The Bishop had promised to provide for his future in the diocese, but nothing had as yet been done. Many of his devoted adherents wanted him reinstated and were thus dissatisfied with the new Dean through no fault of his own. Fortunately, several exciting events transpired during the autumn of 1938 which partially diverted the congregation's attention from this undercurrent of discontent. Beginning in October all the Episcopal churches of Memphis began to focus their attention on the coming meetings of the House of Bishops. The Men's Council was reorganized, and a Board of Directors of the Cathedral Laymen's League was formed (October 9).[6] Special committees were created to assist in the preparations for the Bishops' meeting, which began on October 30, and reached a climax on November 3, with a tremendous Laymen's

---

6. The first members of this board of directors were: D. D. Henderson, C. N. Mabie, P. S. Coate, W. I. Moody, J. W. Burton, J. H. Davis, C. T. Smith, A. J. Warwick, H. Esch, P. C. Clarke, T. Percer. These and the chairmen of the eight usher groups formed what was called an Executive Committee of the Cathedral League. This complex organization did not last long.

Banquet held in the Auditorium—with over fifteen hundred in attendance. It was addressed by the Hon. Francis B. Sayre, Undersecretary of State and son-in-law of President Wilson. The Cathedral was host to several early Eucharistic services. These were celebrated by Bishops Sturtevant of Fond du Lac (October 30), Morris of Louisiana (October 31), and the Presiding Bishop, Henry St. George Tucker. The Presiding Bishop also conducted a great Forward Movement Missionary Mass Meeting in the Cathedral on the evening of November 2. Nearly a thousand persons had to be turned away for lack of room, although an estimated fifteen hundred were packed into the building. Shortly after this, on November 20, Bishop Maxon called for a great mass meeting of Memphis citizens at the Auditorium, to voice a protest against the German persecution of Jews, for these were the ominous days between Munich and the outbreak of World War II.

Meanwhile the supporters of Mr. Noe were rallying their forces, and in January 1939 a large delegation of them attended the diocesan convention, which met in Chattanooga. Their petition for a new Memphis parish was hotly debated, and although the canonical requirement that the petition for a new parish must be in the hands of the Standing Committee sixty days before convention, was not observed, the pressure for the new parish was so great and feeling was so intense that the motion permitting it (in theory to be located outside the city limits) was finally approved 42 to 35.[7]

The formation of this parish, of course, sharply affected the Cathedral. Perhaps a third, or more, of the membership of St. Mary's, consisting for the most part of the former dean's recent converts, and of others who considered him ill-used, followed him into his new and, at the time, highly publicized

---

7. *Journal of 1939* and press accounts for the days of convention for details of the struggle, names of petitioners, etc. The new parish, called St. James, held its first service in Temple Israel. It then moved to 1271 Poplar and later to its present location on Central. It was permitted by the Convention of 1941 to ignore the original stipulation that it be located outside Memphis.

parish. The departure of such a large segment of the congregation meant that those remaining at St. Mary's had to work with renewed energy, and it also meant that the financial situation for the next several years became very stringent indeed.[8]

Dean Hoag tried valiantly to guide St. Mary's through these difficulties for which he was not responsible. He maintained a cheerful and friendly optimism. When he returned from the Convention of 1939 and reported on it in the *Chimes* he never even mentioned the publicized struggle, but instead told of the honors conferred by convention on Cathedral members: of Mr. Patten's being elected to the Standing Committee, and of Mrs. W. E. Barnes being made chairman of a Committee on Rural Work. At the January parish meeting (1939) he lavished praise on Canon Sharp "for his splendid leadership as acting dean," and wrote in the *Chimes,* "we all gave him such an enthusiastic hand that we feel certain he must have heard it way over in Nashville. And he added, "In closing I paid tribute to the untiring devotion, the great ability and the enthusiastic work done for the Cathedral and for the entire Church by our Executive Secretary, Miss Ellen Correll." This was certainly merited praise, for from the mid-1920's until the present Miss Correll as executive secretary, director of religious education and in many other functions (official and non-official) has represented, as various acting-deans, deans, canons, deacons, bishops and coadjutors have come and gone, a "principle of continuity" and of devoted labor.

Dean Hoag also organized a "hospitality committee" under Mr. Herbert Esch to give a warmer greeting to visitors. In the spring of 1939 (April 23-30) he brought an old personal friend, the Rev. Ray Everett Carr of Chicago, to conduct a mission; for he felt that some kind of revival was needed.

8. Chapter minutes for January 9, 1939: "Mr. Lee called attention to the unbalanced budget, and the likelihood of a reduction in income this year." It was decided to have a new Every Member Canvass after the election of a new chapter in January, and also to appoint a new finance committee.

Much effort and prayer went into the preparation for this visit, and the mission proved to be a great success. At just about this time another institution, which has since become "traditional," was launched. On May 2 it was announced in the *Chimes* that Mr. A. J. V. Ware had been persuaded to begin an Adult Bible Class (which is now in its nineteenth year).[9] During the summer months of his first year the Dean assisted at Camp Gailor-Maxon and then took a vacation in Canada in August. Canon Sharp returned to conduct services in his absence, a practice he followed during the whole of Dean Hoag's tenure.

When he returned in the fall Europe was at war; but at first neither the Dean nor the congregation seemed greatly perturbed by this. One repercussion did reach the Cathedral, however, for on October 9 the American Association of Social Workers procured Dr. Muriel Lester (who was on a preaching mission in the United States under the sponsorship of the Federal Council of Churches) to speak in the Cathedral to a large gathering on "The United States and the International Situation." As a pacifist she pleaded, in a powerful address, against American involvement in the conflict.

The Dean tried valiantly to become better acquainted with his congregation. Twice, at least, he ran blank information cards in the *Chimes,* asking that members fill them in and return them to him so that he would know the addresses and birthdays of "his people." The second of these attempts (January 1943) he called a "Family Day" and suggested that on a certain day he and the various church families would meet either at the church or at home to have a private service together. "This," he wrote, "is probably the most difficult task I have undertaken in my ministry." It was too difficult a program to succeed. Earlier, however, he had organized volunteers into thirty teams who made a non-financial every member visitation.

9. Mr. Percy Clarke says the dean asked him to take the Bible Class, but that as he and Mr. Ware were taking a trip to a convention together, he persuaded Mr. Ware to take the class.

The General Convention of 1940 (in Kansas City) adopted an official church flag, and Bishop Maxon gave the Cathedral the first such flag to be used in the diocese. It was carried for the first time in procession at the midnight Christmas Eve service in 1940.

Beginning with the Convention *Journal of 1941,* there has usually been a "Report on St. Mary's Cathedral," in which deans have listed all services of an interparochial or diocesan nature. An analysis of these reports in Dean Hoag's time would show that there were certain "standard" services which reappeared year after year; then there were certain "variable" services held on special occasions. In the former category there always appeared: 1) the service of the Holy Communion and sermon by Bishop Maxon on the Feast of the Circumcision (January 1), which was his birthday; 2) the, by now, "traditional" Feast of Lights on the Sunday nearest the Feast of Epiphany—the Dean added to this a new feature by getting the collaboration of the Hellenic Orthodox Church; 3) an Evensong service at the Cathedral during the Sundays of Lent with the various parishes of the city participating (begun by Bishop Maxon in 1937); 4) a Church School rally of the Memphis parishes on Whitsunday; and 5) an annual corporate communion of the Clericus.

Among the variable, or "special" services listed by the Dean the following may be noted: In 1940 a special Sewanee Sunday observed with an address by the Vice-Chancellor, Dr. Alex Guerry; a big city-wide "Fourth of July Celebration" addressed by Mayor Walter Chandler with the combined Episcopal choirs, representatives of other denominations, and of the Second Army in attendance; and, as the shadows of war lengthened, an interparochial day of meditation and prayer for peace sponsored by the Woman's Auxiliary; also, in the fall of 1940 the Cathedral had as its guests for over two months, the congregations of Grace and St. Luke's which had recently been united, and who were without a home while the remodelling of St. Luke's was under way. The Dean ended his first report on an interesting note, for he called attention to the fact that when out-of-town Episcopalians came to local hospitals they usually called upon the Dean to minister to them and to their families. He therefore suggested that "a canon missioner, as a diocesan official, when someday provided by the diocese, might be able to assist in this all important work." He thus anticipated a later movement which led to the establishment of Quintard House.

On February 13, 1942, Memphians packed into the Cathedral to hear the Rev. Michael Coleman of All-Hallows, Barking, London, tell of the London blitz. During the week of May 4-10 the Rev. Ray Everett Carr returned to conduct his second successful mission. On October 18 (St. Luke's day) there was a great celebration of Bishop Maxon's twentieth anniversary as Bishop. Bishop Dandridge preached, and addresses were made by the Rev. Prentice Pugh for the clergy, by Mr. Edmund Orgill for the laity of the diocese, and by Mr. W. I. Moody for the chapter. On this occasion Mr. Moody presented the Bishop with a beautiful handwrought illuminated Book of Memorials, given by Mrs. Florence Orgill Montgomery, which was then placed on the marble stand given previously by the Woman's Auxiliary of the diocese. Mrs. M. O. Bennett, president of the diocesan Auxiliary, presented a stained glass window to the Bishop as a memorial to his son who had died in service in England on September 19, 1941.[10]

In 1943 the "special events" (as noted by the Dean) were: a visit of the English Ambassador, Lord Halifax; the visit by

---

10. Canon Noll had begun the illumination of the Memorial Book in 1926 and it was about finished before his death in 1930. The leather work on it was done by Miss Nettie Barnwell, and the silver embossing by Miss Louise Fleece. It was to contain the list of Bishops, Deans and Chapter members as well as a list of memorials. It has been put in the vault, and on the stand intended for it is now found a "Standard Prayer Book" donated by Mr. J. Pierpoint Morgan. He donated one to every diocese.

a team of speakers (Bishop Dagwell and Miss A. Nash) from the National Church, who reported on the General Convention of that year, an Armistice Day service of intercession and prayer which lasted from 10 A.M. to 5 P.M., with a different parish in charge of each hour; and the donation of $10,000 to the Canadian diocese of Algonia. One event of 1943, unnoted by the Dean in his report, but which has great significance for Cathedral members, is the fact that in this year Mrs. Thomas Lill returned to St. Mary's and was made the librarian and cataloguer of the Gailor Memorial Library and became a devoted sacristan of the Cathedral. In fact one may say she became the director and guardian of the temple, and in her inimitable way has ever since made clergy, choir directors, janitors and others hew to the line and "keep off the grass."

There were few special services in 1944, but in 1945 as the war was obviously drawing to a conclusion, a tremendous service was held on Ascension Eve at which all the naval and military personnel of the city had representatives. There was a "massing of the colors" and the music was by the eighty-voice Navy choir.

The above listed events were chiefly those of a public and interparochial nature. Let us now observe some of the more important developments within the parish, especially the impact of war, the music situation, and plans or changes connected with the buildings. The conflagration in Europe began virtually with the Dean's coming, but "war psychology" made no strong impact until after Pearl Harbor (December 1941). Soon young men from the parish began to be called away, and soon their names began to be read in prayers for the dead or wounded (see Appendix for names). Gas rationing (November 1942) began to cut into meetings and visitations—and even church going—though the Dean urged the congregation to save enough for that. Sunday School time was moved to eleven so it would coincide with the time of the morning service. Mr.

Russell Perry, who had been superintendent for several years, was called away to service and was replaced first (1943) by Mr. Leon Huddleston, and in the next year by Mr. Hobart Turman. The Dean, as well as the women's organizations, was especially active in war, patriotic and parish work. One guild (St. Martha's) was practically abandoned since so many young wives had to follow their husbands to new locations. One active new guild of young women (St. Elizabeth's) was formed (October 1943). The Dean became the chairman of an executive committee of Memphians which set up a Church Service Men's Bureau at the old Tennessee Club. This became a clearing house for securing invitations for service men residing in Memphis camps to attend church services, meals and other social functions with church members. The Cathedral committee, under Miss Harriette Frank, Mrs. Joe Patten, Jr., and Mrs. J. A. Prewitt, helped staff this bureau, and later to raise funds to procure beds to be given the Y. M. C. A. for the use of service men. The Dean devoted his week day services to prayers and intercessions (by name) for service men. Uniforms began to predominate in the congregation, and many devoted young service men helped augment the Cathedral choir. In the spring of 1945 the Auxiliary, with the help of the Y. P. S. L., undertook the difficult task of filling and sending more than a hundred large boxes (containing concentrated food, sewing kits, socks, towels, adhesive tape, etc., and finally religious pictures—to combat atheism) to the Russians. About the same time Bishop Maxon made a plea for old clothes for European refugees.

The choir, both in its direction and its personnel, went through a period of considerable fluctuation during Dean Hoag's regime. The Dean appreciated and wanted good music, his wife was a talented pianist,[11] and he frequently used the *Chimes* as well as personal appeals in an attempt to recruit

11. She and Mrs. D. C. McCool gave a benefit performance for the Auxiliary on May 3, 1940, at the Nineteenth Century Club. It was at this time the McCools joined St. Mary's.

new choir members. But the music budget was inadequate, and the war caused a constant shift in personnel.

Mr. Meteyarde, who had been organist and choir director since 1930, continued on under Dean Hoag. With the backing of the Men's Council he returned to his original plan of a Boys' Choir, using the Gailor Hall boys. On September 29, 1940, he was honored at a dinner by the Men's Council (and by the organist's magazine, *Diapason*) for his tenth anniversary as organist and choirmaster.[12] The following September he resigned from the Cathedral to accept a post at St. John's Church, Helena. The month in which he departed the Dean announced the coming of Mr. Franklyn Glynn as the new organist and director. Mr. Glynn was well known in Memphis, as he had been the organist at Idlewild Presbyterian Church from the installation of its fine organ in 1928, until 1937. He was an Englishman and had once been assistant organist at Peterborough Cathedral. He was also a composer of hymns and contributed several to the new *Hymnal 1940,* one of which was named for Bishop Maxon. However, he never seemed entirely happy at the Cathedral and failed to create any great musical revival. In a little over a year he moved on to one of the largest churches in Florida.

In the *Chimes* of January 17, 1943, the Dean praised the ministry of music and announced, "On the first Sunday of February I firmly believe that a new era in the ministry of music will start. Miss Helen Pendleton will become organist and choir master." He told of her musical education (B. A. and B. M. in music from Kansas University, and M. M. from Union Theological Seminary), and that she had served with him in Iowa. Miss Pendleton set to work with great vim and enthusiasm, drilled the adults, and reunited the boys' and girls'

---

12. In the chapter minutes there are frequent reports by Mr. Meteyarde on his musical programs, and occasional complaints on the state of the choir room where termites were eating both woodwork and music, and sometimes requests for a raise in salary. These were usually referred to a committee and forgotten.

choirs to again form a single Junior Choir. The year of her coming (1943) coincided with the appearance of the new *Hymnal 1940* (so named because it had been authorized by the General Convention of 1940). It had been well planned and worked on by Canon Winfred Douglas and his commission on church music. Appeals for funds to purchase new hymnals were made in May, but owing to war shortages of paper it was December before the first five hundred hymnals arrived. At Miss Pendleton's suggestion, these were given by the congregation as memorials in honor of past and present choir members. The bookplate listing the names of the donors and honorees was designed by Mrs. Hoag's brother. All musicians were agreed that this hymnal represented a great advance, not only over previous Episcopal hymnals, but over those of other churches, but since many "old favorites" were omitted, since the pointing of the chants and the time value of the "Doxology" were changed, and since new plainsong service music was included, the complaints of certain members of the congregation were loud and numerous. In fact most of the Cathedral organists since the time of the new hymnal's appearance have had to bear the brunt of such criticisms.

Finally, let us observe the changes made in the Cathedral structure, decorations, or plans for the years 1938-1945. By the end of Dean Hoag's time twenty-two windows were completed, leaving only five large, four small, and ten clerestory windows not in stained glass. A new credence shelf designed by Canon Sharp was put on the reredos, a new Bible placed on the lectern, and silver alms basins were donated.[13] In 1940 Mr. Moody and Mr. P. Stenning Coate approached Miss Ann Overton Treadwell with the suggestion that they and some friends would repair the exterior of St. Mary's Chapel (again

---

13. The credence was donated in memory of Miss Lillian Smith by her sister, Mrs. Prewitt. The Bible was donated by Mr. J. M. Patten in memory of his brother, and the silver alms plates by Mrs. A. R. Bliss in memory of her husband, Dr. A. R. Bliss.

in bad shape since Mr. Cairns' restoration) if she and her sisters, Mrs. Elisha Gee and Mrs. Margaret Treadwell Day, would be responsible for rehabilitating and refurnishing the interior. Miss Treadwell accepted the proposal, and the beautifully remodelled and appointed Chapel was dedicated by Bishop Maxon on October 26, 1941. In the ensuing years Miss Treadwell gave many other fine appointments for the Chapel and at her death left an endowment for its upkeep.[14]

In January 1943 Bishop Maxon in his address to convention mentioned the fact that "a group of the members of the congregation (of St. Mary's) has undertaken to raise a fund for completing the building of a Cathedral House, wherein to house the Church School and other activities of the Cathedral Church . . . substantial gifts have been made . . . in amounts upward of $4,000 in the hope of having sufficient funds on hand, when building restrictions due to war are removed, to complete the structure."

The congregation became more fully aware of these plans to build a Church School building on May 16, when in bold type the Dean announced in the *Chimes* "A Challenge to Every Member of the Congregation." He went on to say, "At the chapter meeting this week an announcement was made that a sum of $10,000 would be given St. Mary's Church School Building Fund on condition that the parish itself raises $10,000. The chapter immediately elected Mr. J. M. Patten as chairman of a committee to make arrangements to meet this challenge." In his own letter which followed (under the heading, "A Blockbuster") the Dean said, "My dear people, like a huge bomb coming down upon us unannounced from the sky, the news above dropped into the midst of our chapter meeting

---

14. The Chapel was dedicated to the memory of Mary Overton Snowden Treadwell, the daughter of Colonel Snowden and the mother of Miss Treadwell. Her brother gave the electric organ. Mr. Moody estimated that his committee spent about $3,500 on the exterior, and that Miss Treadwell and her family spent about $14,000 on the interior. She also left a trust fund of $15,000 for upkeep of the Chapel.

last night, causing great excitement." He urged all to get behind the drive. By June it was announced that the old deanery had been sold and proceeds from it added to the building fund. Yet because of war restriction, of uncertainty over where to put the new building and what to include in it, and of changing regimes, the new Church School building had to wait almost ten years.[15]

In the Convention of 1944, the Bishop produced another surprise for the Cathedral. His address contained these words:

> Practically the whole burden of the cost of construction and maintenance of the Cathedral plant, the symbol of the unity of this Diocese, has been borne by the congregation worshipping there known as St. Mary's congregation. Although by repeated resolutions of the Convention, this Diocese not only approved and endorsed the project, but encouraged the Bishop, Dean and Chapter to proceed with the work and called upon the several congregations to make substantial contributions toward the cost, little was contributed by the congregations. Practically the whole burden fell upon the Bishop, Dean and Chapter and the members of St. Mary's congregation.
>
> Recognizing this long deferred obligation, I am particularly pleased that after a careful consideration of the whole matter, the Bishop and Council recommend that this Diocese assume the remaining indebtedness of about $22,000. The Bishop, Dean and Chapter have been paying this indebtedness off, principal and interest, annually. The demands of this obligation have made it impossible for the Chapter and congregation to assume and pay the full mathematical quota of the Diocesan Apportionment. This past year by resolution of Bishop and Council the annual payment . . . of the debt was credited on their quota . . . The Bishop, Dean and Chapter gladly assume the full quota and have pledged it for 1944. I recommend that this Convention, by resolution, assume the remaining obligation of the bonded indebtedness, and make suitable provision for its discharge.

---

15. In the Convention of 1945 the Bishop reported that the Cathedral had $38,000 in bank, "and will begin erection . . . when conditions permit." Mr. Patten says that the original impetus for a building fund came when the delegates to diocesan conventions in the early 1940's agreed to donate their "expense money" to the cause. At lunch meetings of the Financial Committee from then on, Mr. Moody or Mr. Coate would remind the other to contribute and then suggest that Mr. Patten get an equal sum from the congregation.

> I have given . . . much consideration to the completion
> of the Cathedral plant in order that its effectiveness as a
> diocesan agency may be enlarged . . . I trust that before my
> episcopate shall have ended the whole Diocese will rejoice
> in witnessing the completion of the Cathedral plant, with
> sufficient provision for its endowment.[16]

Though the net result of the assumption of the Cathedral
debt by the convention did not alter the Cathedral budget
(since the approximately $2,000 devoted annually to the debt
was now transferred to increasing the Cathedral's apportionment), it did, as the Dean remarked in the *Chimes,* show that
"the action of the convention was prompted by a recognition
of the obligation of the whole diocese for its Cathedral
Church." Since this time the Cathedral has continued its
apportionment pledge to the amount "hoped for."

Dean Hoag had, during his years at the Cathedral, tided
it through a difficult transitional period, and through the trying
years of war. Perhaps both he and the Bishop were disappointed that greater results had not been achieved. In any case
very shortly after the war and after celebrating his seventh
anniversary he announced to the Bishop (on September 27)
and to the congregation (on October 7), "I have been called
to take up my work in the ministry in St. Andrew's Parish,
Tampa, Florida. I accepted the call effective December 11."

At the Bazaar dinner (November 22) farewell speeches
were made by and to the Dean, and his final farewell message
in the *Chimes* appeared in the November 25 issue. Here he
amplified his praise of the congregation and his sorrow at
departing: "This has been a marvelously fruitful vineyard in
which to work. . . . I honestly believe that St. Mary's Cathedral

---

16. *Journal of 1944*, 48. The resolution of Bishop and Council was presented by the Rev. Thorne Sparkman (Ibid. 28). It called for payments of
$1,000 or $2,000 per year until 1955. The debt was paid off by 1951 and the
Cathedral consecrated then. In the same convention the Rev. I. H. Noe presented a resolution to change Canon XII, Sec. 4 so that the dean of the cathedral
"shall be elected by the Cathedral Chapter, with the approval of the Bishop,"
and that "no Dean . . . may be removed from his office except in the same
canonical manner provided for the removal of a parish priest." These
amendments failed to pass.

now stands on the threshold of the greatest period in its history," he remarked prophetically, but added, "I have been called to a larger field of work in the Church, and much to my personal regret, I must leave people . . . whom I have learned to know and love dearly. I must go—God bless you."

The very next Sunday Bishop Maxon addressed the congregation in these words:

> We have bidden farewell to our Dean and his beloved wife . . . now we face the future. Now is the testing time for all of us . . . We are more than a parish, we are a Cathedral Church of the great Diocese of Tennessee. Our fellow churchmen . . . are deeply interested in St. Mary's . . . for our new Dean, whoever he may be, will also be their Dean.
>
> Canon law lays upon the Bishop the selection and appointment of the Dean and of all other clergy of the Cathedral . . . I have asked the Chapter to appoint a committee to advise with me on this appointment [It consisted of the Wardens and Messrs. Huddleston, Turman, Gailor and Patten]. In the meantime, we have been most fortunate in securing the services, as *locum tenens,* of Lt. Col. James E. Clarke, Army Chaplain, who has recently been stationed at Camp Campbell.

After a nine month interval of marking time with various temporary priests while the Bishop and committee sought in vain for a dean, the Bishop finally appointed a recently ordained young priest to act as assistant to a dean as yet unselected. It was this young assistant, The Rev. William E. Sanders, who was destined, in time, to become the dean prophesied by Dean Hoag, who would lead St. Mary's "over the threshold" and into "the greatest period in Cathedral history."

CHAPTER X

THE PRESENT REGIME

I. The Coming of the Dean

CHAPLAIN JAMES E. CLARKE took over as *locum tenens* on November 27, 1945. He was new to the traditions and ways of the Cathedral, but quickly endeared himself to the congregation by his sincerity and kindliness. Miss Ellen Correll planned the usual Feast of Lights, kept the *Chimes* alive, and took charge of most of the routine work of the parish during the kaleidoscopic changes of the ensuing year. A chapter committee was out in search for a prospective Dean, but with little success. In January (1946) it decided to call Mr. Clarke, but too late, as meanwhile he had received an invitation to Christ Church, Glendale, Ohio, which on February 3 he decided to accept. He remained, however, throughout the month. At the first Sunday morning service in March, Mr. W. I. Moody read out the following communication from Bishop Maxon to the congregation:

> Speaking in behalf of you all . . . I desire to express to Chaplain James E. Clarke our deepest appreciation of the service he has rendered as Acting Dean during the past three months. By his forthright preaching of the gospel, his conduct of the service, and his faithful and most helpful ministrations as pastor and friend . . . he has won our hearts. We wish him God speed in entering his new work.
>
> Most happily, I have secured the consent of the Rev. Joseph E. Bernardin, Commander in the U. S. Navy . . . to act as *locum tenens* at St. Mary's. Dr. Bernardin is a highly educated man, a graduate of Yale University and of Oxford University, and with his degree of Doctor of Theology . . . from Union Theological Seminary . . . an unusually well-equipped priest. He is well known to the clergy and to not a few of the laity of the diocese . . . He has agreed to look

after us at St. Mary's until we can secure a Dean. I am delighted that he has been good enough to respond to my request and come to us. He is a friend of long standing . . . We at St. Mary's are truly privileged to have him with us during the Lenten and Easter season. He will be quartered in the Diocesan House and will come to us in time for Ash Wednesday services.

In the meanwhile . . . I will continue to make every effort to secure a well-equipped man as Dean of St. Mary's. I am sure you will all continue to cooperate with the chapter and myself, and each will feel an individual responsibility in building up St. Mary's to an ever-increasing service to Our Blessed Lord and His Church.

Faithfully yours,
James M. Maxon

As the Bishop's letter indicated, Dr. Bernardin was a priest of wide and varied experience.[1] He was also the author of *An Introduction to the Episcopal Church,* a book used throughout the Church for confirmation classes. At St. Mary's he took pains to improve the services. To this end he abandoned the habit of preceding deans of writing personal letters and messages in the *Chimes,* and instead gave brief instructions on Church manners, on the meaning of the Church seasons, or told of gifts needed for the sanctuary or for the improvement of the service. One of the memorable events of his four months' stay was the preparation for and participation in the mission conducted by the Rev. Michael Coleman (March 31-April 5). When Mr. Coleman visited the Cathedral early in the war he had made a profound impact on his hearers. As missioner, one could sense in him the same deep spiritual earnestness. He expressed himself in a simple but moving manner.[2]

---

1. Mr. Bernardin was born June 8, 1899, was B.A. of Yale (1920); B.D. of Eastern Theological Seminary; B.A. and B. Litt. of Oxford (1925); S.T.M. and Th.D. from Union Theological Seminary. He held his first parish in Lamar, Mo., and had been assistant to the Dean of St. John the Divine; a schoolmaster, an assistant at All Angels Church, N.Y.C., then to Kansas, and was for a year rector of the American Church in Munich, Germany. He came to Tennessee in 1940 and served in Knoxville, Maryville and Gatlinburg, was a navy chaplain, and after his period at the Cathedral returned to Maryville.

2. His topics were: 1. Is there a God—What is he like? 2. Is the Bible true—How came sin? 3. Why Jesus—who was He? 4. Redemption and Salvation. 5. Why a Church? 6. Prayer and the Future.

On Ascension Eve Bishop Maxon held another large military service at the Cathedral, this time a Memorial Service for those who gave their lives in the war. The Episcopal clergy of the city, the Knights Templar, and representatives of the armed forces participated in the procession, and as on a previous occasion, there was a "massing of the colors."

Dr. Bernardin retired, during the summer, to East Tennessee where he had served before the war, and again Canon Sharp with the assistance of others mentioned below, took over. On September 1 the *Chimes,* under the heading, "What You Have Been Asking," gave the following information:

> The Reverend William Evan Sanders, a native of Nashville, has been appointed assistant on the Cathedral staff by Bishop Maxon and will be in charge of the parish until a Dean has been named. Mr. Sanders, who holds the degrees of Bachelor of Divinity from Sewanee and Master of Sacred Theology from Union Theological Seminary in New York, served his diaconate at St. Paul's, Chattanooga, and was advanced to the priesthood last June. This summer he has been serving with the City Mission Society in New York, assigned to work in Bellevue Hospital, and will come to the Cathedral after completing this course on September 7. Father Lane, director of Gailor Hall for Boys, will hold the early morning service on Sunday, Dr. John H. Davis will officiate at the late service and Mr. A. J. V. Ware will be the preacher . . .
>
> We are grateful to the clergy who so adequately served the Cathedral during the past two months; to the Reverend Dr. J. B. Bernardin, the Rev. L. D. Brown, the Rev. Vernon Lane, the Rev. H. J. McGehee, the Rev. Malcolm MacMillan, and the Rev. Canon James R. Sharp. The congregations were the largest in many summers. The organizations, with but few exceptions, have maintained regular meetings. To the officers of these organizations as well as to the whole membership much credit is due for carrying on a continuous program of work . . . The Cathedral organization continues as a vital functioning unit, playing its part in the building of the Kingdom.

He began each meeting with an informal hymn sing, directing it himself, and used hymn 429, "To See Thee More Clearly," as a kind of theme song; he also had a question and answer period.

[203]

Mr. Sanders had received this appointment as assistant to a hypothetical dean at the time of his ordination to the priesthood, in June. He arrived, to reside in the "Prophet's Chamber" of the Diocesan House, and to preach his first sermon, on September 15, 1946. The *Chimes* of that date remarked, "the congregation extends to him a hearty welcome." In the next issue Mr. Sanders expressed his thanks and greeting in return:

> Dear Members of St. Mary's:
>
> I want to express my appreciation for the welcome that you have given me. Those of you whom I have met, both old and young, have offered such a warm hand of fellowship that I cannot help but feel completely at home. It has made me look forward more and more toward the future work and worship with you, and toward the deepening of our relationship with one another in God's love.

After reporting on the General Convention which he had visited en route to St. Mary's, he ended with these words: "The congregation of St. Mary's seems to have a unique opportunity. You stand in the fulness of time in your own right. You have the resources, the power, and what already appears to a newcomer, a basic spirit of cooperation and fellowship. You hear about you the urgent cry of persons in need, and a society in many places sick and diseased. 'Who knoweth whether Thou art come to the Kingdom for such a time as this?' "

As it proved, it was Mr. Sanders who had come "for such a time as this." Though young and inexperienced he appealed so instantly to both old and young that before the end of the year the chapter and congregation felt that it could at last discontinue what had proved a long and fruitless search for a new dean. Early in the year Bishop Maxon had announced that he expected to retire at the end of the year. By September he had received permission of the House of Bishops, and it was publicly announced in December. A week before his retirement as diocesan, Bishop Maxon called the members of the chapter to his home for a final chapter meeting. They took with them a parting gift and an urgent request that Mr. Sanders be made

Acting Dean. The Bishop knowing that this was in the air had prepared a letter for the chapter in which he acceded to their request: "After considerable consideration I am appointing the Rev. William Evan Sanders as Acting Dean of St. Mary's Cathedral (Gailor Memorial) effective Monday, December 23, 1946. This appointment is for a year from this date. I feel I cannot bind my successor, Bishop Dandridge, for a longer period than that." He fixed the salary ($4,200), authorized the new Acting Dean to preside at chapter meetings in the absence of the bishop, to have offices and living quarters in the Diocesan House, and to "conduct worship in the Cathedral, subject to the direction of the Bishop." He expressed some doubt as to the wisdom of removing the new appointee from the duty of directing young people's work (for which, at Mr. Coate's request, he had been originally called), although he expressed the "utmost confidence in Mr. Sanders," adding, "He is a cherished son in the Gospel upon whom I lean in my declining years. He will be true . . . He has ability, in my judgement equal to that of any Priest of this Diocese." In conclusion the Bishop expressed his joy in knowing and working with the chapter, and ended with an appeal to them to support their new leader:

> With all his gifts and willingness to spend and be spent, he cannot possibly do this great work alone while others sit by and admiringly watch him . . . It (the congregation) has no right to claim the choicest and give nothing in return . . . This chapter has a solemn responsibility to support Mr. Sanders . . . That support will cost something. It will cost money. It will cost service. It will cost regular and conscientious attendance in the worship of the Church. It will cost earnest effort to bring others to Church, in searching out children and adults for baptism, and confirmation and for the Church School . . . I will watch events for the next year with the prayer that you will go forward.

He reported this event in his diary as follows: "7:30 P.M. in my home held a special meeting of the Cathedral Chapter to appoint the Rev. William E. Sanders as Acting Dean of St.

[205]

Mary's Cathedral. This appointment was unanimously and enthusiastically concurred in by the Chapter. Mrs. Maxon and I were presented with a beautiful silver service by the members of the Chapter."

The chapter and congregation were soon so enthusiastic about the new Acting Dean that long before his year's appointment was up they pleaded with Bishop Dandridge to declare Mr. Sanders "full Dean." Therefore on September 29 Dr. Dandridge wrote the chapter: "In accord with the request of the Chapter, I hereby appoint the Rev. William E. Sanders to be Dean of St. Mary's Cathedral . . . the appointment to take effect December 23, 1947, the same being the end of the time for which he was appointed Acting Dean." He set January 4, 1948, as the official date of installation. In his address to the next convention he referred to the event in these words:

> On January 4, 1948, the churches of Memphis and a great many people outside our communion united in the service of installation, for which occasion the Cathedral was full to the doors. And the stirring nature of the great procession, and the reverent service and the excellent sermon by Dr. Barth, all testified to the place the Cathedral holds in the community and the place Dean Sanders holds in the hearts of the people.

II. RECENT BISHOPS

Having witnessed the rapid rise of Mr. Sanders from assistant to Dean, we shall hold in abeyance the description of his activities (1947-1957) and pause to sketch some of the activities of the several bishops who guided the destinies of the Cathedral and diocese during this decade. Then we shall trace briefly the musical situation at the Cathedral during these years before returning to survey the work of the Dean and the parish. We shall remember that the nearer we approach the present the more complex have Cathedral activities become and the more difficult it is to compress them into one chapter without omitting certain events which to contemporaries involved in them may seem more important than the things mentioned. It may also be wise to reverse the old Roman motto, *de mortuis nil nisi bonum,* and to speak only good things concerning the living.

In the early years of St. Mary's one bishop usually outlasted the tenure of several deans. This picture was now reversed, for Mr. Sanders has already served under three diocesans. Though Bishop Maxon's regime coincided with that of his young appointee for only three months, several important incidents of that time may be noted. Early in October, Mr. P. Stenning Coate, who for nearly fifty years was constantly and devotedly involved in Cathedral affairs, died. Shortly before his death he left a large sum as an endowment for the Cathedral.

Bishop Maxon announced to the chapter on June 12, 1946, that Mr. Coate had set up an "irrevocable trust . . . for the endowment of the Cathedral Church of St. Mary's." Since then other donors have added substantially to the endowment of the Cathedral.[3]

In Bishop Maxon's final year two other events of interest to St. Mary's transpired: St. Alban's mission, which had been founded by the Cathedral in Dean Morris' time (but later entrusted to others), expired. The property was sold and proceeds given the Church of the Good Shepherd. To balance this, the Bishop announced in convention the leasing of DuBose

---

3. The Bishop's Warden, Mr. William Deupree, reports that at present (1957) there are four Trust Funds for the Cathedral: 1) The Coate Fund, "for the extension of Christian work by the Cathedral," (its book value (1957) was $172,697, with a market value of approximately $70,000 more, and an income of $8,393.35); 2) The Treadwell Fund, "for the use and preservation of the Chapel" (with a corpus of $15,000, and an income of $654.26); 3) The Currier Fund started in 1926 by the Currier and Brinkley survivors, the income from which ($197.48) goes one-half to the Cathedral, one-fourth to the Altar Committee, and one-fourth to the Woman's Auxiliary; and 4) the Reserve Fund, "for capital or emergency use by the Cathedral" (this was started in 1942, and now has a book value of $75,645, with a market value of approximately $25,000 more, and income (1957) of $3,155.07).

One should add that there is another fund, outside the regular budget, The Student and Theological Education Fund (now about $1,600 per year) which is contributed to annually by about a dozen members of St. Mary's. This fund is for the support of seminarians, and for paying tuition and expenses of two students at St. Andrew's.

Conference Center. The Bishop's final official act was to plan and participate in the installation ceremony of Bishop Dandridge at the Cathedral on January 5, 1947. The new diocesan made the retired Bishop a Canon of the Cathedral and historiographer of the diocese. Thus Dr. Maxon continued to participate in services at the Cathedral until his death on November 8, 1948.[4]

The Right Reverend Edmund Pendleton Dandridge, who was diocesan from January 1, 1947, to September 20, 1953, quickly let it be known that he intended to maintain his residence in Nashville and center diocesan affairs there, but that he would expect his coadjutor, when elected, to reside in Memphis in the Bishop's House. In his first convention address (1947) he called attention to the shortage of clergy in the state, to his plan for increasing the use of the perpetual diaconate, and to the plans he and Dean Philip Davidson of Vanderbilt had devised of establishing a graduate training center for religious education work. He also pointed out the need of constructing a vault for the storage of diocesan records in the crypt of the Cathedral. (This was finally completed in 1954). The following January he installed the Very Reverend William E. Sanders as Dean, and reverted to Bishop Gailor's habit of conducting the rite of confirmation on Palm Sunday. In the Convention of 1948 he asked for a coadjutor, and at the special convention for this purpose (April 20) the Rev. Theodore Nott Barth was elected. He was consecrated in his old parish of Calvary on September 21.[5] The Cathedral held a reception in

---

4. Bishop Maxon's body lay in state in the Chapel of St. Mary's from Tuesday noon to Wednesday morning, the clergy of Memphis keeping vigil in relays during the night. At the Bishop's request, Canon James R. Sharp, who had been the Bishop's Chaplain throughout his entire episcopate, was the officiant at the funeral. Bishop Dandridge and Bishop Barth assisted in the service. The clergy of Memphis served as active pallbearers, the other clergy of the diocese, the chapter, and diocesan lay officials, as honorary pallbearers. The Bishop was interred near the grave of Bishop Otey in the churchyard of St. John's, Ashwood.

5. Bishop Barth was born in Mt. Savage, Md., July 11, 1898. He was B.A. of the University of Virginia, and B.D. of Virginia Theological Seminary.

his honor on October 21. Early in 1949 he and Mrs. Barth moved into the Bishop's House on Central, and he established his office in the Diocesan House.

By 1949 Bishop Dandridge had established planning commissions for Shelby County and other urban districts. While on a visit to St. Mary's in January 1950 he instituted and wrote the prayer which is said every Sunday at the Cathedral for two churches (or missions) of the diocese. This habit, and later the installation of clerestory windows which contain the shields of all the churches and missions of the diocese, have brought to the Cathedral a feeling of closer relationship with the other parishes of the diocese.

The Convention of 1951 met in Memphis at the Cathedral, and its opening service was a memorable one for St. Mary's. For now after eighty years of existence as a Cathedral, and after more than fifty years since the stone structure was begun, the building was consecrated. This long delay was due, of course, to the fact that since the bond issue of 1906 an indebtedness had remained on the Cathedral which was now at last removed. The *Journal* described the event as follows:

> The opening service at 9:30 (January 24, 1951) consisted of the service of consecration of St. Mary's Cathedral by the Bishop of the Diocese. The certificate of freedom from incumbrance, and request to consecrate being read by Mr. W. I. Moody, the Bishop's Warden, and the sentence of consecration by the Bishop Coadjutor of the Diocese, followed by the celebration of Holy Communion by the Bishop, with the Bishop Coadjutor taking the service to the sermon, the Rev. William J. Loaring Clark reading the Epistle and the Very Rev. William E. Sanders the Gospel. In the place of the sermon the Bishop delivered his annual address.

In this address Bishop Dandridge said, "It has of course already been consecrated by years of reverent worship, but it is

---

He was ordained deacon December 17, 1921, and priest the next year at Mt. Savage, Md. He served in three parishes in Maryland (Mt. Savage, Deer Creek, and at St. Bartholomew's, Baltimore) before coming to Calvary, March 10, 1940. He married Elizabeth P. Ellicott of Baltimore, June 4, 1923, and received the D.D. from the University of the South, Southwestern, and Virginia Theological Seminary.

a happy circumstance that the formal service of consecration could be held now when the whole Diocese is assembled here." Later on he added, "It is not easy to keep clear and make effective the functions of a Cathedral which also serves as a parish church. But I hope and pray the time will come when this Cathedral will serve not only as a center to which the whole Diocese can come, but also as a center from which missionary work and other church activities can go out into many parts of the Diocese. The income from the generous gifts and bequests made by Mr. Stenning Coate is now being used to complete the physical equipment (i.e., the new Church School building). After this is done I hope that this money and other money like it can be used to support missionary and educational work radiating from here."

At this convention the Bishop stated that he felt encouraged by the growing list of postulants and ordinations.[6] But the next year both the bishops were disturbed by the rapid departure of many young priests and deacons to other dioceses, and they expressed the hope that young ministers would feel obligated to remain in the diocese four or five years before heeding calls from the outside. It was in 1951 that the two bishops launched the Summer Music Conference at Sewanee which has done much to improve church music in the diocese, and on the evening of June 25 they joined forces to perform the marriage ceremony for the Dean and Miss Kathryn Schaffer.

In the Convention of 1952 Bishop Dandridge praised Dr. William Rogers Beasley and his wife for going as medical missionaries to Liberia. Though not a communicant of the Cathedral at the time of his going, Dr. Beasley was raised in

---

6. One of his ordinations of the previous year was that of the writer. He noted (for St. James' Day, July 25), "9 A.M. in the presence of Canon Sharp and Dean Sanders examined Dr. John H. Davis for ordination. 10:30 in St. Mary's Cathedral ordained John Henry Davis to the diaconate. The sermon was preached by Dr. Barth . . . Dr. Davis is a member of the Cathedral Chapter and Professor of History at Southwestern. He will serve as deacon on the staff of the Cathedral."

the Cathedral and its members were extremely interested in his work. Bishop Dandridge was in poor health during much of 1952 and for a time his life was despaired of, but fortunately he recovered and since he had reached the canonical age of retirement, did so on September 20, 1953. His retirement, however, only meant a change of activity, for during the previous year a crisis had arisen at the Sewanee Theological Seminary, and in line of duty he went there as Acting Dean. Shortly before this, the Episcopalians of Memphis (September 3) united in a testimonial dinner to him at Hotel Peabody. He described this event in his diary as follows:

> In the evening in the Ball Room of the Peabody Hotel was guest of honor at a dinner attended by about four hundred people. Mr. Walter Chandler presided. Dr. Edward McReady, Bishop Barth and Mr. Edmund Orgill made speeches lauding my virtues and ignoring my faults. They also unveiled a portrait of the "about to retire" Bishop painted by Mrs. Billie Hosmer on the order of the Cathedral Chapter, and presented me with a cheque of $1,000. I made a speech of thanks.

Bishop Barth was installed as diocesan in an imposing ceremony at the Cathedral on September 21, 1953. He had lived in Memphis since 1940, but as coadjutor his duty as supervisor of missionary activity of the diocese had often taken him away. As early as the convention of 1953, when it became known that he would become diocesan during the year, he divulged his plans for the Diocesan House:

> It is a lovely dignified old house, so well suited to be, with the Cathedral group, the diocesan frontispiece. It is not my intention to make it the center of every activity, but I hope to gather around me there the various offices and officers who ought to be near at hand. The treasurer of the Diocesan House Committee tells me the present amount of money allocated for its upkeep is not much more than sufficient to take care of routine expenses . . . There is not enough to keep it in proper repair. Therefore I have asked for an increased allotment for this purpose . . . I am going to spend my working hours there. But in a very real sense it is your house . . . We want to look our best when company comes.

This promise was soon fulfilled. The House was renovated without and within and assumed a more dignified appearance. Soon Canon Sharp began to move the diocesan records to the newly prepared office and vault in preparation for his retirement from the office of Executive Secretary (which he had held for 35 years) and from that of Secretary to the Convention (held for 28 years).[7]

Bishop Barth then announced that Mr. M. C. Nichols, a Chattanooga business executive, was giving up his own work to become the Bishop's administrative assistant. In February 1956 Mr. Nichols took up his new duties in the Diocesan House and soon fell heir to many of Canon Sharp's titles and tasks. He was ordained a perpetual deacon on December 21, 1956, was made Secretary to the convention (January 1957), and quickly became a valued member of the Cathedral staff.

Bishop Barth requested the Convention of 1954 to elect a suffragan rather than a coadjutor. In the special convention for this purpose (April 22, 1954) the Rev. R. F. McGregor was elected, but declined (May 2). Another election was held on November 9, at which time the Rev. John Vander Horst, rector of St. Paul's Chattanooga, was chosen. He was consecrated in his home church on March 2, 1955.[8]

Among the many things that Bishop Barth has forwarded and accomplished as diocesan only a few can be mentioned

---

7. In his address to the convention (1955) Bishop Barth told of the completion of the vault and of his plans for it: "Already records of the episcopate of Bishop Maxon and of Bishop Dandridge are stored, and other legal and historical documents." He wisely suggested that mission and parochial records not in current use be deposited there and suggested a canon which might make the deposit of certain classes of documents mandatory. He praised Canon Sharp as a man "whose devotion has uplifted us, whose courage has strengthened us, whose knowledge and good sense have so many times saved us from making fools of ourselves."

8. The Rt. Rev. John Vander Horst was born in Orange, N. J., January 10, 1912. He studied Theology at St. Stephen's House, Oxford, England, and at the Virginia Theological Seminary. He was ordained deacon, June 1938, and priest, June 1939. He was rector of St. John's Church, Ellicott City, Md., (1938-42); St. Paul's Church, Macon, Ga., (1942-45); the Church of the Good Shepherd, Philadelphia, Pa., (1945-51); and of St. Paul's Church, Chattanooga (1951-55) before his election as Suffragan.

here. He pushed the Builders for Christ campaign, and the Diocesan Survey (both sponsored by the National Church). He and the Suffragan have promoted a Revolving Fund (for aid to church building), the Capital Fund Drive (1956) and created a new "Seven-Point Mission Program."[9] In Memphis three of the Bishop's programs have been strongly supported (morally and financially) by the Cathedral: the rebuilding of Emmanuel Church, to which St. Mary's contributed over $5,000; the establishment of a new medical center at Quintard House, which though supported by all Memphis parishes was a movement conceived by and growing out of work begun at the Cathedral; and the work of the Planning Commission of Shelby County in establishing All Saints' mission (Mr. William Ray of the Cathedral was an active member of the commission, and Mr. Robertson Eppes, its first priest, a former Cathedral Canon).

III. MUSIC

In the spring of 1946, while Dr. Bernardin was still *locum tenens,* Miss Helen Pendleton resigned, her resignation to take effect on July 1. Before going she procured Miss Frances McFadden of Memphis as a summer replacement. Miss McFadden quickly won the confidence of the choir. During September and early October the music committee tried out several other organists and choir directors, but by October 20 decided, after consultation with the choir, to employ Miss

---

9. The Bishop explained the "Builders for Christ" campaign in his address to the 1954 Convention. Briefly, it was a campaign, authorized by the 1952 General Convention, to procure funds ($4,150,000) during the triennium for a) improving facilities at the Church's theological seminaries; b) for aiding new building in the foreign mission fields, especially in Japan and the Philippines and c) aiding Negro churches. Tennessee's share was approximately $60,000 (and St. Mary's about $2,800).

The Capital Fund Campaign was to obtain $500,000 for special needs of the diocese, especially for rehabilitation of DuBose; for work (in the nature of Tyson and Quintard House) in the various colleges of the State; and for the building of All Saint's Chapel at Sewanee.

The "7 Point Program" for Missions is fully explained in the *Journal of the Convention of 1956,* 34-37. It refers to the necessary steps required for the progression of a "mission" to "organized mission" and to "parish" status.

McFadden. Thus her coming almost coincided with the coming of Dean Sanders. She attended several summer music conferences in Evergreen, Colorado, and worked well with the Junior Choir (In 1948 they recorded Mr. Glynn's hymn, "Maxon," as a gift to the Bishop). It was almost a year after her coming that she gave her first organ recital (November 1947), assisted by Miss Helen Parker and Mr. James Byerly. She followed the tradition established by Miss Pendleton of describing in the *Chimes* the hymns and anthems which would be sung on Sundays, and she often gave instructions, in this column, on singing and chanting. She was cooperative with other organists and choir directors, for example for Ascension Day, 1950, she invited Mr. Vernon Perdue-Davis of Southwestern to bring his liturgical choir to the Cathedral, where, with the cooperation of the Dean, the complete Merbecke setting of the Mass was sung. The next year she joined Mr. White of St. John's Church in a hymn festival in celebration of the four hundredth anniversary of the Geneva Psalter.

There is a certain irony in the fact that a program enthusiastically launched by the Dean in cooperation with the music committee of the chapter, with the avowed purpose 1) of improving congregational singing, 2) of seeing more clearly the musical heritage of the church and 3) of "sharing the fellowship of learning and singing together," should have ended by making life unpleasant for the choir director, but such proved to be the case. The plan was for congregational groups of fifteen to meet weekly for five weeks in six different homes to study the new hymnal and the pamphlets put out by the National Church about the hymnal. Some groups did sing, learn and enjoy, but sometimes these sessions degenerated into indignation meetings (on the part of some members) against the hymnal, hymn selection, the singing of the chants, or the tempo of the doxology. Miss McFadden, already overworked by preparation for the Christmas program and by her many private classes, felt so discouraged that she decided to resign and devote full time to teaching. The chapter "regretfully accepted her resignation" and praised her for her five years of efficient service.

As a replacement was needed quickly, it was fortunate that the music committee was able to obtain from Southwestern College two young music majors who stepped into the breach on January 13, 1952. On that date Mr. Robert Matthews became the choir director with Mr. Douglas Barnett as organist. Mr. Matthews had had experience as assistant conductor of Dr. Burnet C. Tuthill's college choir, and as a young man of ability, charm, and excellent musical taste, quickly won the choir's allegiance. His own interest in church music led him meanwhile to become a postulant for the ministry, and as he graduated from college in June and entered seminary in September his stay was necessarily brief. After his departure Mr. Barnett carried on for another year as both organist and choir director before going into the service.[10]

The Dean and the committee were aware that Mr. Barnett's tenure was temporary, so in the spring of 1953 they began a serious and intensive search for a full-time organist and choir director. Many applicants were heard but the committee was unanimously impressed with the playing of Mr. William Brice, then organist of Holy Trinity Church of

---

10. During this period of the early 1950's several unusual and beautiful musical services were presented at the Cathedral by the Southwestern Liturgical Choir, directed by Mr. Vernon Perdue-Davis, a talented young musician and composer, then teaching at Southwestern. As these services were unheralded and unannounced, few members of the Cathedral were aware of their existence. He and his liturgical choir presented: 1) the Merbecke Mass on Ascension Day 1950; 2) Evensong in French with French carols and the reading of Claudel's religious poetry (in the Chapel, in Lent, 1953); 3) Litany in procession with the sung Passion for Tuesday of Holy Week (1953); 4) French evensong with a French mystery play, a cantata of Bach and a reading of Spanish religious poetry (Rogation Day, 1953); 5) Office of Instruction with sung Litany and three newly composed hymns (In the Chapel, April 7, 1954); and 6) Litany in procession with the sung Passion for Wednesday in Holy Week (April 14, 1954).

Decatur, Georgia.[11] He accepted the invitation of the committee and came to the Cathedral in August 1953, to assume direction of the choir.

It had been obvious to recent organists and to the music committee that the Coate organ was in a serious state of disrepair. Various damages to the tower by lightning and the resultant water damage to the organ, as well as its dusty and inadequate chamber, meant that breakdowns or ciphers could be expected at any time. Dr. Dick McCool, chairman of the music committee, and others began an "educational campaign" to inform the chapter and congregation that a new instrument, plus complete revision of the old, was needed for adequate Cathedral music. In June 1954 the chapter agreed that a new organ should be one of the first steps in the projected Centennial Program (which will be discussed later). Meanwhile Dr. and Mrs. McCool, Mr. Brice, and other members of the music committee began to visit various churches to hear and inspect different kinds of organs. The committee received bids from various organ companies, and eventually decided upon a Schantz organ. The old one was removed in November 1955 and for several months the congregation was faced by a gaping open space where the organ had been (Mr. Brice used this most effectively on Christmas Eve, 1955, for an "echo" choir). Finally in the spring of 1956 the pipes of the new organ began to arrive and be put in place and the congregation was soon amazed (and most were delighted) by the innovation of having the pipes of the "great" and "positiv" sections showing in the open, thus forming pleasing geometrical patterns and color

---

11. See *Chimes*, July, 1953. The Dean told of the music committee's work in interviewing applicants, and said, "the committee selected Mr. Brice instead of other men of greater years and training because of his outstanding musical talent and his impressive work in his present church. Mr. Brice is a native of Knoxville and confirmed in St. John's Church, Knoxville, by Bishop Maxon . . . He studied piano at seven and organ at twelve years of age. He has studied under Maurice Pederson in Knoxville and Richard Thomasson in Atlanta. He took academic work at Emory University."

combinations, instead of being hidden and muffled by dummy pipes or screen work as was traditional.

The strains of the new instrument were first heard on Palm Sunday, 1956. On the following Sunday, Easter afternoon, Mr. Brice played his first recital on it, and the organ was dedicated by Bishop Barth on May 13. Mr. Brice had, even before the installation of the new organ, by his assiduous work, by his fine musicianship, by regular letters and phone calls to choir members, built up a wonderful *esprit de corps* in both the Junior and Adult Choirs. During the Lenten seasons of 1954 and 1955, he led these choirs on pilgrimages to the missions in Collierville and Somerville for special sung Evensongs. After the installation of the new organ he began regular monthly organ recitals (September-May) on the second Sundays. These have been marked by a fine taste in the selection of programs (where the great organ literature of the past and present has been explored) and by his excellent playing. On several occasions when baroque music was played he has been assisted by the "St. Mary's recorder group." Mr. Brice has also brought several outstanding organists to the Cathedral. The quality of the singing has improved so markedly under the present director that St. Mary's choir is now considered one of the most outstanding in Memphis. The *Commercial Appeal* recognized this fact (May 12, 1957) and devoted a front page feature article in its Sunday edition to the work of Mr. Brice and the choir.[12]

---

12. In the report of the chairman of the music committee to the Chapter (for 1957) some statistics are of interest. The Adult Choir now contains 50 members, the Junior Choir 20. They participated in seventeen special services in the course of the year. One outstanding organist, Dr. Marilyn Mason, gave a recital in January. Twice the local Chapter of the A.G.O. has held meetings at the Cathedral. Nine public recitals were held at St. Mary's, four by guest recitalists. Many famous organists, Dr. Ragatz, Dr. Noehren, Dr. D. M. Williams (to name a few) have visited St. Mary's to hear and play the organ. Mr. Brice attended the International Congress of Organists in London, and was a recitalist at the Southern Convention of the A.G.O.

IV. Finishing the Buildings

The increase in membership, in parish religious work and in building activity have been so considerable during the past ten years that although these have progressed simultaneously, we shall, as in treating the work of previous deans, revert to the habit of separating the Dean's work into the dichotomy of building activity and religious (or parish) activity and consider the former phase first.

During the first few years of his regime, while the Dean was "getting the feel of things," and attempting to bring in new blood, neither he nor the chapter were prepared to launch into any ambitious building plans. The only alteration of the Cathedral fabric in the late forties was a minor renovation of the crypt, when an acoustic ceiling and fluorescent lighting were installed.[13] Not until 1950 were the postponed hopes of a new Parish Hall revived. (Mr. Moody had started raising funds for this in 1942 and by now had approximately $100,000 on hand). In February it was openly announced that the chapter hoped to bring the total building fund to $135,000, which was then thought sufficient for the building. Mr. Russell Perry and Mr. Joseph Patten, Jr., were chosen to head the committee in charge of securing this amount. By summer this additional $35,000 was raised, and with full ceremony ground was broken on July 23.[14] But as so often happened in the past, by the time everything seemed in readiness, and money raised for a project, a war or depression (this time the Korean War) would intervene to hamper hopes, impose restrictions, or bring rising

---

13. The *Chimes* of June 27, 1948, says, "The number one problem and eyesore in the Cathedral structure is well known as being the Crypt." It said the "sentiment to improve began last fall." It was planned to spend $7,000 and a committee for raising funds was created (Russell Perry, Mrs. Leroy Taylor, Miss Harriette Frank, John McCarroll, H. O. Turman).

14. *The Commercial Appeal,* July 24, 1950. The headline read, "Site is consecrated as Choir lifts voice." The chief participants in the ceremony were: the Dean; Mr. J. M. Patten, Sr. (Chapter's Warden); Mr. Morris Cobb (president of the Men's Council); Mr. Leroy Taylor (representing the Church School staff) and Mrs. Allen Hughes (representing the Woman's Auxiliary).

prices. Thus within a year it became necessary to elevate the sights from $135,000 to $180,000 (and eventually to $200,000). Another drive had to be launched for the necessary supplement, and this was undertaken (April to June 1951) under the leadership of Mr. Leon Huddleston.[15]

As the Parish Hall was in process of construction, the ceremony of the consecration of the Cathedral gave a boost to the morale of the congregation (January 24, 1951). Building restrictions did, however, delay the completion of the Parish Hall for almost a year. Thus it was on March 30, 1952 that a Thanksgiving Service was first held in the new building, and on April 24 it was formally dedicated by Bishop Dandridge. The Dean, the Superintendent of the Church School and the Director of Religious Education as well as the architects had put much thought into the design of the building, but since some old pianos were repainted to match the room colors, this was the feature which attracted most attention in the press. *The Press-Scimitar's* headline for the dedication read: "St. Mary's Church School Building, Wonderland with Pink Pianos." The article did, however, fully describe how the new building integrated "a basement, a chapel and a cloister," and it described the new parish hall, the Sunday School rooms, the club rooms, and the child-sized lavatories. It quoted Miss Correll as saying, "It represents faith in the future, and meets the challenge of changing conditions in the parish and in the church neighborhood. Instead of the church moving from its downtown location as some have done before, St. Mary's is launching a new program that will provide better facilities for all."[16]

---

15. The original estimates of $155,000 were increased to $183,000. Even after the second drive, the Cathedral was between $25-30,000 short of the sum required. The finance committee got the permission of the Bishop to use the income from the Coate Trust for several years. This was later repaid.

16. See *Chimes* for April 27, for list of committees for the Reception and Open House. Walk C. Jones, Sr., and Jr., were the architects and Robert C. Crouch the contractor. The building contains a large hall (seating 250) and

In January 1954 the chapter purchased a new deanery at 2246 Court (the Dean and Mrs. Sanders had resided previously in an apartment on Poplar), and during this same year the Bishop refurbished the Diocesan House. In spite of recent expenses, discussions about the need for a new organ revealed that there were many other pressing needs as well; it was necessary to repair the Cathedral roof, to repaint and replaster the badly weathered plaster of the interior, to plaster and redecorate the unsightly crypt, and many—accustomed to the comforts of modern living and to "meet competition"—wanted air conditioning. Mr. Moody, Mr. Patten, and the Dean, by inaugurating (June 1954) a meeting of present and former chapter members at a fishing lodge at Bear Creek, Arkansas, hit upon an extremely happy device for bringing the Cathedral's executive group together in an atmosphere of relaxation and informality.[17] It was at this first meeting that the idea of a Centennial Program germinated. Before this there had been much discussion as to which improvement should have priority—if repairs should be undertaken piecemeal. Now the idea developed that the Cathedral should raise a sufficient fund to care for all its pressing needs, to have the work done more or less simultaneously, and to have it completed and in readiness for the centennial year.

The original goal of the centennial fund was $100,000 but was later increased. A few hard workers, without much fanfare, began the campaign early in 1955 and by the end of

---

stage, a completely equipped kitchen, 12 class rooms, a library, and office, 6 lavatories, storage closets, a large recreation room and club room.

The Building Committee decided to call the Parish Hall "Moody Hall" in honor of Mr. W. I. Moody, who had worked for so many years on the project. When he found that his name was cut in the stone over the door, he sent out workmen and had it removed and resurfaced.

17. Bishop Barth, who attended the 1955 meeting, approved heartily as may be seen from his *Journal*, "At Bear Creek with St. Mary's chapter. A great idea this, giving the men an opportunity to discuss and think through long-range spiritual goals, and do a little fishing on the side."

the year most of the money had been pledged.[18] As we have seen, by the fall of 1955 the old organ was removed, and during the spring of 1956 the chambers for the new one were prepared. That spring the interior of the Cathedral was a maze of scaffolding as replastering, repainting, and air conditioning were in progress. While the scaffolding was still up the final twelve stained glass windows were installed.[19]

Three other significant changes in the Cathedral ensemble have occurred since the centennial program was launched. It was discovered that certain "eye-sore" property next to the Cathedral was for sale, and a small group of Cathedral members raised the money to purchase these. The houses were soon demolished and the space thus provided has permitted the construction of a convenient parking lot to the west of the Diocesan House (completed 1956). In the fall of 1956 the crypt was at last renovated, plastered, given a tile floor, and provided with attractive lighting. Mr. Roy Cotner, a Cathedral member and former teacher at the Art Academy who had already demonstrated his decorative talents by helping choose the tone of the cathedral paint and in planning the decor of the bookstore, now

---

18. The original expenses contemplated in the Centennial Program were:

Painting and decorating	$ 5,000	
Organ	39,400	
Air Conditioning	40,950	
Engineers Fee	3,000	
Air Conditioning S.S. Room	3,000	
	$91,350	$ 91,350

In 1956 and 1957, these were added:

Parking lot and landscaping	8,111	
Renovation of Crypt	9,915	
Curtains, Ventilation, etc.	856	
	$18,982	$ 18,982

Total pledges to the Centennial Fund (Nov., 1957)........$110,338
$115,173

Over and above this, the Chapter has partly raised and partly borrowed $30,000 to pay for the property (Novarese and Bilbo) now converted into the parking lot.

19. On March 7, 1952, previous gifts of two large and four small windows had been dedicated. The final twelve (10 clerestory and 2 in the nave) were dedicated on April 24, 1955. (See appendix on Memorials). The *Chimes* of February 17, 1952, and April 24, 1955, give a full description of these windows.

advised on the colors and hangings in the crypt. The "new crypt" was ready for the parish meeting and for the diocesan convention which met in the Cathedral in January 1957. The parishioners of St. Mary's certainly owe a deep debt of gratitude for the strenuous and devoted work of the Chairmen of the Building and Grounds Committee of these active "building years." The men most responsible for the oversight of the work have been Messrs. Carter B. Lyon, William Lea and William Hudgins. Finally in the fall of 1957, by a series of munificent gifts, Mr. and Mrs. C. N. Johnston and Mr. and Mrs. S. K. Jones have supplied cushions for all the pews and elegant new lighting fixtures with which the Cathedral will greet its centennial year.[20]

V. Parish Activity

There has been a remarkable growth in the religious activities of the parish during Dean Sanders' tenure. Before attempting to enumerate his work in detail, I shall indicate what have seemed to me to have been his major aims and objectives. Some were of his own devising; in some he was aided by the fact that the National Church (e.g., by its Teaching Series and New Curriculum) happened to be emphasizing the same aims. To this writer, then, the Dean has tried to promote: 1) a spirit of fellowship; 2) corporate activity, centered both in the church and in the home (by means of "family groups," "family nights," etc.), not just as activities for activity's sake, but for educational or devotional ends; 3) a realization of the responsibility of a downtown church toward the ever-changing community around it, which in St. Mary's case has meant an interest in the neighborhood and work in the

---

20. The cushions and lights were given in memory of Augusta Johnston, and of Purcell Johnston. (They were formally dedicated by Bishop Barth on January 5, 1958.) The firm of Walk Jones, Jr., supervised the work. The six large lights were created by Rambusch of New York. The Scruggs Electric Co. installed them.

Four of the old lights were donated by the Cathedral to ex-Canon Sheldon Davis for his church at Ravenscroft.

medical areas; and 4) a great concern for an increase in the ministry. These have been his major interests over and above the regular conduct of services, pastoral duties and civic duties in which he has been active.

We shall now try to observe how and when these various types of activity were developed. Mr. Sanders arrived in September 1946 and his first few months were devoted to becoming acquainted with the congregation. One of his first "activities" was to launch (January 19, 1947) St. Mary's Forum. This was a Sunday evening discussion group, at the Diocesan House, designed for young married couples or those of college age. For the first year or two the Dean kept this group going but in 1949 turned it over to Mr. William Ray, an active worker and a natural discussion leader. He kept the Forum flourishing, supplying many topics and many outside speakers.

On January 7, 1948 the Cathedral (under the sponsorship of the Woman's Auxiliary) launched its first "Coffee Hour." This quickly caught on, for it gave members and visitors a time to become better acquainted after the morning service. It has flourished since its inception, and from time to time various new features have been introduced. Thus in May 1949 there was an interesting exhibit sponsored by the Church School, of old Prayer Books, and during 1951-52 an experiment was made of having a table of religious books from the Cathedral Library on display, so that members might be tempted to borrow them. The Y.P.S.L. has used the coffee hour for various of its fund raising projects, and Youth Service has usually conducted its annual membership drive during the February coffee hour. In May 1954 the location of the coffee hour was changed from its original home in the Diocesan House to the Parish Hall where it has since remained.

It was in October 1948 that the Dean organized his first Parent's Class ("Religion in the Home") in the Church School. He began this several years before the National

Church's "new program" made parents classes an integral part of church school instruction. In February 1949 he and Dr. McCool began some Tuesday evening discussions on "marriage." Later, during Lent, the Dean continued the Tuesday evening class on the subject, "The Prayer Book speaks to an uncertain Age" (this was the year of the four-hundredth anniversary of the Prayer Book). By 1950 the Church's Teaching Series was beginning to appear. On October 20 of that year, with the assistance of the Auxiliary and the Men's Council, the first experiment in home study groups was begun. The plan was for groups of about fifteen each to meet in six homes scattered throughout various parts of the city. With the help of a prepared discussion guide, "Consider the Bible," six leaders (the Dean, Miss Correll, W. Ray, A. J. V. Ware, Dr. Richard Overman and J. H. Davis) led the groups in discussions of the Bible based on Denton's *The Scriptures.* This experiment proved so successful that the ensuing Lent it was decided to combine all the groups into one large group (of over 100) for the discussion of P. M. Dawley's *Chapters in Church History.* This time the entire group met together in the crypt once a week for five lectures (given by the Dean, Mr. Ware and Mr. Davis on different phases of church history). These lectures were followed by the group being divided into four smaller sections for discussions led by Mr. Ray, Mr. McGee, Dr. Overman and Miss Correll.

In the fall of 1951 the Dean and his assistants reverted to the 1950 plan of again organizing group meeting in private homes. This time the plan was to meet in six homes under the leadership of the choir director, Miss McFadden, assisted by five musically trained members of the congregation in order to study the *Hymnal 1940* (described above in the section on Music). In Lent of 1952 the subject studied was *The Faith of the Church.* The last series of Lenten meetings devoted to the Church's teaching series was in 1953 when Massie Shepherd's

Worship of the Church was the text. All groups again met at the Cathedral on Monday evenings to discuss topics prepared by Mr. Ray.

Soon after this last series (on April 12-14) a team of three leaders from the National Church visited the Cathedral to conduct a three day "Christian Living Conference." Visitors from other parishes attended and between seven and eight hundred were at each session.[21] These early and tentative experiments with groups meeting in homes or the entire group meeting in the Cathedral led the Dean and his advisors, shortly before the Lenten season of 1954, to launch into a really ambitious program, namely, the division of the city and its environs into forty-five (later forty-two) regions with a group leader for each. The Dean, aided by a Committee of Cathedral Women under the chairmanship of Mrs. William Jones, provided an outline for a devotional program which was to be followed by each group. After the devotional and educational program there was to be a social hour; and an effort was made to get the members of each group to meet in several different homes during the course of the Lenten period. This program had a most stimulating effect. Many people who lived within a few blocks of each other now for the first time became acquainted and were inspired to work for the common cause. Some groups were so enthusiastic over the idea that they continued to hold meetings regularly after Lent. The Dean and chapter have continued to modify the group idea and to employ it in a variety of ways ever since. Groups, or group leaders, have taken part in the visitation of new members, have called on the sick, and acted as telephone agents for other projects. Recently groups have been combined into districts, under dis-

---

21. The leaders of this conference were: the Rev. Grant Morrill, Mrs. Cornelia Haines and Miss Helene Schnurbush. The topics discussed were: 1. Religion is meaningless to many—why 2. God's redemptive pattern. 3. You fit into God's pattern. The team also had a large display of Church literature, much of which had already been used at St. Mary's. The meeting was, in a sense, preparatory for the "new curriculum."

trict chairmen. The present chairman general, Mr. Joseph M. Patten, Jr., has organized regular weekly meetings with his district chairmen (a Monday noon luncheon at the King Cotton Hotel), and these dedicated laymen have extended the work of the church by planning the visitations, sick calls, and other pastoral services performed by the groups. Partly as a result of the enthusiasm generated by this device, partly because of the chapter's Bear Creek experiment, the Dean and chapter decided to launch the Centennial Program in 1955. It was in this same year that the Dean decided to channel the attention not so much to the homes and regions as to the church as the central focus, and to widen the base from adult participation to family participation. Thus in Lent 1955 the first of the "Family Nights" was launched. Here the technique was for group chairmen to alert and make reservations for a weekly family dinner in the crypt (a tremendous undertaking for the Woman's Auxiliary, which often had to feed over 400 at each meeting). Dinner (5:30-6:30) was followed by a short period of hymn singing as members gathered in the Cathedral; then from 7-7:20 there was a service of Evening Prayer. After this the adults remained for a meditation by Dean Sanders. The children and young people went to their departments for a period of instruction. (This took the place of the weekly mission for children that the Cathedral formerly had held during Lent.)

The same pattern was followed in 1956, but in 1957 some new features were added. During the final instruction period, instead of a message from the Dean the congregation was somewhat surprised to find three characters in the pulpit, one in an alb, one in a business suit and one in a black cloak. These were the three participants in a trialogue called *Man in the Middle,* written by Dean Pike and Howard A. Johnson of St. John the Divine, which portrayed "the conversation of a tempted soul and two voices (one a heavenly voice and one a satanic voice) on the seven deadly sins." The three roles were taken by the Dean and his two deacons, James Coleman and John Davis. Though they reversed roles each week, many felt that the one playing the satanic voice acted most realistically. Another and more significant change than the substitution of a trialogue for a monologue was made in the family nights of 1957, for this was the year the Dean "took the women out of the kitchen." It had become obvious since the first family night that in spite of the good accomplished, the strain of preparing so many meals was a wearing one on the Auxiliary. After many consultations and much planning, it was decided to employ a regular caterer for this (and for many of the other meals now seemingly such an integral part of church life). This was a real revolution, and it remains for the future to prove how much good the women will accomplish on their "released time."

Before leaving the subject of regional groups and family nights two recent activities emanating from them need be mentioned. In the diocesan Convention of 1955 it was decided to import a team of sociological experts from the National Church to make a thorough survey of the diocese. To this end every parish had to furnish certain pertinent data and a census containing some required information on each member to the visiting team. At the Cathedral this task was entrusted to a committee headed by Mr. C. L. Springfield and Mr. W. Clark Williams. In November they entrusted to the group leaders the job of collecting the census information. The final Survey was completed in 1956. It contains fascinating information about religious, educational and population trends in the diocese, the city of Memphis and St. Mary's parish, and made recommendations on the problems that seem to confront these places. At the Bear Creek chapter meeting of 1956, Mr. Williams and the Dean made a detailed report on the findings of the Survey and posted the interesting charts it contained.

At the time of this writing, the most recent aspect of the family night is in operation as one phase of St. Mary's Centennial Celebration. Heretofore, family nights have been confined to the Lenten season. This year (1957-58) they are being held monthly, on the second Wednesday night of each month, and follow the same general pattern. The unique feature of this series, however, is that each meeting is conducted by a different young priest who has gone into the ministry (as postulant and candidate) from St. Mary's during the past decade. The Dean has often referred to this increase in the ministry as "the most thrilling aspect" of his own work. He has every reason to be humbly proud of the Cathedral's record and boastfully proud of the men who are conducting these services. They are: The Rev. Fred C. Wolf, Jr., rector of St. John's Church, Corsicana, Texas; The Rev. Warren Haynes of St. Mary's, Dyersburg; the Rev. Robert J. Matthews of St. Barnabas', Tullahoma; the Rev. William Ray of St. Paul's, Franklin; the Rev. C. Allen Cooke of St. Mark's, Copperhill; and the Rev. L. Anderson Orr of the Church of the Redeemer, Shelbyville. One should also mention that in addition to these priests the Cathedral now has three postulants for the ministry. Two of them, Robert Rickard and Donald Williamson, are now in seminary, and the third, Hubert Jones, who so ably directed youth work at the community center, intends to enter seminary this fall (1958). This is a truly remarkable record for the past ten years, when we consider that during the preceding ninety years not more than three or four men had gone into the priesthood from this parish.

During the Dean's regime several new guilds were organized or reorganized.[22] The attendance of many members of the Auxiliary at the DuBose summer conference did much to strengthen the women's activity and devotion. A group of young women, inspired by the 1956 conference, returned to the Cathedral and, anxious to make a contribution to the spir-

---

22. The *Chimes* (March 11, 1947) tells of the reorganization of St. Martha's. St. Elizabeth's and St. Dorcas were also reactivated, and a "new guild of young women" (St. Anne's) was formed February 17, 1952.

itual life of the parish, conceived the plan for launching a Cathedral Bookstore. During the late summer months they negotiated for the purchase of the small Episcopal Bookshop in the Arcade building and had the old choir room in the crypt transformed into an attractive shop and, retaining Miss Juliette Allein as manager, opened for business on October 1, 1956.[23] This has been a venture of faith and hard work which has been enormously beneficial and has indirectly helped inspire the movement to redecorate the crypt. Of course the bookstore represents but one of the many phases of the constant and sacrificial work of the Auxiliary. Its general program is one of worship, service, study and giving. The particulars of this program are so varied it is impossible to mention all, for besides what might be called its routine activities—caring for the altar, the grounds, the kitchen, the coffee hour, and giving medicines, clothes, books, etc., to hospitals and missions—the Auxiliary has within the past few years furnished a group of trained women who have gone as visitors to the Western State Hospital, and has another group which have been active in making

---

23. The Dean, in the *Chimes* of September 16, 1956, gives the following account of the transaction: "The past few weeks have been exciting and busy weeks for the Cathedral Auxiliary as they have been studying, planning, and working toward the purchase of the Episcopal Book Shop . . . Quarters for the new bookshop will be in an entirely renovated room entered through the west door of the crypt. This move has caught the imagination and enthusiasm of the members of the Woman's Auxiliary as well as of the whole Cathedral . . . Many people have been called on and have responded . . . with great generosity. Mrs. William Lea has accepted the role as chairman of the Book Shop —the aspects of organization had to be dealt with and were carried out by the tireless efforts of Mrs. J. M. Patten, Jr., and Mrs. Ben Adams. The taking of inventory of the stock and the setting up of the financial procedures have been under the direction of Miss Harriette Frank. The preparation of the room . . . has involved many. Mrs. Lea . . . has spent many hours and has been wonderfully assisted and guided by Mr. Roy Cotner. Mrs. William E. Sanders has organized a committee to work with the manager in the method of purchasing the stock and Mrs. Clark Williams is in charge of the important program of publicity. Mrs. Allen Hughes and Mrs. Jeff Brown are in charge of the volunteers. Mrs. Bert Stegall has served on the General Committee. Many others have played a part in this work. I am deeply confident it will be of real spiritual benefit to the life of our parish and to the church in Memphis . . . It remains now for us to put our energy and interest behind this good work and I know that this will be done." The women obtained a loan of $4,000 from the Chapter's Reserve Fund for the undertaking.

clerical vestments and altar decorations for young clergymen and for mission churches.

Two offshoots of the Men's Council developed during the early fifties. In November 1952 a Cathedral Brotherhood was organized.[24] This was a small group willing to work at almost anything the Dean needed, from repairing church furniture to calling on new members. Not long after this (1954) another group reactivated the Cathedral chapter of the Brotherhood of St. Andrew. Within recent years, however, the work of groups such as these, and even of the Men's Council, has been merged into the broader activities of the groups and of the "Family Nights." During the 1950's laymen from the Cathedral became greatly interested in the DuBose Laymen's Conference. The large group which went to the 1954 conference won the coveted cedar bucket, the prize to the parish with most men in attendance. They have run second since, which means that St. Mary's sends more men than do the majority of the larger parishes.

Unfortunately lack of space and lack of early records has meant that the fine and outstanding work of the Church School has had to go mainly unrecorded (in Appendix G will be found a list of former superintendents and a list of the present Church School organization). It should be pointed out, however, that from its earliest years St. Mary's has always laid great emphasis on its Church School. Many important innova-

---

24. Although the Cathedral Brotherhood merged its activity into the "group organization," its members still carry their signed pledge cards. These read as follows: Desiring to more effectively discharge my duties as a Christian and to assume my personal responsibility for the furtherance of the work of the Cathedral, I agree with a group of my fellow members to faithfully perform the following to the best of my ability, with the help of God:
1. Attend church services every Sunday.
2. Bring at least one new person into active membership each year.
3. Represent St. Mary's Cathedral in inter-parish and diocesan meetings.
4. Cooperate with men's work of the Cathedral.
5. Set up and follow a personal rule to strengthen my spiritual life daily.
6. Prayerfully consider and give my proportionate share for the support of St. Mary's Cathedral.

tions have been launched (teacher's training, kindergarten, Vacation Bible School, Lenten Missions, etc.). The school has always kept in close contact with the National department of Religious Education. Thanks also to the fact that its superintendents have usually been prominent and active chapter members (e.g., Messrs. Moody, Patten, Huddleston, Turman, Perry), the chapter has maintained an active interest in its work. One significant change of recent years must be mentioned. For years the National Church has been preparing a "new curriculum" for the Church School. In the early 1950's Miss Ellen Correll, Mr. Russell Perry, and the Dean began to attend diocesan and interparochial conferences to study the new approach and to read the new literature. In the spring of 1955 they began the task of explaining the program to the Church School staff and of incorporating it into the school. The family aspect of the Church School has long been stressed at St. Mary's, but the renewed emphasis on having families worship together led the Bear Creek chapter meeting of 1955 to authorize a new schedule of church services in order to make the program more effective (it is still in force). Thus early Holy Communion remained at 7:30, but at 9 A.M. a new "family service" was inaugurated. Parents could thus bring their children to this service before attending Church School (9:30-10:20), or start with Church School and remain for a 10:45 service (which replaced the former 11 o'clock service). The Cathedral has found both the "new curriculum" and the new time of services helpful.

Two achievements of the present regime, mentioned early in this section, remain to be considered: The Cathedral's part in community work and the establishment of Quintard House as the focus for work in the nearby medical center. Practically every dean since the Civil War has felt a sense of responsibility for aiding in the spiritual and physical development of the residents of the crowded and decaying region near the

Cathedral. Father Klein began a gymnasium, a soup kitchen and a hospital in the 1880's but these were later abandoned. His successors in the early years of this century tried clubs, kindergartens, ball teams, scout groups and the like. The Auxiliary has also nearly always had an active Social Service Committee which has rendered aid and comfort. But Dean Sanders has striven to put less emphasis on the charity and Social Service aspect of this work and instead to bring the neighborhood into the life of the parish. It was the completion of the new Parish Hall building, with its gymnasium and other recreational facilities, that gave him and his helpers the physical plant from which to launch a really significant program. This building was dedicated in April 1952. In July of that year Mr. Robertson Eppes, a newly ordained deacon, was sent by Bishop Barth (and partly paid by the diocese) to be an assistant to the Dean in two spheres of work: community activity and mission work.[25] The Dean did not have enough time when he was sole priest in charge at St. Mary's to keep very close supervision on this neighborhood activity. The Rev. Mr. (soon Canon) Eppes could undertake this, and with the help of a staff partly of paid and partly of volunteer workers, he supervised and developed the clubs for boys and girls of all age groups which had already been started earlier by the Dean and by volunteer workers.[26] On Sundays Mr. Eppes, with the

25. Mr. Eppes was born in South Carolina, received an engineering degree from North Carolina State College (1943), was a 1st Lieutenant in the Army Signal Corps, and worked for a time with the Tennessee Eastman Corporation. In 1949, he entered Virginia Theological Seminary and was ordained deacon July 15, 1952, and priest on February 28, 1953.

26. For many years prior to the opening of the Community Center, Miss Ellen Correll, Miss Lillian Smith, Miss Sarah Sadler and Mr. and Mrs. Robert Clark labored in the Cathedral neighborhood, and paved the way for the later organized activity. The work in Dean Sanders' time seems to have had its beginning when Mrs. Fred Bryson and Mrs. DeWitt Johnston organized a "Friendly Girls Club" in the crypt. Soon thereafter Messrs. J. M. Patten, Jr., Clark Williams, Elton Burrows and William Deupree began to meet with boys on Thursday nights. Then James Monteith, Russell Douglas, Jack Davis began to assist with basketball and other sports. Often in the summer young seminarians (Sidney Sanders, Allen Cooke, Robert Rickard) have helped with the ball teams and clubs. By the time the new Parish Hall was completed it was decided to procure salaried supervisors for the work. These have been: Allene

help of Cathedral lay readers (A. J. V. Ware, William Ray, Clark Williams) and with some from other parishes, took charge of three neighboring missions; Collierville, Somerville, and LaGrange (and often others). Canon Eppes (ordained priest at the Cathedral on February 28, 1953, and married to Miss Nelsie McGehee on October 21, 1953) rendered the Dean and the Cathedral valiant service until he left (July 1956) to take charge of All Saints, one of the new east Memphis missions which the Bishop and the Shelby Planning Committee had by then established. He was replaced, for one year, by an able and consecrated deacon, the Rev. James Coleman. Mr. Coleman devoted almost his entire time to community work and to the young people of the Cathedral. However, he had been sent by the Bishop for only a year, and though the members of the Cathedral rejoiced with him in his ordination to the priesthood (May 6, 1957), they watched him depart for his new assignment (Gallatin and Lebanon) with regret and sorrow (July 1957).

Due to its location the Cathedral was a logical place for work with the great medical center which has grown in the heart of the city and now extends from Union Avenue to Washington Avenue. In Bishop Maxon's time, when he and the National Church were pushing the formation of Canterbury Clubs in colleges and universities, Dean Noe and Dean Hoag had been given general supervision of the clubs formed for student nurses and medical students. The Dean of the Cathedral was often the person whom out-of-town Episcopal patients or their families called on for consolation or advice. The Canterbury Club died out during the war. After Mr.

Ogden and her mother, Mrs. F. E. Ogden, Barbara Fox, Hubert Jones and Pat Baskin. By the time Mr. Eppes left, with the help of many volunteer assistants, the following educational and recreational clubs were in existence: 1) Beginners Girls Club; 2) Story Hour; 3) Middlers Girls Club; 4) Senior Girls Club; 5) Music Appreciation Class; 6) Junior Boys Club; 7) Middlers Boys Club; 8) Junior High Boys Club; 9) Senior High Boys Club; 10) Cub Scouts; 11) Teen Time; 12) Poplar Teens. When the center is in full operation some club is meeting every afternoon and on Friday and Saturday evenings.

Sanders became dean several young doctors from the University of Tennessee joined St. Mary's, and as early as 1949 the Dean and Dr. McCool brought some of them into discussion groups held at the Cathedral. It would seem (from the *Chimes*) that the first specifically "Medical Group" was organized in 1952 by the Dean and Dr. McCool, assisted by Dr. James Biles, Dr. Jack Von Lackum and Dr. Jesse Perkinson.[27] Originally the class met both Sunday morning and evening, but it soon became an evening discussion group which met at the Diocesan House for a light collation and for the consideration of many of the problems in which medicine and religion overlap. As a result of consultations of the Bishop with the St. Mary's group, the Memphis clergy, and with doctors from the medical center, a house was rented on the corner of Washington and Dunlap which, when redecorated and furnished, was christened Quintard House in honor of Tennessee's famous doctor bishop. Bishop Barth was fortunate in securing as its first director the Rev. H. Sheldon Davis (October 1954).[28] He was soon made a Canon of the Cathedral, and in the two years he remained at Quintard House did a wonderful work in creating a real place at the medical center for Quintard House, in visiting and ministering to the sick, and in letting the parishes of Memphis and the diocese know of this new work. He endeared himself to the Cathedral congregation, where he often celebrated Holy Communion, preached, and became one of the family. It was a hard blow to the work he had organized and to his many friends in Memphis when he decided that his true vocation lay in a country parish. In June 1956 he removed from Quintard House to Quintard parish. Unfortunately, the Bishop and the

27. One of the first committees entrusted with the task of planning for the group consisted of the Dean, Dr. Perkinson, Dean Ruth Neal Murry, Dr. Charles Clark, Mr. A. W. Shelby, Dr. McCool, Dr. John Wood and Dr. T. S. Hill.

28. Howard Sheldon Davis was born at Bethayre, Pennsylvania, April 14, 1912. He received his B.A. from Amherst, and B.D. from the Philadelphia Theological Seminary. He was ordained priest in December 1943, served in Brookline, Pennsylvania, and as a chaplain before becoming rector of the Church of the Good Shepherd in Forrest City, Arkansas (1946-1954).

committee on Quintard House had great difficulty in finding a successor to Canon Davis, and the House lay dormant during the entire academic year of 1956-57. On June 2, 1957, Bishop Barth announced the appointment of Canon Rue Moore to Quintard House. He arrived in the late summer and with the help of an active Auxiliary committee began to repair, to repaint and redecorate his headquarters. He has created an Oratory of St. Luke at Quintard and is hard at work in his new cure reactivating and expanding the work begun in 1954.

The chapter had long recognized the fact that the work at St. Mary's was too heavy for one man, even for a young one. True, since 1952 the Dean had (besides his perpetual deacon) first Canon Eppes and then deacon Coleman, but these young men who were attached only temporarily to the Cathedral had so many specific duties that they were unable to assist in general parish work. In the spring of 1957, even before Mr. Coleman left, the chapter began an active search for an assistant to the dean, one whose duties would be primarily parochial. By March 31 it was able to announce that it had located the "ideal assistant" (one recommended by the Dean himself) in the person of the Rev. Frank Cayce of Mayfield, Kentucky.[29] Mr. Cayce met the chapter in the May Bear Creek meeting, and moved his family to the new home procured for him at 1868 Vinton in June. His energy and organizational ability are already in evidence, one of his first efforts being to promote an adult education program in the Church School.[30] The new Canon has also been helpful in the latest reorganization of the cathedral

29. Frank Quarles Cayce was born in Hopkinsville, Kentucky, July 4, 1915. He was educated at Emory University and was in business before entering the ministry. He received his theological training at Virginia Theological Seminary, was ordained deacon in January and priest in November 1954. He served in missions centering in Mayfield before coming to the Cathedral.

30. His program, announced by letter and in the *Chimes* of September 15, 1957, elicited an amazing response. About two hundred adults registered for the five classes: 1) Heroes of the Faith (A.J.V. Ware), 2) New Testament Study (Dean Sanders), 3) The Episcopal Church (J. H. Davis), to be followed by a Prayer Book Study (Canon Knox), 4) Families and the Church (Canon Cayce), and 5) The Church in Literature (Professor Dan Ross).

office. The Dean gave the following explanation of this needed step in the *Chimes* of October 20, 1957:

> All of you who have even a faint inkling of the work and program of the Cathedral have realized how desperately we have needed a more adequate office staff. For many years, Miss Correll, who was listed as Director of Religious Education, worked night and day alone to keep up the records, the bookkeeping, the correspondence and all the other manifold details that are essential in the operation of a Parish Church.
>
> A few years ago, we took the first step toward this end by adding Mrs. Mary Van Zandt to our staff. Mrs. Van Zandt took over the secretarial work, the files and general office routine, while Miss Correll still had to take care of the financial records, the supervision of the buildings and staff . . . The work was more than two human beings could do. Still these two women gave unsparingly and devotedly of themselves and their time . . . I am personally deeply grateful for them. Unfortunately during the late summer Mrs. Van Zandt became ill . . . and has moved to Mason . . .
>
> At a meeting of our Cathedral Chapter in September, leaders of the Woman's Auxiliary and other church groups were invited to discuss our needs for a more adequate office staff, and to develop plans to meet them. Though we had gathered merely to discuss the possibility of long-term planning, this group unanimously came to the conclusion we should act now to remedy the situation . . .
>
> All of this is a long but exciting way of getting to the point that I am today happy to introduce to you our present office staff. Miss Correll is being freed from all work except that of her special love and talent, Religious Education. Miss Margaret Crump has accepted the position of Parish Secretary and Mrs. Ethel Crawford the position of Financial Secretary. Mrs. Crawford will also supervise the housekeeping and kitchen . . . Both Miss Crump and Mrs. Crawford come from the business world. Both are Churchwomen and their devotion to the Church was the determining factor of their entrance into their present vocation.

After the departure of Mr. Coleman, the chapter decided to employ a full time priest to have charge of community activity. The Rev. Robert Knox was persuaded to accept this post of Canon for Community Work. His coming was announced in the *Chimes* of September 8, 1958. Father Knox arrived in Memphis in October and has been furnished one of the old "landmark houses" on Adams and is launching into his new duties as the centennial year dawns.[31] It was in November that the Bishop announced the appointment of Father George Fox of Chattanooga to be a diocesan canon missioner who will conduct retreats, preaching missions, etc., throughout the diocese, working from Nashville. The year 1957 may well go down in Cathedral history as "the year of canons."

The first century of St. Mary's is ending (and this sketch of its history is ending on New Year's Eve). In this hundred years it has lived through many vicissitudes, wars, woes, pestilences and setbacks. By contrast the past decade has been remarkable for almost continuous advance. Ten years ago the Dean was the sole priest in the parish, now there are two canons in residence and two diocesan canons (one in Memphis and one in Nashville) and two perpetual deacons to assist in various aspects of Cathedral work. The Cathedral structure is completed and refurbished; the active membership has increased greatly between 1947 and 1957; the budget has increased from $28,000 in 1948 to over $100,000 in 1958. The Cathedral now stands on the threshold of its second century. Let us hope that it needs no Amos to warn against the dangers of prosperity, no Greek dramatist to warn of the sin of *hybris*. Instead, may it continue to serve, to attempt to solve the ever-changing problems of our complex age, to clarify and strengthen its relationship to the diocese, and to further the Kingdom of God, else its builders have labored in vain.

---

31. Robert Walter Knox was born June 22, 1918, at Thomaston, Georgia. He is a B.A. from Emory University, B.D. from Nashotah House and studied at New College, Oxford (1952-4). He was ordained deacon in October 1944 and priest, September 1945. He has served at Grace Church, Cherry Valley, New York, and in the Church of St. Michael and All Angels, Baltimore, before coming to St. Mary's.

In attempting to write the history of the first hundred years of St. Mary's, it has been painfully obvious to the writer how many important events, organizations, and people have had to be omitted (though some may equally claim that too many have been included). But a historian is compelled, to a great extent, to follow his sources, and since the sources deal primarily with the bishops, deans and chapters—in other words, the "High Command," the reader may complain that the role of the "humble private" (and it is the ordinary communicant who really gives life and meaning to a parish) has been neglected.

I confess there is justification for this complaint, and I concur in it, for church histories, like military histories, are usually written from the viewpoint of the generals and as many have pointed out, it is the behavior of the unnamed private in the ranks which makes or breaks the best laid plans of the commanding officers. Thus I feel that I have neglected not only the roles of the privates of the church (the devoted guild members, choir members, altar guild workers, acolytes, church school teachers, ushers, Y.P.S.L. janitors, cooks, etc.) but even those of the noncommissioned officers (Auxiliary, Guild, Church School, Men's Council officials). But they are partly to blame for leaving poor records. I hope that anyone who feels offended by the omission of his (or her) name will have the consolation of knowing that it will have been duly recorded in a book far more important than any earthly history.

APPENDIX

The Episcopate In Tennessee

JAMES HERVEY OTEY, D.D., LL.D.

Born January 27, 1800, Bedford County, Virginia. Ordained by Bishop Ravenscroft (North Carolina): Deacon 1825, Priest 1827. Consecrated as First Bishop of Tennessee, 30th in American Succession, in Philadelphia, January 14, 1834; chief consecrator, Presiding Bishop William White. Died April 23, 1863.

CHARLES TODD QUINTARD, MD., D.D., LL.D.

Born December 22, 1824, Stamford, Connecticut. Ordained by Bishop Otey: Deacon 1855, Priest 1856. Consecrated as Second Bishop of Tennessee 75th in American Succession, in Philadelphia, October 11, 1865; chief consecrator, Presiding Bishop John Henry Hopkins. Died February 15, 1898.

THOMAS FRANK GAILOR, S.T.D., LL.D., D.D. (Oxon)

Born September 17, 1856, Jackson, Mississippi. Ordained by Bishop Quintard: Deacon 1879, Priest 1880. Consecrated as Bishop Coadjutor of Tennessee, 170th in American Succession, Sewanee, St. James' Day, 1893; chief consecrator, Bishop Quintard. Third Bishop of the Diocese, February 15, 1898. Died October 3, 1935.

TROY BEATTY, D.D.

Born November 12, 1866, Tuscaloosa, Alabama. Ordained: Deacon by Bishop Gregg for Bishop Quintard, 1891; Priest by Bishop Quintard, 1892. Consecrated as Bishop Coadjutor of Tennessee, 301st in American Succession, in Memphis, September 18, 1919; chief consecrator, Presiding Bishop Daniel Sylvester Tuttle. Died April 23, 1922.

JAMES MATTHEW MAXON, D.D., LL.D.

Born January 1, 1875, Bay City, Michigan. Ordained by Bishop Fawcett (Quincy): Deacon 1907, Priest 1907. Consecrated as Bishop Coadjutor of Tennessee, 323rd in American Succession, in Nashville, St. Luke's Day, 1922; chief consecrator, Bishop Gailor. Fourth Bishop of the Diocese, October 3, 1935. Resigned January 1, 1947. Died November 8, 1948.

EDMUND PENDLETON DANDRIDGE, D.D.

Born September 5, 1881, Flushing, New York. Ordained (West Virginia): Deacon by Bishop Gravatt, 1906; Priest by Bishop Peterkin, 1908. Consecrated as Bishop Coadjutor of Tennessee, 407th in American Succession, in Nashville, September 20, 1938; chief consecrator, Presiding Bishop Henry St. George Tucker. Fifth Bishop of the Diocese, January 1, 1947. Resigned September 20, 1953.

THEODORE NOTT BARTH, D.D.

Born July 11, 1898, Mount Savage, Maryland. Ordained by Bishop Murray (Maryland): Deacon 1921, Priest 1922. Consecrated as Bishop Coadjutor of Tennessee, 482nd in American Succession, in Memphis, St. Matthew's Day, 1948; chief consecrator, Presiding Bishop Henry Knox Sherrill. Sixth Bishop of the Diocese, September 20, 1953.

JOHN VANDER HORST, D.D.

Born January 10, 1912, Orange, New Jersey. Ordained by Bishop Helfenstein (Maryland): Deacon 1938, Priest 1939. Consecrated as Suffragan Bishop of Tennessee, 534th in American Succession, in Chattanooga, March 2, 1955; chief consecrator, Presiding Bishop Henry Knox Sherrill.

First Communicants

A list of the first communicants of St. Mary's, as they appear in the *Register*, with the remarks attached.

Mrs. J. M. McCombs	Removed to St. Louis, May 1872
Miss Estelle Lamb	
Mrs. C. M. Gailor	Removed to Pulaski, 1879
Mrs. S. H. Brooks	
Mrs. Julie Howe	Removed to Texas, summer of 1875
Mrs. E. Finley	Died September 5, 1901
Anne M. Hilson	
Mrs. A. Hilson	
Thomas F. Gailor	Removed to Pulaski, ordained deacon May 1879
Eliza C. Quintard	
Clara E. Quintard	
Charles T. Quintard	
Lizzie DuBose Thorn	Reported lapsed to Convention of 1876
Mrs. James Meigs	Removed to Grace Church
Mrs. R. C. Brinkley	
James M. Brinkley	Does not commune
Mrs. Richard Hines	
Rev. Richard Hines	Removed
Richard Hines, Jr.	Removed
Mrs. E. Yerger	
Jenny Yerger	Removed to Somerville
Avery Lamb	
Sidney R. Lamb	Died August 18, 1882
C. A. S. Richardson	Died August, 1880
Mrs. C. A. Richardson	
Mrs. James Woods	Removed June 1871, returned 1872, died March 14, 1889
Peter Wager	April 26, 1871 ordained deacon by Rev. C. T. Quintard
Mrs. P. Wager	
Mrs. Hugh Rose	Removed to Grace Church, 1871
Miss Fanny Rose	Removed, reported to Convention of 1876
Miss Emma Rose	Removed to Grace Church, 1872
Miss Anna Rose	Removed to Grace Church
Mrs. M. H. Skipworth	Reported removed to Convention of 1876
Mrs. G. P. Fouts	Reported removed to Convention of 1877
Miss Ethel Fouts	Reported removed to Convention of 1877
Ed Fegan	Removed 1872
Anna Fegan	Removed 1872
Henry Fegan	Removed 1872
Mrs. Harrison	Removed to Grace Church, 1879
Mrs. Leroy Pope	Removed
Dr. Voorhies	Reported lapsed to Convention of 1876
Mrs. Voorhies	Reported lapsed to Convention of 1876
John P. Trezevant	Died of yellow fever, September 1878
Mrs. Thomas Hunt	Removed to Calvary Church
Thomas Hunt, Jr.	Reported lapsed to Convention of 1876
Mrs. Clemmons	Removed to Missouri, 1880
Katy Russell McComb	Removed to St. Louis, 1872
Liza Nash McComb	Removed to St. Louis, 1872

The Deans and Acting Deans of St. Mary's

Richard Hines, D.D., Rector 1857-1868; listed as Dean, 1868-1871

George C. Harris, D.D., listed as Assistant Minister 1871, 1872; as Dean, 1873-1880

William Klein, listed as Canon, 1881; as Dean, 1882-92

Howard Dumbell, Dean 1893-1894
(Dr. Tupper, 1895)

Charles H. B. Turner, Dean 1895-1897
(J. P. McCullough, 1897)

Stephen H. Green, Dean 1898-1901

James Craik Morris, Dean 1901-1916
(Arthur H. Noll, 1916)

Frederick DuMontier DeVall, Dean 1917-1921
(Arthur H. Noll, A. C. Killefer, C. P. Parker, 1921)

Israel Harding Noe, Dean 1921-1938
(James R. Sharp, 1938)

Harold Brown Hoag, Dean 1938-1945
(James R. Clarke, Joseph Bernardin, 1946)

William Evan Sanders, Assistant, 1946; Acting Dean 1947; Dean 1947-

Canons, Archdeacons, Assistants and Lay Readers

A list of (A) Clergy who have been appointed Canons of the Cathedral; (B) Archdeacons of West Tennessee; (C) Assistants on the Cathedral staff; (D) Lay readers. This list is probably incomplete.

A. CANONS

Charles C. Parsons	Spruille Burford	Hiram Douglass
George White	Arthur H. Noll	Robertson Eppes
V. O. Gee	Paul Williams	H. Sheldon Davis
Ridley Gray	Charles S. Ware	Frank Q. Cayce
William Klein	T. Porter Simpson	Rue L. Moore
G. C. Harris	James R. Sharp	Robert W. Knox
George Patterson	James M. Maxon	George A. Fox

B. ARCHDEACONS

Alexander McCabe	Benjamin F. Root	Charles K. Weller

C. ON THE STAFF (*indicates "perpetual deacon")

James Vaulx	F. A. Juny, Sr.	Stanley Young*
Alfred Todhunter	F. A. Juny, Jr.	David S. Rose
Louis Schuyler	R. Calder Young	Sterling Tracy
William Dalzell	G. R. Cadman	John H. Davis*
W. B. Huson	Alfred Loaring-Clark	James Coleman
G. S. Fisse	Guy Usher	M. C. Nichols*

D. LAY READERS

C. B. Coate	J. E. Deupree	Hobart Turman
Frank Baum	Sam Loring	Fred Wolf
Duncan Martin	William Deupree	William Ray
Stanley Young	J. H. Davis	Clark Williams
Joseph R. Murphy	A. J. V. Ware	

Vestries and Chapters of St. Mary's

(Omitting Names of Bishops, Deans and Chancellors)
From 1880 new names appearing will be in italics.

1858-1866 No records

1867 J. P. Trezevant (SW), E. Bradley, W. L. Henderson, E. J. Walton, J. A. Omberg, B. S. Stewart, W. Goodman, W. W. Carnes, H. Forrester (Sect.), J. A. Hayes, Jr., W. R. Scott (JW)
(E. Bradley resigned, and E. Fegan elected; J. W. Scott removed and Robert Steele elected; Mr. Swingley replaced W. Goodman; Carnes removed, and replaced by F. P. Wolcott; Mr. Fegan made JW)

1868 J. P. Trezevant (SW), E. Fegan (JW), S. Lamb, H. Forrester, B. S. Stewart, J. H. Haynes, W. L. Henderson, J. Weld, James Stuart, A. L. Swingley (Fegan resigned, S. Lamb made JW; J. Stuart removed from town)

1869 J. P. Trezevant (SW), E. Fegan (JW), Dr. A. H. Voorhies, Dr. R. S. Green, J. A. Hayes, Jr. (Hayes resigned, P. Wager elected Sect.)

1870 John P. Trezevant (SW), E. Fegan (JW), S. H. Lamb, Dr. S. P. Green, Peter Wager

1871-1879 No records

1880 S. H. Lamb (SW), George Faxon (JW), R. F. Phillip, Spence Finlay, B. W. Crow.

1881 S. H. Lamb (SW), *George Yerger,* Spence Finlay, *F. W. Cruse, Malcolm McDowell, C. B. Coate, James Richardson, C. C. Currier*

1882 S. H. Lamb (SW), *Thomas Morgan, W. Shuttleworth,* S. Finlay, F. Cruse, *C. C. Currier, J. B. Dallon,* J. W. Richardson, G. Yerger, M. McDonald, C. B. Coate

1883 *F. W. Royster,* S. H. Lamb, W. Shuttleworth, T. Morgan, J. W. Richardson, C. C. Currier, C. B. Coate, G. Yerger, S. L. Finlay, F. Cruse, M. H. McDowell

1884 Not listed

1885 S. H. Lamb, F. Royster, W. Shuttleworth, C. B. Coate, C. C. Currier, G. Yerger, M. McDonald, S. Finlay, J. Richardson, *T. J. Clarke*

1886 S. H. Lamb, W. Shuttleworth, F. Royster, *T. Counsell,* C. B. Coate, *J. N. Scott,* T. J. Clarke

1887 S. H. Lamb, W. Shuttleworth, F. W. Royster, T. G. Counsell, T. Clarke, C. C. Currier, M. McDowell, C. B. Coate, *R. G. Brown, T. M. Scruggs*

1888 S. H. Lamb, F. Royster, T. Counsell, T. J. Clarke, C. C. Currier, M. McDowell, C. B. Coate, R. G. Brown, *W. R. Overman*

1889 S. H. Lamb, F. Royster, W. Overman, C. B. Coate, M. McDowell, C. C. Currier, T. J. Clarke, R. G. Brown, *A. J. Warwick*

1890 S. H. Lamb, C. C. Currier, A. J. Warwick, T. J. Clarke, C. B. Coate, *F. Schas,* M. McDowell, R. Brown, *P. S. Coate*

1891 No record

1892 No record

1893 S. H. Lamb, M. McDowell, P. S. Coate, C. B. Coate, T. J. Clarke, A. J. Warwick, C. C. Currier, R. G. Brown, *M. S. Buckingham*

1894 S. H. Lamb, M. Buckingham, C. B. Coate, C. C. Currier, A. J. Warwick, P. S. Coate, *G. B. Faxon*

1895 S. H. Lamb, M. Buckingham, C. B. Coate, C. C. Currier, T. J. Clarke, A. J. Warwick, P. S. Coate, G. B. Faxon, F. Schas, *F. J. Baum*

1896 Missing

1897   *P. Friedel,* M. Buckingham, C. B. Coate, C. C. Currier, T. J. Clarke, A. J. Warwick, P. S. Coate, G. B. Faxon, F. Schas, F. Baum, *Bolton Smith*

1898   (Chapters began to be listed in the Convention Journal.) S. H. Lamb (SW), G. B. Faxon (JW), C. B. Coate (Clerk), M. S. Buckingham, F. J. Baum, P. S. Coate, T. J. Clarke, C. C. Currier, P. R. Friedel, F. Schas, A. J. Warwick

1899   G. B. Faxon (SW), P. R. Friedel (JW), C. B. Coate (Treas. and Clerk), F. J. Baum, M. S. Buckingham, T. J. Clarke, P. S. Coate, C. C. Currier, F. Schas, B. Smith, A. J. Warwick

1900   The same members

1901   The same members

1902   The same members

1903   The same members, except G. B. Faxon (clerk) and F. Baum (treas.), C. B. Coate, off.

1904   The same members

1905   The same members

1906   The same members, adds *W. I. Moody*

1907   G. B. Faxon (SW and clerk), P. R. Friedel (JW), F. J. Baum, M. Buckingham, T. J. Clarke, P. Stenning Coate, C. C. Currier, F. Schas, B. Smith, A. J. Warwick, W. I. Moody, F. Baum (Treas.)

1908   B. Smith (SW), P. R. Friedel (JW), F. Baum (clerk and Treas.), P. S. Coate, M. Buckingham, *Charles Faxon,* F. Schas, T. J. Clarke, W. I. Moody, C. C. Currier, A. J. Warwick

1909   The same members

1910   The same members

1911   B. Smith (SW), P. R. Friedel (JW), F. Baum (clerk and Treas.), P. S. Coate, M. Buckingham, T. J. Clarke, W. I. Moody, A. J. Warwick

1912   B. Smith (SW), P. R. Friedel (JW), F. Baum (clerk and Treas.), W. I. Moody, A. J. Warwick, P. S. Coate, T. J. Clarke, M. S. Buckingham, *J. A. Evans*

1913   B. Smith (SW), P. Friedel (JW), F. Baum (clerk and Treas.), M. S. Buckingham, *C. N. Burch, T. B. Blake,* T. J. Clarke, P. S. Coate, C. C. Currier, J. A. Evans, W. I. Moody, A. J. Warwick

1914   The same members

1915   The same members

1916   B. Smith (SW), P. Friedel (JW), F. Baum (clerk and Treas.), C. N. Burch, P. S. Coate, C. C. Currier, T. B. Blake, J. A. Evans, W. I. Moody, A. J. Warwick

1917   B. Smith (SW), P. Friedel (JW), F. Baum (clerk and Treas.), M. S. Buckingham, C. N. Burch, T. B. Blake, T. J. Clarke, P. S. Coate, C. C. Currier, J. A. Evans, W. I. Moody, A. J. Warwick

1918   B. Smith (SW), P. Friedel (JW), J. A. Evans, P. S. Coate, A. J. Warwick, *W. R. Friedel,* W. I. Moody, *Thomas Jackson,* C. C. Currier, M. S. Buckingham, C. N. Burch

1919   B. Smith (SW), P. Friedel (JW), *Herbert Esch* (clerk), *P. C. Clarke* (Treas.), C. C. Currier, J. A. Evans, P. S. Coate, A. J. Warwick, W. I. Moody, C. N. Burch, M. S. Buckingham, W. Friedel, A. H. Noll, Canon

1920   B. Smith (SW), J. A. Evans (JW), H. Esch (C), P. C. Clarke (T)

1921   P. S. Coate, *J. Beley,* T. H. Jackson, *W. N. Reed,* W. Friedel, A. J. Warwick, W. I. Moody, *A. S. Caldwell,* P. Friedel, *S. Loring, W. E. Barnes*

(For the period 1922-1936, I shall adopt the system used in St. Mary's *Memorial Book* and list only the names which appear for the first time on the chapter rolls.)

1922 *C. I. Barnett, Wayne Deupree, Robert N. Throckmorton, Frank Ward, Robert Wilkerson*

1923 *William D. Kyser, A. S. Petit, R. L. Taylor*

1927 *Shubael T. Beasley, Frank Fisher*

1928 *Joseph M. Patten*

1930 *Richard Bliss, Jr., Finley Faxon, Whitfield King*

1934 *H. S. Buchanan, W. R. Smith-Vaniz*

(In 1936, the new Canon XII created the new larger elected Chapter, with fifteen elected members, plus three appointed by the Bishop, plus three elected by Convention. The following abbreviations will be used: BA—Bishop's appointee; C—elected by Convention! E—elected by parish meeting; BW—Bishop's Warden; CW—Chapter's Warden.)

1936 BA—P. S. Coate (BW), *J. B. Lee, Rowlett Paine*

E—W. I. Moody (CW), L. M. Patten, P. C. Clarke (S and T), *Leroy Taylor, Amiel Brinkley, Joe Dean, J. W. Burton, R. L. Stratton, R. S. Christie, Allen Hughes, J. D. H. Meyer, Jr.,* A. J. Warwick, Whitfield King, H. S. Buchanan, A. R. Bliss

1937 BA—P. S. Coate (BW), J. B. Lee, W. R. Smith-Vaniz

C—J. W. Burton, *Martin Dunkin, O. Holly*

E—W. I. Moody (CW), P. C. Clarke (S and T), J. M. Patten, Joe Dean, R. S. Christie, Allen Hughes, *W. A. Haglin,* R. L. Stratton, A. J. Warwick, Leroy Taylor, Rowlett Paine, Whitfield King, A. Brinkley, H. S. Buchanan, J. D. H. Meyer, Jr.

(1938-1945, new names only)

1938 *Frank Hoyt Gailor*

1939 *Russell Perry, Dudley Henderson, Julian P. Williams*

1940 *J. G. Gordon, Jr., A. Leon Huddleston, Carter B. Lyon*

1941 *Matthew J. Erlicher, A. J. V. Ware*

1942 *R. R. Carrington, Louis Furbringer*

1943 *G. C. Connell*

1944 *Clifford Kulp, Hobart Turman*

1945 *D. C. McCool*

1946 BA—P. S. Coate (BW), F. H. Gailor, C. B. Lyon

C—M. J. Erlicher, R. L. Stratton, Leroy Taylor

E—W. I. Moody (CW), P. C. Clarke (S, T), G. C. Connell, H. Esch, L. Furbringer, D. Henderson, A. Hughes, C. Kulp, D. C. McCool, R. Paine, J. M. Patten, R. Perry, H. Turman, A. J. V. Ware

1947 BA—W. I. Moody (BW), F. H. Gailor, C. B. Lyon

C—M. J. Erlicher, J. G. Gordon, Jr., *John McCarroll*

E—J. M. Patten (CW), P. C. Clarke (S, T), G. C. Connell, H. Esch, L. Furbringer, D. Henderson, L. Huddleston, A. Hughes, *Franklin Kimborough,* C. Kulp, D. C. McCool, R. Perry, L. Taylor, H. Turman, A. J. V. Ware

1948 BA—W. I. Moody (BW), J. McCarroll, M. J. Erlicher

C—F. H. Gailor, C. Lyon, J. B. Lee

E—J. M. Patten (CW), P. C. Clarke (S, T), G. C. Connell, H. Esch, L. Furbringer, D. Henderson, A. Hughes, F. Kimborough, C.

Kulp, D. C. McCool, R. Perry, L. Taylor, H. Turman, A. J. V. Ware

(As may be seen from the above the elected Chapters became about as fixed as the appointed Chapters, therefore in 1949 a new method of rotation was begun. Five were elected for three years, five for two years, and five for one year. Thereafter in subsequent years five would go off the chapter, and five would be elected each year. In the remaining listings, therefore, after 1949 only the five newly elected members will be given.)

1949 BA—W. I. Moody (BW), C. Lyon, G. C. Connell

  C—J. B. Lee, *Julien Fulenwider,* M. J. Erlicher

  E—(for 3 years) J. M. Patten (CW), A. Hughes, L. Furbringer P. C. Clarke (S, T), L. Taylor

   (for 2 years) D. C. McCool, R. Perry, F. Kimborough, H. Esch, J. McCarroll

   (for 1 year) L. Huddleston, H. Turman, C. Kulp, A. J. V. Ware, *J. M. Patten, Jr.*

1950 BA—W. I. Moody (BW), C. Lyon, J. B. Lee

  C—*Mercer West, C. N. Johnston, Morris Cobb*

  E—(for three years) *Winston Braun, H. Brent Cooke, Jr., J. H. Davis, William Hudgins, Chester Perry*

1951 BA—W. I. Moody (BW), C. N. Johnston, *Leland Cranford*

  C—*E. T. Holloway, John Morris, William Deupree*

  E—C. B. Lyon, L. Huddleston, J. M. Patten, Jr., M. West, *Earl McCarroll* (and A. J. V. Ware to replace J. H. Davis now deacon)

1952 BA—J. M. Patten, Sr. (BW), E. T. Holloway, W. Deupree

  C—C. N. Johnston, J. W. Morris, *William Barr*

  E—L. Cranford, H. Esch, J. M. McCarroll, D. C. McCool, R. Perry

1953 BA—J. M. Patten, Sr. (BW), *William Ray,* P. C. Clarke (T)

  C—W. Barr, *Prentice Fulton,* J. W. Morris

  E—W. Deupree, E. T. Holloway, A. Hughes, L. Taylor, *Clarke Williams*

  By Chapter election, R. Paine, W. I. Moody

  Clergy—J. H. Davis

1954 BA—J. M. Patten, Sr. (BW), W. Ray, P. C. Clarke (T)

  C—H. B. Cooke, Jr., *Jesse Perkinson, Edward Reuter*

  E—W. Barr, *W. Embry, W. Lea,* C. Perry, *Clyde Washburn*

  Clergy—J. H. Davis, *Robertson Eppes*

1955 BA—J. M. Patten, Sr. (BW), W. Ray, P. C. Clarke (T)

  C—C. Lyon, C. N. Johnston, M. West

  E—H. B. Cooke, Jr., L. Huddleston, J. M. Patten, Jr., *R. Poole, Ray Strong*

  Honorary—W. I. Moody, R. Paine

  Clergy—R. Eppes, *H. Sheldon Davis,* J. Davis

1956 BA—J. M. Patten, Sr. (BW), C. N. Johnston, C. B. Lyon

  C—L. Cranford, *Rembert Donelson,* M. West

  E—*Tom East,* H. Esch, J. M. McCarroll, D. C. McCool, R. Perry (CW)

  Clergy—Same

1957 BA—W. Deupree (BW), C. B. Lyon, C. N. Johnston

  C—L. Cranford, E. T. Holloway, *C. L. Springfield*

  E—R. Donelson, W. Hudgins, M. West, C. Williams, *Arthur Woodside*

  Clergy—*James Coleman, F. Q. Cayce, R. Knox,* J. Davis

Lay Delegates and Alternates to Convention

* indicates did not answer roll call.
( ) indicates alternates

1858　William Armour, J. A. Anderson, John P. Trezevant
1859　William Armour, R. C. Brinkley, J. P. Trezevant
1860　No record
1861-1864　No convention *Journals*
1865　P. Wager, Z. Grey, S. Dashiell*
1866　J. P. Trezevant,* John Hines, Dr. Henderson
1867　J. P. Trezevant, B. S. Stuart, John Hines*
1868　Dr. S. P. Green, J. P. Trezevant,* B. S. Stuart*
1869　S. H. Lamb, J. P. Trezevant, S. P. Green
1870　John P. Trezevant, S. H. Lamb, A. H. Voorhies
1871　None listed
1872　None listed
1873　S. H. Lamb, E. Fegan, J. P. Trezevant
1874　George Freeman, S. H. Lamb, W. C. Wilton
1875　B. Crow, Henry Wilton, Dabney Scales
1876　S. H. Lamb, James A. Anderson, Benjamin Crow*
1877　S. H. Lamb, B. Crow, D. Scales
1878　S. H. Lamb, D. Scales, George Faxon
1879　S. H. Lamb, G. Faxon*
1880　S. H. Lamb, G. Faxon, D. M. Scales
1881　S. H. Lamb, M. H. McDowell,* Spence Finlay
1882　S. H. Lamb, S. Finlay, George Yerger
1883　S. H. Lamb, S. L. Finlay
1884　S. H. Lamb, F. W. Royster, Albert Thumel*
1885　S. H. Lamb, C. C. Currier, H. C. Wilton*
1886　S. H. Lamb, William Shuttleworth, C. B. Coate
1887　S. H. Lamb, F. W. Royster, C. C. Currier
1888　S. H. Lamb, C. B. Coate, W. H. McDowell*
1889　S. H. Lamb, C. B. Coate,* W. A. Everman*
1890　S. H. Lamb, F. Schas, A. T. Warwick
1891　None reported
1892　S. H. Lamb, C. C. Currier, A. T. Warwick
1893　S. H. Lamb, C. B. Coate
1894　S. H. Lamb, G. B. Faxon, C. C. Currier*
1895　S. H. Lamb,* G. B. Faxon, C. B. Coate*
1896　S. H. Lamb, G. B. Faxon, C. B. Coate*

1897 None reported

1898 C. C. Currier, C. B. Coate, G. B. Faxon

1899 P. R. Friedel,* F. H. Carlile, G. B. Faxon

1900 G. B. Faxon,* C. B. Coate, Duncan Martin

1901 G. B. Faxon, C. B. Coate, George M. Darrow
(F. Schas,* B. Crow,* F. J. Baum*)

1902 G. B. Faxon, D. Martin, F. J. Baum
(F. Schas,* W. E. Barnes,* Gwyn Yerger*)

1903 P. Friedel,* F. J. Baum, G. B. Faxon
(F. Schas,* T. Clarke,* Cannon)

1904 G. B. Faxon,* C. C. Currier,* P. S. Coate*
(G. Yerger,* A. J. Warwick,* W. T. Moody*)

1905 G .B. Faxon,* W. I. Moody,* D. Martin*
(Arthur Crownover)

1906 G. B. Faxon, G. Yerger,* W. I. Moody

1907 W. I. Moody,* G. B. Faxon,* C. C. Currier*
(F. Schas,* D. Martin,* W. R. Friedel*)

1908 W. I. Moody, P. Stenning Coate,* A. J. Warwick*
(D. Martin,* James Veley,* W. E. Barnes*)

1909 Bolton Smith,* W. I. Moody, F. Schas
(M. S. Buckingham,* P. S. Coate,* D. Martin)

1910 Stanley Young, W. I. Moody,* F. Schas*
(F. Baum,* D. Martin,* G. Yerger*)

1911 W. I. Moody,* W. R. Friedel,* Dr. Thomas Bailey*
(D. Martin,* W. E. Barnes,* John W. Apperson*)

1912 W. R. Friedel,* A. J. Warwick,* E. O. Gillican
(B. Smith,* W. E. Barnes,* W. I. Moody*)

1913 Bolton Smith, J. A. Evans,* Charles N. Burch
(T. Blake,* G. Yerger,* C. C. Currier)

1914 J. A. Evans, C. N. Burch, W. I. Moody
(B. Smith,* G. Yerger, T. Blake)

1915 T. B. Blake, W. R. Friedel,* W. I. Moody*

1916 T. Blake, James P. Krantz, C. N. Burch*
(P. S. Coate,* J. A. Evans,* A. J. Warwick*)

1917 C. N. Burch,* B. Smith, P. S. Coate*

1918 J. A. Evans, T. H. Jackson,* Herbert Esch
(P. S. Coate,* W. I. Moody,* A. J. Warwick

1919 B. Smith, J. A. Evans,* C. N. Burch*
(G. Yerger,* T. H. Jackson,* P. S. Coate*)

1920 Herbert Esch

1921 C. N. Burch, B. Smith, P. S. Coate
(J. A. Evans, G. Yerger,* T. H. Jackson*)

1922 J. A. Evans,* C. J. Barnett, A. J. Forbes

[247]

1923 A. S. Caldwell, C. N. Burch,* B. Smith*
1924 B. Smith,* C. N. Burch,* A. S. Caldwell*
       (P. Clark,* J. A. Evans,* P. S. Coate*)
1925 None listed
1926 None listed
1927 None listed
1928 P. S. Coate,* W. D. Kyser,* J. M. Patten*
       (C. D. Montgomery, S. Beasley,* W. Gilfillan*)
1929 C. D. Montgomery, Dr. A. R. Bliss,* B. Smith*
1930 W. D. Kyser, W. I. Moody, P. S. Coate
       (S. Beasley, J. M. Patten,* P. C. Clarke)
1931 W. D. Kyser, A. R. Bliss, Whitfield King
       (J. M. Patten)
1932 Whitfield King, Dr. A. R. Bliss, W. D. Kyser*
       (J. M. Patten)
1933 W. I. Moody,* Dr. A. R. Bliss,* J. M. Patten
1934 Hal Buchanan, P. C. Clarke,* A. R. Bliss
       (R. L. Stratton)
1935 P. C. Clarke,* J. M. Patten, A. R. Bliss
1936 J. M. Patten, P. C. Clarke, H. W. Dunkin
       (Herbert Esch)
1937 P. S. Coate, W. I. Moody, J. M. Patten
1938 P. S. Coate, P. C. Clarke, Amiel Brinkley
1939 P. S. Coate, W. I. Moody, P. C. Clarke
1940 J. M. Patten, P. S. Coate,* W. I. Moody*
       (P. C. Clarke)
1941 P. S. Coate, W. I. Moody, J. M. Patten
1942 Russell Perry,* A. J. V. Ware, J. M. Patten
1943 W. I. Moody, Leon Huddleston, P. S. Coate
1944 J. M. Patten,* L. Huddleston, Clifford Kulp
       (William Hudgins)
1945 W. I. Moody, M. J. Erlicher, G. C. Connell
1946 W. I. Moody,* L. Huddleston, C. Kulp
       (G. C. Connell)
1947 C. Kulp, L. Huddleston, G. C. Connell
1948 W. I. Moody, C. Kulp, L. Huddleston*
       (Leroy Taylor)
1949 C. Kulp, L. Huddleston, L. Taylor
1950 Louis Furbringer, J. M. Patten, Jr.,* Franklin Kimborough*
       (Herbert Esch, Dr. D. C. McCool)
1951 L. Huddleston, L. Furbringer, R. Perry
1952 L. Huddleston, D. C. McCool, J. M. Patten, Jr.*
       (H. Esch)
1953 R. Perry, J. M. Patten, Jr., W. Deupree
1954 L. Huddleston, W. Deupree, J. M. Patten, Jr.
1955 J. M. Patten, Jr., L. Huddleston, W. Deupree
1956 W. Deupree, William Embry, D. C. McCool
1957 J. M. Patten, Jr., W. Embry, Clark Williams*
       (W. Deupree, W. Lea)

Superintendents of The Church School

I. A List (incomplete) of the Superintendents of the Church School (early dates are often uncertain)

Dr. Richard Hines (1860's)
Alfred Todhunter (1870's)
Dr. S. H. Collins (1880's)
Arthur Baum (1890's)
William Friedel (1890's)
Frank Baum (ca. 1900)
William I. Moody 1906-1916
Mrs. William Omberg 1917-1921

Mrs. Leroy Taylor 1921-1924
Miss Ellen Correll 1924-1925
Joseph M. Patten, Sr. 1925-1938
Russell Perry 1938-1943
Leon Huddleston 1943-1945
Hobart Turman 1945-1951
Russell Perry 1951-present

II. Church School officers and teachers for 1957-1958

SUPERINTENDENT ....Russell Perry
SECRETARIES..................................Mrs. J. M. Barron, Mrs. Leon Huddleston
TREASURER ....Leroy Taylor
RECORDS ....John How
COORDINATORS....................John McCarroll, Sam Dawson, William Hudgins
BIRTHDAY SECRETARY..Miss Margaret Hamlet
ORGANIST ....William Brice
DIRECTOR OF CHRISTIAN EDUCATION..............................Miss Ellen Correll

CHILDREN FROM BIRTH TO 12 YEARS

Pre-School and Nursery
    Guild of the Christ Child—Mrs. Orston Coe, Mrs. O. H. Skinner
    Nursery—Mrs. Douglas Harstick, Mrs. Richard Peece
Beginners (3 year olds)—Mrs. W. W. Melton, Jr., Miss Sara Mae Randolph, Miss Lucy B. Lea
Kindergarten A (4 year olds)—Mrs. Wilson Carruthers, Mrs. Basil Mitchell, Miss Ada Gilkey
Kindergarten B (5 year olds)—Miss Frances Beeson, Mrs. Russell Perry, Mrs. J. Guerry Wilson
Primary: Grade 1—Miss Helen Moore, Miss Jo Lynn Palmer
    Grade 2—Mrs. John McCarroll, Mrs. John H. Davis
    Grade 3—Mr. and Mrs. Charles J. Loverde
Juniors: Grade 4—Mr. and Mrs. Jeff Hanna
    Grade 5—Mrs. Duncan Williams, Miss Dorothy Cooke
    Grade 6—Mrs. L. J. Larkey, Miss Doris Threlkeld

YOUTH FROM 12 TO 18 YEARS

Junior High: Grade 7—Mr. and Mrs. H. Brent Cooke
    Grade 8—Mr. and Mrs. Sam Hollis
    Grade 9—Mrs. Ernest G. Kelly, Mrs. James D. Biles
Senior High: (Grades 10, 11, 12)—Miss Ellen Correll, Ray Monteith

ADULTS

Heroes of the Faith: Mr. A. J. V. Ware
New Testament Study: Dean Sanders
The Episcopal Church: Dr. John Davis, Canon Knox
The Family at Church and Home: Canon Cayce
The Church in Literature: Dr. Danforth R. Ross

[249]

Officers of The Woman's Auxiliary, From 1939
To 1957

(*Abbreviations:* P—president; 1VP—first vice-president; RS—recording secretary; CS—corresponding secretary; T—treasurer)

1939 P, Mrs. J. D. H. Meyer; 1VP, Mrs. Charles Dillard; 2VP, Mrs. Julien P. Williams; RS, Mrs. B. M. McKnight; CS, Miss Adelene Gilfillan; T, Miss Perlie Moody.

1940 P, Mrs. Charles Dillard; 1VP, Mrs. J. D. H. Meyer; 2VP, Mrs. Allen Hughes; RS, Mrs. B. M. McKnight; CS, Miss Adelene Gilfillan; T, Miss Perlie Moody.

1941 P, Mrs. Charles Dillard; 1VP, Mrs. Allen Hughes; 2VP, Mrs. J. D. H. Meyer; RS, Mrs. B. M. McKnight; CS, Miss Adelene Gilfillan; T, Miss Perlie Moody.

1942 P, Mrs. W. E. Barnes; 1VP, Mrs. Allen Hughes; 2VP, Mrs. J. D. H. Meyer; 3VP, Mrs. Walter Medding; RS, Mrs. John H. Davis; CS, Mrs. John Maxon; T, Mrs. H. R. Schwarzkopf.

1943 P, Mrs. R. S. Caradine; 1VP, Mrs. H. R. Schwarzkopf; 2VP, Mrs. W. R. Medding; RS, Mrs. John Davis; CS, Mrs. R. B. Dubberly; T, Mrs. J. D. H. Meyer.

1944 P, Mrs. R. S. Caradine; 1VP, Mrs. W. Medding; 2VP, Mrs. D. C. McCool; CS, Mrs. William H. Chandler; T, Mrs. J. D. H. Meyer.

1945 P, Mrs. D. C. McCool; 1VP, Mrs. Frank Gailor; 2VP, Miss Harriette Frank; RS, Mrs. H. Brent Cooke, Jr.; CS, Mrs. W. H. Chandler; T, Mrs. J. D. H. Meyer.

1946 P, Mrs. H. Brent Cooke, Jr.; 1VP, Mrs. Duncan Williams; 2VP, Mrs. J. Lister Skinner; RS, Mrs. J. M. Barron; CS, Mrs. W. H. Chandler; T, Mrs. J. D. H. Meyer.

1947 P, Mrs. H. B. Cooke; 1VP, Mrs. W. C. Catron; 2VP, Mrs. J. L. Skinner; RS, Mrs. J. M. Barron; T, Mrs. J. D. H. Meyer.

1948 P, Mrs. Leroy Taylor; 1VP, Miss Harriette Frank; 2VP, Mrs. H. Brent Cooke; RS, Mrs. J. M. Barron; CS, Miss Mildred McIntyre; T, Mrs. J. D. H. Meyer.

1949 P, Mrs. Leroy Taylor; 1VP, Mrs. Allen Hughes; 2VP, Miss Harriette Frank; RS, Mrs. V. H. Smith; CS, Miss Mildred McIntyre; T, Mrs. J. D. H. Meyer.

1950 P, Mrs. Allen Hughes; 1VP, Miss Harriette Frank; 2VP, Mrs. Leroy Taylor; RS, Mrs. V. H. Smith; CS, Miss Elizabeth Martin; T, Mrs. J. D. H. Meyer.

1951 P, Mrs. Allen Hughes; 1VP, Mrs. L. B. Alexander; 2VP, Mrs. Alice Henry; RS, Mrs. Leon Huddleston; CS, Miss Elizabeth Martin; T, Mrs. J. D. H. Meyer.

Note: To this time Auxiliary elections were usually held in November or December, the officers being installed in January. In 1952 the officers were elected in the spring and installed soon after Easter. While this change was being made, the *Chimes* seems to have neglected to give the full slate of officers.

1952 For the first four months—Mrs. Duncal Williams, president.

1952-53 Mrs. Carl Fischer, president.

1953-54 Mrs. Joseph Patten, Jr., president.

1954-55 P, Mrs. J. M. Patten, Jr.; VP, Mrs. Roy Collins; RS, Mrs. D. C. McCool; CS, Mrs. Walker Richardson; T, Miss Harriette Frank.

1955-56 P, Mrs. L. B. Alexander; 1VP, Mrs. Allen Hughes; 2VP, Mrs. Max Lucas; CS, Mrs. Charles Van Hook; T, Miss Harriette Frank.

1956-57   P, Mrs. L. B. Alexander; 1VP, Mrs. William Lea; 2VP, Mrs. Julian Phelan; RS, Miss Lucy Lea; CS, Mrs. Charles Van Hook; T, Mrs. Miles Nevin.

Note: For 1957-58, the Centennial Year, I shall list the entire Executive Board.

President—Mrs. Ben Gilliland
1st Vice-President—Mrs. William Lea
2nd Vice-President—Mrs. J. C. Loverde
Secretary—Mrs. William Bullock
Treasurer—Mrs. Miles Nevin
Corresponding Secretary—Miss Adelene Gilfillan
Devotions—Mrs. William E. Sanders
Education—Mrs. William Morse
Missions—Mrs. Arthur Woodside
United Thank Offering—Mrs. Chester Perry
Christian Social Relations—Mrs. Charles Van Hook
Church Periodical Club—Mrs. O. B. Stegall
Personnel and College Work—Miss Ellen Correll
Altar—Mrs. Charles Roe
Youth Service—Mrs. Duncan Williams
Church Home—Mrs. James Prewitt, Mrs. A. B. Treadwell
Office Representative—Mrs. Sam Latta
Adviser—Mrs. Ludwell Alexander
Parliamentarian—Mrs. D. C. McCool
Hospitality—Miss Harriette Frank
Chimes—Mrs. Elmer Johnson
Coffee Hour—Mrs. Charles Dillard
Grounds—Mrs. D. C. McCool
Book Store Representative—Mrs. William Lea
Memorials—Mrs. Lanier Perkins
Publicity—Mrs. Rembert Donelson
Shut-ins—Mrs. Clark Williams
Visiting—Mrs. J. M. Patten, Jr., and Mrs. Allen Hughes
Honorary Member—Mrs. William E. Barnes

Besides the above officers, the Executive Board includes the presidents of all Guilds—listed below:

Cathedral Guild—Mrs. Turner E. Sledge
Dean's Guild—Mrs. Allen Hughes
Gailor Guild—Mrs. Lloyd Calhoun
St. Anne's Guild—Mrs. C. R. Hughes
St. Catherine's Guild—Mrs. William Bullock
St. Dorcas' Guild—Mrs. Charlie Crawford
St. Elizabeth's Guild—Miss Mary George Coward
St. Martha's Guild—Mrs. Guy Northrop
St. Mary's Guild—Mrs. A. Barlow Treadwell
St. Pricilla Guild—Mrs. Elizabeth P. Shaw
St. Faith's Altar Committee—Mrs. Charles A. Roe

Parish Facts and Figures

(from Convention *Journals*)

It should be remembered that the report for each year is made to the Convention and refers to data of the previous year.

Year	Total Communicants	Sunday School	Budget (collections)	Salary (or parish expenses)	
1858	38		$ 475.31	$ 1,500 "entitled to receive"	
1859	50	40	605.45	Hines	
1860	55	30	1,319.22		
1861					
	No records				
1865					
1866	No report from St. Mary's				
1867	No *Journal* in our files				
1868	90	80	1,105.93	1,400 arrears on salary	
				3,500 debt on parish	
1869	75	70		1,350 arrears on salary	
1870	70			3,000 debt	
1871	68				Harris
1872	118	75	2,186.85		
1873	146	70	3,837.36*	982.77	
1874	173	70	3,833.58**	1,075.95	
1875	201	100	1,906.00		
1876	220	131	1,896.79		
1877	181	130	2,050.41	990.00	
1878	217	130	2,170.80	936.43	
1879	168	125	2,875.52	992.52	
1880	200		4,661.38		
1881	177	116	1,161.48	519.54	Klein
1882	189	140	2,061.57	851.31	
1883	189	121	2,612.90	723.57	
1884	208	124	2,585.91	895.05	
1885	246	106	2,927.84	997.38	
1886	310	148	3,430.44	1,065.37	
1887	324	145	4,182.67	1,239.33	
1888	284	152	3,096.58	1,143.72	
1889	312	155	4,543.23	1,450.00	
1890	305	145	4,060.98	1,550.00	
1891	315	145	3,055.11	1,800.00	
1892	290	145	4,068.67	1,800.00	
1893	345	104	3,170.64	1,450.00	
1894	377		3,769.67	1,500.00	Dumbell
1895	No report				
1896	287	75	3,043.03	2,131.98	Turner
1897	303	97	3,857.59	2,539.63	(all salaries)
1898	303	100	3,684.52	2,801.85	Green
1899	339	120	27,107.43	2,511.32	
1900	377	130	9,412.86	3,144.47	
1901	420	166	5,000.78	4,194.74	
1902	452	160	5,438.18	3,196.31	Morris
1903	472	151	6,084.87	3,024.40	
1904	487	233	3,753.05	3,141.11	
1905	495	200	6,087.06	2,150.50	
1906	520	277	7,287.42	4,413.07	
1907	532	195	17,674.43	1,800.00	(dean's)
1908	539	166	5,174.66	1,800.00	

Year	Total Communicants	Sunday School	Budget (collections)	Salary (or parish expenses)
1909	520	163	8,775.97	1,800.00
1910	538	166	7,514.37	1,800.00
1911	540	166	13,167.65	1,800.00
1912	552	161	7,886.52	2,140.00
1913	592	185	8,090.36	2,100.00
1914	608	188	6,080.56	2,100.00
1915	626	160	6,328.82	2,400.00
1916	604	250	10,265.05	2,449.60
1917	No report			DuVall
1918	604			
1919	604	169	10,779.65	6,767.43 (all parish exp.)
1920	597		11,753.31	6,623.89
1921			11,991.66	3,300.00 (dean) Noe
1922	603		13,882.64	3,458.32
1923	638	174	16,349.63	14,850.00 (parish expense)
1924	733	252	13,940.66	4,500.00 (dean)
1925	750	254	17,886.72	10,886.00 (all salaries)
1926	No report			
1927	870			
1928	907	337	21,731.39	11,690.00
1929	915	280	25,200.32	13,593.00 (parish expense)
1930	816	305	23,805.75	13,604.25
1931	820	302	23,896.06	14,064.83
1932	834	355	23,632.56	18,053.06
1933	832	364	20,870.09	15,058.00
1934	822	327	16,297.00	12,702.32
1935	798	371	16,067.00	13,530.89
1936	833	317	17,315.00	12,350.00
1937	855	333	16,054.80	12,500.00
1938	865	311	17,648.53	14,127.90
1939	841	405	18,722.00	15,151.03

*—indicates it includes "special offering of $2,364.59."
**—indicates it includes "Offering for yellow fever sufferers, $1,942.59.

Year	Comm'ts	Ch. S.	Total Receipts	Assess. & Apport.	Parish	
1940	599	365	$17,657.50	$3,449.96	$12,118.58	Hoag
1941	653	310	17,037.24	2,884.85	12,532.00	
1942	668	284	16,533.84	2,219.05	12,283.78	
1943	687	210	19,473.48	3,294.98	12,273.72	
1944	728	175	27,620.78	11,000.00	13,129.77	
1945	779	175	23,104.32	7,502.91	13,661.13	
1946	749	184	23,907.29	7,565.55	13,667.64	
1947	740	176	31,572.95	13,772.84	12,573.45	interim
1948	712	165	27,992.97	8,943.74	15,964.03	Sanders
1949	688	213	36,555.74	9,069.90	15,835.68	
1950	711	179	32,328.00	9,300.92	18,024.94	
1951	719	199	39,251.32	9,375.83	17,714.21	
1952	709	244	36,667.65	10,034.42	19,278.83	
1953	762	322	41,010.56	10,052.66	24,909.40	
1954	795	312	44,536.94	13,448.96	26,545.43	
1955	848	328	52,979.75	15,158.68	32,258.85	
1956	818	378	63,633.85	20,995.16	34,550.73	
1957	839	397	68,461.77	19,087.30	35,043.41	

Group Leaders for 1957

(The names in parentheses indicate moved from the city or resigned because of illness.)

DISTRICT A: Mr. and Mrs. Rembert Donelson
Group 1.   Mr. and Mrs. Ed L. Reuter
      2.   Mr. and Mrs. Charles Van Hook
      3.   Mr. and Mrs. J. Jeff Brown
      4.   Mr. and Mrs. Tom F. East and Mr. and Mrs. Clyde Washburn

DISTRICT B: Mr. and Mrs. Arthur Woodside
Group 5.   Mr. and Mrs. Basil Mitchell
      6.   Mrs. Jack Baldwin
      7.   Mr. and Mrs. Chris T. Ellis
     41.   Dr. and Mrs. James Biles

DISTRICT C.   Mr. and Mrs. W. Clark Williams
Group 8.   Mr. and Mrs. Murry Jack Cord
     10.   Mr. and Mrs. Leland Cranford
     11.   Dr. and Mrs. W. L. Whittemore
     12.   Mr. and Mrs. George Partin

DISTRICT D: Mr. and Mrs. Miles Nevin
Group 13.   Mr. and Mrs. Russell Perry
     14.   Mr. and Mrs. Chester Perry
     16.   Mr. and Mrs. C. Roy Hughes
     17.   Mr. and Mrs. H. Brent Cooke
     18.   Mr. Paul Lee

DISTRICT E: Mr. and Mrs. William Hudgins
Group 15.   Dr. and Mrs. William H. Morse
     20.   Dr. and Mrs. O. B. Stegall
     21.   Mrs. J. M. Barron
     28.   (Dr. and Mrs. Jess Perkinson)
     29.   Mr. and Mrs. E. Tom Holloway

DISTRICT F: Mr. and Mrs. William Lea
Group 23.   Mr. and Mrs. John McCarroll
     24.   Mrs. William Bulloch
     25.   Mr. and Mrs. John McCarroll
     26.   Dr. and Mrs. D. C. McCool
     27.   Mr. and Mrs. A. J. V. Ware

DISTRICT G: Mr. and Mrs. William Deupree
Group 30.   Mr. and Mrs. Robert S. McKnight, Jr.
     31.   Mr. and Mrs. William Deupree
     33.   Miss Louise Fleece
     34.   Mr. and Mrs. Charles D. Crawford
     38.   Mr. and Mrs. J. Otto Nolte

DISTRICT H: Mr. and Mrs. M. C. Nichols
Group 22.   Mr. and Mrs. Leon Huddleston
     32.   (Mr. Owen D. Massie) Miss Jacqueline Stanford
     35.   Mr. and Mrs. Raymond Strong
     40.   Dr. and Mrs. John H. Davis
     43.   Mr. and Mrs. H. Brent Cooke III

DISTRICT I: Mr. J. M. Patten, Sr.
Group 9.   Mr. and Mrs. Frank Krotzer
     39.   (Miss Mary Coward) Mr. and Mrs. Raymond Simmons
     44.   (Mr. and Mrs. Herbert Esch) Mr. P. C. Clarke

Honor Rolls

Honor Rolls (posted in the Cathedral) of those who participated in the First and Second World Wars, and the Korean War.

FIRST WORLD WAR

Arthur Hackett (killed in France, December 12, 1915)
Thomas Guy Bragg (killed in France, April 6, 1918)
Albert Cohen (killed in France, October 1918)

George William Jenkins
Maury Jenkins
James S. Clarke
Trezevant Collier
Benton D. Edgington
Hugh Edgington, Jr.
N. Falls Austin
Winchester H. Bennett
Louis Wood
Bertram M. Bates, Jr.
Silas McBee, Jr.
Samuel Loring
Thomas W. Deupree
Frederick Charles Deupree
William H. Chandler, Jr.
Green Chandler
Hugh Campbell Chandler
Frank Hoyt Gailor
John Early Burgess
Fred G. Jones
Bennett Doty
Robert Gilfillan
L. T. Kavanaugh
William E. Barnes, Jr.
Jesse Forrest
Victor A. Hundley

Mason Frederick Percival
H. Neil Percival
Jack Creighton Percival
Rowan Greer
Kenneth E. Johnston
Ernest Sutton
Clarke W. Thornton
Ludwell Alexander
Robert E. Townes
Henry G. Buckingham
John Royster Thurman, Jr.
Maxwell H. Noll
Arthur H. Bower
George P. Friedel
James A. Friedel
William S. Jett
Charles Marable
Guy Bedford Bruce
Enoch Ensley
Walter Rucks
Arthur Rucks
William P. Hammer
Fred S. Perry
Albert S. Caldwell
Charlotte Gailor

SECOND WORLD WAR (* indicates killed in action)

James M. Maxon, Jr.*
Walter Munding, Jr.
Robert DeWar
William Moody Shaner
John Poe
Robert D. Mulette
Jack Ringger
J. D. Henry Meyer, Jr.
Frederick C. Wolfe, Jr.
George A. Paine, Jr.
Robert Callahan, Jr.

John P. McNamara, Jr.
John B. Tacker
Robert H. Shaner, Jr.
Fred W. Holmes
Edwin Howe
Leonard Goff
Thomas Van Zandt
William Lea, Jr.
Bruns McCarroll
James Thomas Shaw
Robert W. Wyman

[255]

Milton C. Mendle
Thomas E. Mitchell, Jr.
Johnson Rhem
Samuel D. Rhem, Jr.
William Aurand
Clarence Cole
Franklin Gossett
John How
Thurman Crawford
Lant Abernathy
Clifford N. Mabie, Jr.
Frederick Fischer
Clare Boyd
Austin James Calhoun
Joseph E. Dean
Clinton W. Starr
Stephen Naggfy
Ludwell Alexander, Jr.
Clayton Stearns
Edward Lee Lyon
Hector G. McAllister
Muriel Clare Lloyd
Harold P. Donle
Richard Drake, Jr.
Robert Edwards
Ralph Graham
Thomas Griffin
Franklin Kimborough
George F. Ham
Lloyd Hudson
Dabney Hull Lea
Henry Mitchell III
Russell Perry
Charles Dillard*
Walter Medding

Charles A. Roe, Jr.*
Ceylon B. Frazer
Maurice Hill
James Washington
Alfred Hardin
Stevenson Bledsoe
Verner H. Smith, Jr.
Glenda Moore
Richard J. Oliphant
Emmett L. Abington
Daniel Hanley, Jr.
Hays Brantley, Jr.*
Roscoe Yancey
Alfred W. Hardin
Rembert Donelson
Robert McKnight, Jr.
John B. Maxon
E. Kent Jones
Robert S. Ramsey, Jr.
Bartlett F. Hanson
Joseph M. Patten, Jr.
Odell Hamlett
Richard Medding
Joseph R. Adams
James I. McKnight, Jr.
Frank M. Glover
John M. Perkins
John S. Finlay, Jr.
Andrew J. Donelson, Jr.
Aubrey L. Powell
W. Poindexter Hastings
Robert B. Hutton
Ronald M. Birchler
Winston Braun

KOREAN WAR

Austin Calhoun
H. Brent Cooke III
Earl Cooley
Victor Cordes III
Russell Douglas
Alfred Hardin
William H. Jones

W. L. Medding
Walter Medding
Donald Roe
Richard Schultz
William F. Smith
Robert R. Willis

The Centennial Organ

GREAT

8'	prinzipal
8'	bordun
8'	viole
8'	gemshorn
4'	octav
4'	hohlfloete
4'	gemshorn
2⅔'	nazat
2'	superoctav
III rk.	mixtur
8'	harmonie trompete
4'	harmonie trompete

POSITIV

8'	nason floete
4'	koppelfloete
2⅔'	rohrnazat
2'	blockfloete
1-3/5'	terz
III rk.	cymbel
8'	schalmei

PEDAL

32'	untersatz
16'	contrabass
16'	brummbass
16'	bourdon doux
16'	dulciana
10⅔'	quintenbass
8'	octav
8'	bordun
8'	bourdon doux
8'	gemshorn
8'	dulciana
4'	superoctav
4'	gemshorn
2'	gemshorn
II rk.	mixtur
16'	bombard
8'	harmonie trompete
4'	harmonie clarion

SWELL

16'	bourdon doux
8'	montre
8'	bourdon
8'	salicional
8'	voix celeste
4'	prestant
4'	flute harmonique
2'	doublette
III rk.	plein jeu
16'	sous-basson
8'	trompette
8'	basson
4'	clairon
	tremulant

CHOIR

16'	double dulciana
8'	concert flute
8'	quintadena
8'	dulciana
8'	unda maris
4'	viol principal
4'	flute
2'	flute
1⅓'	larigot
8'	harmonie trompete (GT)
8'	clarinet
8'	english horn
	harp
	tremulant

ECHO

16'	bourdon
8'	quintadena
8'	flute
8'	vox angelica
8'	vox celeste
4'	flute
2'	flute
8'	vox humana
	chimes
	tremulant

ECHO PEDAL

16'	echo bourdon
8'	flute

Schantz Organ—1956

Cathedral Windows

I had originally intended an appendix on Memorials, but discovered that this involved too many complexities; for memorials have been given in so many forms—money, flowers, candles, books, music, parts of the structure—and records are so extensive and kept by so many different organizations, that it is impractical and impossible to name all. It might be best to name none, but I decided to make an exception in the case of the windows. (This list is furnished by the Memorial Committee.)

WINDOWS

A) *West end*

2 large	Given by Mr. and Mrs. J. Axson Evans in memory of Marion Boyle Evans and Jacob Axson Evans
1 medium	Given by subscription in memory of James M. Maxon, Jr.
1 medium	Given by Mrs. Roe and Mrs. Dillard in memory of Charles S. Roe, Jr., and Charles Dillard
2 small corner	Given by the Chandler family in memory of W. H. and Knoxie Clift Chandler
2 small corner	Given by Mr. and Mrs. J. M. Patten in memory of Anne T. Carter and William Clay Swope

B) *Epistle-aisle*
(beginning at west)

1)	Given by Mr. W. I. Moody in memory of Edmund Orgill, his wife Lucy Willing Orgill, their sons, Joseph, Frederick, William, their daughter, Florence
2)	Given by Mr. and Mrs. Whitfield King in memory of Sarah Lea Taylor
3)	Given by Bishop T. F. Gailor in memory of Charlotte Moffett Gailor
4)	Given by Mr. Robert L. Taylor in memory of William Lea

C) *Gospel-aisle*

1)	Given by Mr. William I. Moody in memory of Grace Prestige Moody
2)	Given by Mrs. C. C. Currier in memory of Charles Cruse Currier and his wife Elizabeth Brinkley Currier
3)	Given by her children in memory of Nellie Cunningham Gailor, wife of Thomas Frank Gailor
4)	Given by Sister Hughetta Memorial Committee in memory of All the Sisters of St. Mary's who have labored in this diocese since 1873.

D) *Epistle-clerestory*

1)   Given in memory of Bishop James Craik Morris— donor anonymous

2)   Given by Mr. John Morris in memory of John Shelton Morris

3)   Given by Mrs. J. J. Busby in memory of Nancy Busby and Andrew Jackson Donelson

4)   Given by Mrs. E. T. Holloway and Mr. John How in memory of Emily Hopkins and Henry John How

5)   Given by Mr. and Mrs. Julien Brode in memory of Frederick William Brode II

E) *Gospel-clerestory*

1)   Given by Mr. and Mrs. J. M. Patten, Jr., and Mrs. Tempe S. Patten

2)   Given by Dr. Winston Braun

3)   Given by Mr. Walter Chandler and family in memory of Greene C. and Ellen Ogden Chandler

4)   Given by Mrs. G. W. Spain in memory of Herbert M. Sparrow

5)   Given by Mr. C. N. Johnston and Mrs. S. K. Jones in memory of Augusta Rodgers Johnston

F) *Transept—gospel side*

1) Facing west   Given by Miss Perlie Moody

2) Round window and   Given by Mrs. J. A. Evans in memory of Jacob Axson Evans and Jane Eliabeth Boyle

3) Two large

G) *Transept—epistle side*

1) Facing west   Given by Mr. W. I. Moody and Mr. J. M. Patten in memory of P. Stenning Coate

2) Round window   Given by Will J. Brinkley of Iuka, Miss., in memory of Elizabeth M. Brinkley, her sister Lucile, and her daughter Lucile

3) Two large   Given by Mr. George M. Darrow in memory of Tempe Swope Darrow and William D. Kyser

H) *Sanctuary*

        Given by Mr. Whitfield King in memory of John Smith King, Sallie L. King, John Robert King, Mrs. R. L. Taylor, Robert Lee Taylor, James Wilson Bell, Nancy F. Bell

[259]

INDEX

DeVall, Dean Frederick D., 114n, 132-135, 139
Diocesan House (see also Bishop's House), 178, 187, 209, 211, 220, 221
Diocesan Survey, 213, 227
Division of the Diocese (discussed), 39, 86, 172
DuBose Conference Center, 208, 228, 230
DuBose, William P., 119, 119n, 120
Dumbell, Dean Howard, 89, 91, 105, 106n

Emmanuel Church, 64, 78n, 81, 82, 116, 213
Eppes, Robertson, 213, 232, 232n, 235
Esch, Herbert, 135, 150, 174n, 187n, 189
Evans, Jacob Axson, 124, 134, 148, 152, 164
Every Member Canvass, 47, 78, 126, 140, 168, 189n

Family Nights, 226, 227, 228, 230
Faxon, George, 95, 97, 101
Feast of Lights, 169, 176, 191, 201
Fleece, Louise, 167n, 192n
Fox, George, 237
Frank, Harriette, 194, 218n
Friedel, P. R., 96, 96n, 100n

Gailor Guild, 169
Gailor, Bishop Thomas F., 21-23, 32n, 48, 73, 89, 90-93, 99, 102, 105-120, 130, 136-38, 144, 152, 159, 161, 171, 172
Girls Friendly Society, 126, 127, 135n
Gloster, Mrs. Mary H., 10, 11, 12, 12n
Glynn, Franklin, 195
Grace Church, 17, 18, 42, 52, 56, 115, 136, 146, 185n, 191
Green, Dean Stephen H., 90, 97-101, 108-10, 111n, 118
Green, William M., 9, 17, 18, 19, 35n, 38n, 93

Harris, Dean George C., 55-76, 78
Harris, Mrs. G. C., 55, 56, 69, 71
Haynes, Warren, 228
Higbee School, 85, 127
Hines, Dean Richard, 26, 31-53, 55
Hoag, Dean Harold B., 185-200, 233
Hoffman Hall, 81, 82, 116
Holy Trinity Church, 114, 146
Honesty, Dr., 81, 82n
Howard Association, 61, 61n, 64
Howard, Len, 161
Hudgins, William, 222
Huddleston, Leon, 194, 219
Hymnal 1940, 123, 195, 196, 224

Immanuel Church (LaGrange), 12

Jackson, Andrew, 2, 3
Jackson, George, 64, 65, 65n, 81
James, George, 48, 49n
Jenny Wrens, 78
Jones, Hubert, 28, 233n
Jones, Mr. and Mrs. S. K., 169, 222
Jones, Mrs. William, 225
Johnson, Mr. and Mrs. C. N., 222
Junior Guild (or Auxiliary)—later Deans Guild, 110, 168n
Juny, F. A., Sr. and Jr., 80

Keating, *Memphis,* quoted, 20n, 24, 24n, 38
Killefer, A. C., 139, 139n
Klein, Dean William, 64-66, 72, 76-89, 90
Knox, Robert, 236, 237n
Kopper Kettle Tea Room, 141, 141n, 151
Kyser, W. D., 152, 154, 162n, 168n

Ladies Aid Society, 78
Ladies Educational and Missionary Society, 21, 22
Lambeth Conferences, 46, 66, 87, 130
Lea, William, 222
Lill, Mrs. Thomas, 77, 193
Litton, Samuel, 11n, 12
Loaring-Clark, Alfred, 167, 168
Loring, Sam, 135, 139
Loomis, Helen, 129, 148
Lyon, Carter B., 222

Madison College, 18, 23n
McCullough, J. P., 108, 114
McCool, Dr. and Mrs. D. C., 194n, 216, 224, 234
McFadden, Frances, 213, 214
Matthews, Robert, 215, 228
Maxon, Bishop James M., 39, 143, 146, 147, 151, 172, 178-80, 182, 184, 192, 200-204, 207, 208n
Memphis, founding of, 3-5
Men's Council, 169, 187, 230
Meteyarde, Lawrence, 160, 183, 195
Moody, W. I., 125, 141, 146, 150, 152, 162, 164, 174n, 183n, 187n, 192, 196, 201, 209, 218, 220n
Moore, Rue L., 235
Morris, Dean James Craik, 99, 105-131, 188
Morris, Mrs. J. C., 120-125

National Church (Episcopal), 7, 8, 111, 115, 136-39, 167, 214, 222
Negroes, work among, 44, 64, 65, 81, 82, 116, 117
Nichols, M. C., 212

Snowden, Col. R. B., 84, 97, 100n
Stephens, William, 43, 50

Tate, S., 95-97
Taylor, Mr. and Mrs. Leroy, 162, 218n
Tennessee (early settlement), 1-5
Todhunter, Alfred, 65
Tracy, Sterling, 176, 180, 183, 184
Treadwell, Anne Overton, 196, 197n
Treadwell Fund, 207n
Trezevant, J. P., 16n, 27, 33, 48, 71
Turman, Hobart, 194, 218n
Turner, Dean C. B. H., 90, 98, 105-06

United Guild, 134
University of the South (or Sewanee), 23n, 40, 46, 66, 86, 90, 109, 118, 119
Usher, Guy, 183, 184

Vander Horst, Bishop John, 212, 212n
Vaulx, James J., 41, 42n, 45, 53, 62, 114n

Wager, Peter, 39, 51, 53, 57, 63n, 114

Ware, A. J. V., 190, 224, 233, 235n
Ware, Charles S., 167
Warwick, Arthur J., 82, 83, 96, 187n
Weathers, L. M., 95, 102, 103
Weller, George, 11n, 17
Wells, Holly, 108n, 114n, 119n, 123
West Tennessee Historical Society Papers, 16, 22
Wheelock, J. A., 42, 43
White, George, 34n, 39, 43, 56, 67, 69, 71
Williams, W. Clark, 227, 228, 232n, 233
Williamson, Donald, 228
Winchester, Marcus, 4, 5
Wolf, Fred C., 228
Wood, W. Halsey, 92-95, 102, 103
Woman's Auxiliary, 87, 107, 110, 134, 169, 182, 192, 194, 223, 226, 229
Wright, Thomas, 11n, 12, 13, 14

Yellow Fever epidemic, 57, 60, 74
Young, R. Calder, 80
Young, Stanley, 167, 168, 183, 184